M000281101

MRS GUINNESS

MRS GUINNESS

THE RISE AND FALL OF
DIANA MITFORD
THE THIRTIES SOCIALITE

LYNDSY SPENCE

The History Press

'Tis the set of a soul
That decides its goal,
And not the calm or the strife.

– Ella Wheeler Wilcox

Cover illustrations
Front: Mrs Bryan Guinness, formerly Diana Freeman-Mitford (1910–2003) and later Diana Mosley. © Illustrated London News Ltd/Mary Evans. *Back*: The Mosleys after their release from prison. (Private collection)

First published 2015

This edition published 2017 by
The History Press
The Mill, Brimscombe Port
Stroud, Gloucestershire, GL5 2QG
www.thehistorypress.co.uk

© Lyndsy Spence, 2015, 2017

The right of Lyndsy Spence to be identified as the Author
of this work has been asserted in accordance with the
Copyright, Designs and Patents Act 1988.

All rights reserved. No part of this book may be reprinted
or reproduced or utilised in any form or by any electronic,
mechanical or other means, now known or hereafter invented,
including photocopying and recording, or in any information
storage or retrieval system, without the permission in writing
from the Publishers.

British Library Cataloguing in Publication Data.
A catalogue record for this book is available from the British Library.

ISBN 978 0 7509 7051 8

Typesetting and origination by The History Press
Printed and bound by CPI Group (UK) Ltd

CONTENTS

Acknowledgements   7

1   She Can't Live Long   9
2   Clever by Association   16
3   A Demi Paradise   19
4   An Age without a Name   25
5   The Unhappy Youth   33
6   Coming Out   40
7   A Deb's Delight   47
8   The Engagement   54
9   A Society Wedding   62
10 Mrs Bryan Guinness   67
11 He-Evelyn   72
12 Confinement   76
13 A Gilded Life   80
14 An Interval in Friendships   83
15 The Bloomsbury Set   86
16 The Happy Foursome   89
17 Life and Death   93
18 The Age of Reason   97
19 The Man, Mosley   101
20 The Demon King   106
21 Turmoil   110
22 Courting Scandal   113

23	A Clean Break	118
24	Social Pariah	124
25	The Devil and the Deep Blue Sea	127
26	Detour	134
27	The Golden Month of October	140
28	The Fall of Fascism	145
29	Munich: An Idyllic Life	154
30	A Series of Unfortunate Events	163
31	The Importance of Unity Mitford	171
32	A Life Together	176
33	The Upper Hand	180
34	Decline and Fall	188
35	A Token Gesture	192
36	Lady Mosley	196
37	Fate	201
	Epilogue	209
	Notes	211
	Select Bibliography	217
	Index	220

ACKNOWLEDGEMENTS

When Diana Mosley died on 11 August 2003, the obituaries printed in British newspapers echoed public sentiment when they proclaimed her to be 'the most hated woman in England'. Prior to her death, Diana had not resided in England for more than fifty years, and yet she remained something of an arch-villain; the aristocrat who stepped away from the establishment, perhaps intent on tearing it down.

Osbert Sitwell quipped, 'Sooner or later, everyone marries a Guinness.' From its intermarriages between the brewing and banking branches of the family to the dazzling society marriages, it was a family that produced philanthropists, politicians, artists, writers and socialites. At the age of 18, Diana could have been forgiven if her brilliant in-laws eclipsed her, but with her beauty and intelligence, she became a shining star in an age when the foundation of celebrity was carved out of frivolity.

It is this period of Diana's life that intrigues me most: the interval between her Mitford childhood and her downfall in becoming Lady Mosley. The prominent players of this saga are long dead, and although from the outset it may have seemed a hindrance, it has allowed me to write without being influenced. I hope I have remained objective in the telling of Diana's story.

Two biographies have been written about Diana. The first, *Diana Mosley: A Life* by Jan Dalley, published during Diana's lifetime, extensively relates the Mitford childhood. And the latter, *Diana Mosley* by Anne de Courcy, had the advantage of Diana's co-operation, on the agreement that it should remain unpublished until after her death. De Courcy's conversations with Diana and her external sources, such as Irene Ravensdale's diaries, have proved invaluable.

I am thankful to the following people for their support and helpful insights: Diane Banks, Olivia Morris, Robyn Drury, Mark Beynon, Miriam Crozier, Debbie Catling, Stephen Kennedy, Isobel O'Neill, Tania Todd, David Platzer, Lee Galston, Christopher Warwick, Joseph Dumas, Meems Ellenberg, Diana Birchall, Rastko Podestà, Terence Pepper, Tracey Spence, Shirley Jaffe, Andrew Budgell, Terence Towles Canote, Kimberly D. Davis, Meredith Whitford, and Victor Olliver. And to the members of my immediate family who encouraged the idea of this book.

I am especially grateful to Michael Bloch for his kind permission to quote from the letters of James Lees-Milne and Diana Mitford, published in his biography *James Lees-Milne: The Life*. And to Christopher Holmes for making available his collection of photographs. As always, I am indebted to followers of The Mitford Society for their continued support.

1

SHE CAN'T LIVE LONG

Tears of gloom greeted Diana Freeman-Mitford on the day of her birth, on 17 June 1910. After a long and punishing labour, the baby, who was previously referred to as 'him', was delivered in the lull of a violent thunderstorm, eventually giving way to a gruelling hot afternoon.

The exhausted mother, Sydney, cried, for she had wanted another son. In sympathetic unison the inhabitants of the family's tiny London house on Graham Street, relatives and staff alike, were solemn when they learned of the news. The father, David, received his newborn daughter with an air of indifference – a girl was no cause for celebration. They already had two girls, Nancy and Pamela, and each parent longed for another boy to balance out the family. Tom was to be their only son, born ten months previously, and the thought of going through the ordeal of childbirth again in the hope of producing a son, weighed heavily on Sydney. She wanted seven boys and perhaps one girl; she was to have six girls and one boy. As the family and servants gathered to look at Diana, aged about an hour old, the nurse peered down at her newest charge and hissed: 'She's *too* beautiful; she can't live long.'

Diana was born as the curtain fell on the Edwardian era, a decade forever romanticised in history for its place across the abyss of the First World War and the roaring twenties. In years to come it was remembered with an air of nostalgia; a golden age of endless summers, basking in the sun that never set on the British Empire. The death of King Edward VII and the ascent of King George V to the throne, a month before Diana's birth, brought change and an air of uncertainty to British society. A new king pushed the monarchy into the twentieth century and a Liberal government quickened society's pace. The threat of war looming on the horizon and the family's dwindling finances, meant life for the Mitfords was rapidly changing, too.

David Freeman-Mitford belonged to the British aristocracy. He was loosely tied to the peerage through his father, Bertie, the first Baron Redesdale, and his mother, Lady Clementine Ogilvy, daughter of the 10th Earl of Airlie. Despite this impeccable pedigree, David was not a rich man and he depended on financial handouts from his father-in-law, Thomas Gibson Bowles, known as 'Tap'.

A self-made man, Tap Bowles was the illegitimate son of a Victorian Cabinet minister, Milner Gibson, and a servant, Susan Bowles. Owing to social mores and her lowly position in domestic service, Susan surrendered the boy to his father. She vanished from Tap's life and, given his illegitimacy (his half-siblings were born in wedlock), his father sent him to boarding school in France. It was a small consolation to Tap that his father's wife, a kind and tolerant woman, loved him as though he was her own son. Regardless of his stepmother's benevolence, when he came of age, Tap knew he would have to make his own way in the world.

Launching a career in freelance journalism, Tap wrote a column for the *Morning Post*, where, using balloon and pigeon post, he covered the Siege of Paris. At the age of 26, the ambitious young man borrowed £200 to found *Vanity Fair* in 1868, which he sold nineteen years later for £20,000 following the untimely death of his wife, Jessica. His second magazine, *The Lady*, was conveniently founded to give his mistress, Rita Shell (known as 'Tello'), a job. Prior to that, Tello was employed by Tap as a governess for his four children, and she eventually bore him three illegitimate children. With little interest in *The Lady* except for its financial turnover, Tap's attention was absorbed in editing *The Candid Quarterly*, a magazine that gave him a platform to criticise the government.

Perhaps given Tap's unfortunate start in life, the wealth he accumulated from his own merits served to turn him into a more tolerant and charitable man than his daughter's father-in-law, Bertie Redesdale. Tap gave David his first job as manager of *The Lady*, a highly unsuitable position for a man who once sailed to Ceylon on a tea-planting venture and who had gallantly fought and lost a lung in the Boer War. The refined tone of the magazine – 'for elegant women with elegant minds' – did not compliment David's own philistine views. Although grateful for Tap's generosity and the salary which afforded his family their house on Graham Street, he was not happy.

It remains unclear what David planned to do to remedy his restlessness, but with an ever-increasing family, he was not in a position to resign. The outbreak of war in 1914 seemed to provide the answer; he rejoined his old regiment, the Northampton Fusiliers, and went to the front line in France. His army pay was significantly less than his salary from *The Lady* and Sydney's allowance from Tap was greatly reduced when his vast earnings suffered as a result of the Liberal government's heavy taxation.

Sydney was not one to wallow in self-pity – a trait Diana inherited – and she set off for Paris to visit David when a spell of leave presented itself. With her typical resourcefulness, she returned to London with yards of the pale blue cloth from which the French officers' uniforms were made. Using the fabric for the children's winter coats, first Diana's, then Pamela's and eventually Nancy's, they were handed down and lasted six winters. Sydney was also pregnant with her fifth child and with the harrowing reality of another mouth to feed in the family's already dire financial situation, another compromise had to be reached. Their London house was let and Sydney and the children went to live at Malcolm House, near the church at Batsford, belonging to David's father. At her young age, Diana knew they were poor, and she also knew there was no help for it.

The family's circumstances were further changed when, only one year into the war, David's eldest brother, Clement, was killed in the Battle of Loos. The shock of losing his firstborn son shattered Bertie and despite the bitter blow of losing a brother, David sought comfort in knowing that should he survive the war, he would inherit Bertie's title and estate.

With the freedom of living in the 'real' countryside for the first time, Diana became an alert child, sensitive to her surroundings and the behaviour of others, particularly the grown-ups. Nursery life was still a shielded world that could not be intruded upon by the sadness of war or the imminent death of her grandfather, Bertie. The kaleidoscope of childhood memories – the vague presence of Sydney, and the comings and goings of nannies and governesses – was momentarily displaced, creating a void for an experience that would strengthen Diana's future beliefs in predestination.

On a hot summer's day in 1916, whilst playing in the garden of Malcolm House, Diana paused and looked up at the sky. The blinding sunlight strained her vision, but she kept her gaze fixed upon the clouds, when before her eyes, the heavens opened and a flock of angels appeared. A few seconds later, this eerie phenomenon was over. Racing off to find her siblings and bursting with excitement, she spoke of her experience. Nancy, Pamela and Tom fled inside Malcolm House and moaned in unison to Sydney: 'Oh, Muv, it's so unfair, Diana's seen a *vision*!' Their mother, much too logical for such supernatural tales, brushed it aside. There could have been numerous reasons why Diana saw what she did and Sydney did not pander to mystery. Having repeated the tale so often, Diana wondered if she had, in fact, dreamt the entire thing.

Far from having forgotten this vision, it was brought back to Diana when, not long after her sixth birthday, her grandmother, Lady Clementine, fetched her from the garden where she played with Pamela. 'Come, I will take you to visit grand-father,' the stately old lady announced to the curious children. This personal interaction was not unusual as Lady Clementine was 'deeply interested in her children and grandchildren and governesses and nurses and households' and Diana, along with Pamela, obediently followed her into the house.

After a lengthy walk up the staircase and down a never-ending landing, Lady Clementine opened a door and gently pushed the children into the semi-dark-ened bedroom. A small, frail man looking quite unlike their grandfather, sat bolt upright in bed, his jaundiced face emphasised by the shock of white hair standing on end. He muttered a few pleasantries to the spooked children, but Diana could barely comprehend what he had said, for she could not take her eyes off his face. The visit was soon over and Bertie died a month later, aged seventy-nine.

David succeeded the barony of Redesdale, and upon his father's death he inherited Batsford Park, the sprawling estate Bertie had so loved that he plunged the majority of his fortune into restoring it. Diana adored Bertie's Japanese gardens with the Buddha statues, koi fish ponds and exotic plants. Along with David's inheritance, Diana and her siblings were now fashioned as Honourable. This elevation in society could potentially change the course of her life in the future; she was now the daughter of a lord, a far more respectable status than the daughter of an impoverished second son on the fringes of the aristocracy.

Despite the peerage and the properties, David inherited little money, the bulk of which was tied up in land in the neighbouring village of Swinbrook. With a large household staff to pay, the upkeep of Batsford and maintaining the dowager cottage on the other Redesdale estate in Northumberland, David's expenditures were greater than he could afford. The solution to their problem was obvious – Batsford Park would have to be sold. The money garnered from the sale would allow David to purchase Asthall Manor, an attractive Jacobean manor house where Diana's character thrived and her imagination flourished.

Those who encountered Diana were not quick to forget her. A precocious child, she spent her days in the musty library amongst the polished mahogany book-shelves cluttered with books. Her straight, blonde hair hung around her waist and her limpid blue eyes scoured the pages of Byron, Shelley, Keats and Coleridge, understanding not one word. Although already a great beauty, she lingered in the shadows and her inconspicuous position as the middle child permitted her to manoeuvre through the minefield of everyday family life, emerging relatively unscathed from sibling squabbles and nursery politics.

SHE CAN'T LIVE LONG

Diana did not attract the attention of Nancy, the eldest, whose acid wit and quick temper made her someone to fear. Pamela, born three years after Nancy, consumed their mother's attention with her bouts of infantile paralysis. Tom, the family's cherished boy, was granted more freedom than his sisters. 'That's different, Tom is a *boy*,' the girls were often reminded when they protested against the lenience shown towards him. Due to his schooling at Lockers and then on to Eton, Tom was largely removed from family life. The three youngest girls – Unity, Jessica and Deborah – born in 1914, 1917 and 1920, respectively, completed the family.

Diana hovered between the restricted worlds of nursery life and lessons in the schoolroom. Each day was repetitive, with lessons presided over by an English governess who covered a limited curriculum deemed acceptable for a girl's education. During the holidays a French governess was engaged and the children were supposed to speak French, which subsequently resulted in long silences in the dining room. Her education was sparse and, unlike Nancy, Unity and Jessica, Diana did not harbour an ambition to attend school. In her youth, Sydney had considered the idea of going to Girton, a women's college in Cambridge, but for unknown reasons she had declined the opportunity. Regardless of her fleeting interest in education, Sydney was quick to dismiss her children's pleas.

School was also strictly forbidden by David, who feared the rigorous PE lessons would cause his daughters to develop 'legs like gateposts'.[1] Education, to David, was most unattractive in a girl – a view held by many men and women of his class. Although Diana was terrified of being sent away to boarding school – an underlying fear which plagued her – David often reminded his daughters, 'I have no money to give you.' Sydney added to Diana's misery when she conformed to his reasoning. 'Of course, not,' she agreed. 'Girl's don't expect it.' Diana realised the prospect of failing to find a good husband meant she may have to earn her own living, a thought which filled her with dread. Adding to her turmoil, the girls were forbidden to shave their legs or to wear lipstick. Jessica questioned why, and decided that her parents 'disliked the idea of trying to attract men by these artificial means'.

Diana heeded David's warning and spent sleepless nights mulling over her future. Diana's worries were not eased when, hoping to instil modesty in the young beauty, the governess often reminded her, 'Now Diana, try to remember that you are the least important person in the room.' The morbid thoughts of an uncertain future and the boredom from her inadequate school lessons, inspired Diana to firmly attach her attentions towards anything that took her fancy. The first fancy of which came in the form of organised religion.

The Mitfords were not a God-fearing family, in spite of David and Sydney supporting the Church of England, an act they viewed as their patriotic duty. Until the age of 11, Diana loathed church and resentfully proclaimed it a waste of her Sunday. She also thought it unjust when the clergyman, Mr Ward, frequently used his sermons to complain about the Mitfords' riotous behaviour. He once preached on the evils of 'people who run shouting with their dogs through God's holy acre'. Diana told her father, but he only laughed. There were lighter moments, when Mrs Ward sprang to her feet to sing the solo, much to the delight of Diana who screamed with laughter at her powerful, contralto voice.

Diana's outlook towards religion was changed when she noticed that her new governess, Miss Price, owned a Roman Catholic shrine. There was little explanation for this religious conversion, except that she was drawn in by Miss Price's crucifix, brass candlesticks and brass vases. Having lost her head to religion, Diana attended church several times a day, she declared her family heathens and claimed that time spent anywhere other than church or praying in her bedroom were wasted hours. Diana eagerly learned the New Testament, the lives of the saints, the history of the early church and the meaning of the sacraments. She fully believed in transubstantiation, original sin and the Immaculate Conception as well as the virgin birth and the real presence. She learned to turn to the east and curtsy at the right moment during the creed.

The obsession was not to last. After four terms – about the limit of time any governess could tolerate the children – Miss Price packed up her shrine and departed. Diana abandoned her religious ways, but she was grateful to Miss Price for igniting the phase; it taught her how deeply one could feel about their convictions, regardless of opposition.

Although this fixation with religion proved to be a mere phase, Diana still possessed an inquiring mind and her desire to learn could not be quelled. The schoolroom lessons could not satisfy her thirst for knowledge and she looked to the library to hone her intellect. This love for books stemmed from Nancy's example, when at the age of 7, Diana spied her eldest sister reading a large leather bound book. Questioned about her literary taste, the 13-year-old Nancy's triangular green eyes sparkled and her shrill voice boasted, 'My favourite book is *King Solomon's Mines* or *The Chaplet of Pearls*.' At the time, Diana glanced inside the books to sample their complex text and found herself completely baffled. Feeling defeated, she returned to her old favourites, *Mrs Tiggy Winkle* and *Herr Baby*.

The boredom of family life was interrupted by a surge of unexpected excitement, though at Diana's expense. For some time she had been complaining about feeling unwell and moaned of a twinge in her lower abdomen, but as always,

Sydney dismissed any mentions of ill health. When the pain became unbearable, her mother finally relented and summoned the doctor for a check-up. Diana's suffering was diagnosed as acute appendicitis and the doctor promptly ordered an emergency appendectomy. The news of Diana's operation spread through Asthall, with siblings and servants alike baffled by Sydney's approval of the procedure. Believing 'The Good Body' would eventually heal itself, Sydney opposed operations, and as with medicine, they were almost taboo. Without an ounce of squeamishness, David stood in the sterile visitors' room, transformed into a makeshift operating theatre, to supervise the operation.

When the anaesthetic wore off, Diana found herself in a huge brocade bed, surrounded by presents. The proclamation on the day of her birth: 'She can't live long,' haunted her siblings. Pamela, quite distressed by the premonition, spent all of her pocket money on a paint box for the patient. For a fleeting moment, Diana was the centre of attention – something, she felt, she could get used to.

2

CLEVER BY ASSOCIATION

The limited surroundings of Asthall Manor and the Oxfordshire countryside was the only world Diana had known. Few outside influences could intrude on her quiet routine which, by the age of 14, included endless hours spent in the library.

During the Eton school holidays, Tom returned to Asthall, bringing with him a fellow pupil. The shy, unassuming 16-year-old introduced himself as James Lees-Milne, known to his friends as Jim. By the end of the visit, his small circle of friends included Diana. Both Jim and Diana were intrigued by one another, and he was bewitched by her beauty as he silently observed her sitting next to Tom as he played the piano. Diana, too, thought Jim quite possibly the cleverest person she knew. She was impressed by his loathing of games and his preference for sitting indoors, listening to classical music and conversing about art and literature. Tom seemed to share an easy-going, brotherly type of affection with Jim, but this schoolboy camaraderie concealed a discreet affair.

The close bond between Diana and Tom reminded Jim of his loneliness and lack of familial ties – he despised his father, saw little of his mother and had nothing in common with his siblings. Adding to this misery, all through his childhood and early adolescent years, Jim wished he were a girl. Society's expectations placed on him as a boy, and his countrified father's disapproval, conspired to make him 'feel desperately ashamed' of his wish. Adding to Jim's feelings of shame was the guilt of his affair with Tom and he desired to replace him with Diana, a socially acceptable catalyst for romance.

After his stay at Asthall, Jim immediately sent Diana a letter, asking her, 'May I treat you as a much cherished sister to whom I can say everything? You don't realise how essential they are to boys. Why are you so amazingly *sympathique* as well as charming?'[2] Surrounded by six sisters and an all-female staff – David and Sydney disapproved of male servants, believing them to be drunken, dirty and unreliable – Diana was unsure of how to respond to such flattery. She acted with indifference, which could have been mistaken as modesty – an appealing attribute in one so beautiful.

Jim returned to Asthall, and soon he, Tom and Diana became a peculiar trio. When the other Mitford children were outside riding and hunting, they spent their days indoors, lapping up joyous hours in the library where Jim expressed his devotion by teaching her to read the greats. They read poetry and fantasised about going to live in Greece, where they 'would scorn material things and live on a handful of grapes by the sea'.

Jim appointed himself as Diana's faithful correspondent and the letters exchanged during this precarious time provide an insight into her outlook. As her intellect developed, she felt comfortable to confide her innermost thoughts to Jim. 'There will never be another Shelley. I wish I had been alive then to marry him. He was more beautiful physically and mentally than an angel.'[3] Her philosophy on life was extremely modern for a sheltered teenager in the 1920s; 'why on earth should two souls (I wish there was a better word, I think SPIRIT is better). Why on earth should two spirits who are in love a bit have to marry … and renounce all other men and women?' Monogamy, to Diana, was 'SUPREMELY foolish', but she was quick to acknowledge that speaking of 'free love is almost a sin'. And, to dispel any hint of romance, she quickly informed Jim of his platonic place in her life, 'I sometimes feel that I love you too much, but you are my spiritual brother.'[4]

It was not only Diana's beauty which served to enchant those who met her; her outward qualities attracted solitary individuals, and those of a lonely or melancholic disposition were drawn in by her friendly demeanour. Her sparkling intelligence, sincere interest in others and natural conversation eased any initial feelings of awkwardness. A victim of Nancy's critique, and used to being reminded that she was the 'least important person in the room', Diana knew only too well the burden of feeling unwanted and unworthy of attention.

Jim was not the only admirer competing for Diana's affection. Clementine and Winston Churchill's only son, Randolph – known as 'The Chumbolly' – had fallen madly in love with her during a visit to Asthall. Clementine was David's first cousin, though it was whispered in family circles that she was the product of a lengthy affair between Bertie Redesdale and his wife's sister, Lady Blanche Hozier. Such rumours remained unfounded, but the eldest Churchill children, Diana – known as Dina – and Randolph were brought up alongside their Mitford cousins. Dina, a year older than Diana, was a highly nervous child prone to dark moods. She tagged alongside Randolph who, with his boisterous behaviour, was often on the receiving end of the grown-ups' disapproval. Randolph was unlike Jim in every way: he lacked Jim's refined aesthetic tastes and, being a year younger than Diana, he held no charm for her.

Relatives falling in love with Diana was not an unusual concept. When she was aged 10, her 16-year-old cousin, Michael Bowles, fell violently in love with her. This disturbing obsession came about after a visit to Asthall, where he had spent the weekend in the company of his rambunctious Mitford cousins. Despite being closer in age to Nancy and Pamela, it was Diana's enthusiasm for life that had a lasting effect on the lonely schoolboy. Like Jim, Michael felt isolated in his home life, and this loneliness was emphasised by his unhappy experience at Marlborough.

Diana was oblivious to the true nature of Michael's passion and she politely received his letters with an air of detachment. Michael went to great efforts to ensure his letters escaped the attention of David and Sydney, and he convinced the family's parlour maid, Mabel, to act as his channel to Diana. To the horror of Mabel, David learned of this infatuation with his daughter, when Michael wistfully wrote: 'I suppose we must wait six years and then you will be old enough to marry.'

Without questioning Diana about the correspondence – entirely one sided on Michael's behalf – David stormed into Marlborough with the intention to kill the boy. Intruding into the dorm that Michael shared with his friend Mitchell, David roared, 'Is this Michael Bowles's room? My name is Redesdale and I want to talk to him!' David's temper so terrified Mitchell that he ran off to find his lovelorn friend. 'Somebody called Redesdale has come to see you,' he said, hardly taking a moment to catch his breath. 'You've got to hide for a couple of hours until he goes away, otherwise I think he'll kill you.' Michael successfully hid and David departed. Michael was so disturbed by David's reaction that he ceased contact with Diana for forty years.

The story of Michael Bowles was a cautionary tale for future suitors, and Randolph, already wary of David's quick temper, restrained his admiration during visits to Asthall. Randolph would have to wait until Diana was old enough to visit his family home before openly pursuing her.

Soon, the trivialities of family life evaporated into the background. James Lees-Milne once said, 'My world was the only real world.' But Diana was not content to live vicariously through the characters in the books that she read and she looked further afield to broaden her horizons.

3

A DEMI PARADISE

The Churchill family home, Chartwell, situated on a heavenly, tree-crowned hill overlooking a view to the south over the Weald of Kent, served as a portal of escapism for Diana during her first visit in the summer of 1924. The regal history of the house captured her imagination: Henry VIII had stayed there during his courtship of Anne Boleyn, whose family seat, Hever Castle, was located close by. Winston Churchill commissioned the architect Sir Phillip Tilden to modernise the exterior of the house, and he extended the building between 1924 and 1926, but the original red brick remained intact, complete with tile hung gables and tiny oriel windows.

With an outburst of impulsive critique, Diana crushed Randolph when she announced that Chartwell was not as aesthetically pleasing as Asthall. Though, as the stay progressed, she realised the freedom granted to the 'brats' – a Churchillian term of endearment – compensated for its cosmetic shortcomings. This freedom came in the form of a tree house, constructed in the fork of a great lime on the front driveway. Access to the house was by a rope ladder, quickly pulled up to preserve the privacy of 'the big ones': Randolph and Diana Churchill and Diana and Tom Mitford. When they were not hiding in the tree house, Randolph proudly held court with Diana.

They made a striking pair, with Randolph the eager suitor standing several inches shorter than Diana, who at 14 was already edging towards her adult height of 5ft 10in. As Diana grew older – perhaps there was a hint of truth in the rumours surrounding Clementine's paternity – she strongly resembled his mother, with whom he had a complicated relationship.

Ever the hospitable companion, Randolph delighted in showing Diana the beautiful grounds surrounding the house. A hillside fell away to a lake fed by a spring, the Chartwell, and alongside the valley was a scattering of beech woods sheltering the house from the north and east. They explored the house together and no rooms were off-limits to the children, with the exception of Churchill's bedroom and study. When the children were sent to the study, often on an errand to deliver a message, they were instructed to remain completely silent, as noise of any variety, especially whistling, was met by a thunderous roar of displeasure from Churchill.

Diana was fond of 'Cousin Clementine', whom she praised as 'beautiful and kind', and 'Cousin Winston' made an impression on her as 'a perennial wonder'. To her own children – most especially Randolph and his sister Diana – Clementine was a difficult character to fathom. She was extremely demanding when it suited her and the children dreaded the emotional storms that lurked beneath her otherwise aloof personality. Churchill was largely absent, but when present he would indulge his attentions onto Randolph, treating him as though he were his most cherished possession, and the affection bestowed by his father gave the boy an air of arrogance. Struck by Diana's extraordinary beauty, Churchill thrilled her with the nickname 'Dina-mite'.

Randolph's immature sense of humour struck a familiar chord with Diana. Nancy, too, verged on childishness; it was a form of escapism for a generation that had seen its elder brothers and fathers killed on the battlefields of the Somme. Although quite the norm in behaviour for debutantes of the twenties when an entire decade was caught up in an everlasting adolescence, Diana found Randolph's stunted personality exasperating and unattractive. Despite his idiosyncrasies, she praised the lighter side of Randolph's character, especially his eagerness to please her. In an attempt to keep Diana to himself, Randolph invited her to watch Clementine play tennis and they spent endless hours alone strolling in the gardens.

The visits to Chartwell corresponded with school holidays, but for Randolph they always seemed painfully short. A feeling reciprocated in Diana, but for unromantic reasons. When she returned to Asthall, she longed for the comforts of Chartwell with its pretty rooms, indulgent food and fascinating guests. 'I loved the [Churchill] family,' Diana said, fifty years later. 'When people say Clementine was so cold, well, she was particularly kind to us and, to me particularly, wonderful.' To the outside world, Clementine was the picture of serenity and self-control, something Diana could mimic. Their personalities were alike; Clementine's coldness was also apparent in Diana's own nature and as she matured she honed this side of her personality to contrast with her extreme kindness, which she would overindulge onto those she liked best.

Randolph wrote to Diana, inviting her to return to Chartwell – a lure she could never resist. 'My darling Diana, I am so longing to see you before I go back to Eton.' Inviting her to stay for the weekend, Randolph boldly informed her that his parents and siblings were staying elsewhere (the Churchill family's nanny, Cousin Moppet, would be on hand as a suitable chaperone). 'I will come and pick you up and deposit you again on the Monday ...' Should an air of indecency lurk in his suggestion, he advised Diana to tell her mother three significant things: she had visited the previous year under similar circumstances; they were, after all, family; and 'Darling Randolph' – as he referred to himself – was returning to Eton soon, before which, he would be all alone. Randolph's sympathetic appeal floundered once Diana mentioned it to Sydney.

Sydney decided that Diana's visits to Chartwell had been plentiful. Diana often said that her mother took pleasure in saying no to her children, without bothering to explain the reasoning behind her decision. Both Sydney and David were mindful of their children indulging in a liberal sense of fun, and enjoyment outside of Asthall was to be dispensed in frugal measures. This lack of enthusiasm for Chartwell was founded on Diana's endless chatter about the procession of guests spilling through the front door for supper, tennis matches with Cousin Clementine and private political conferences with Cousin Winston, then a hub of excitement for the impressionable teenager. 'I'm sure Chartwell's lovely,' Sydney often said, as she stretched out her arms, yawning to demonstrate her boredom. 'Clementine is so clever,' was about all she could muster.

When referring to their father's absence from parliament, the Churchill children often hypothetically asked, 'What is the use of a WC without a seat?' By the time Sydney permitted Diana to return to Chartwell, Winston Churchill was back in parliament as Chancellor of the Exchequer in Stanley Baldwin's Conservative government. Interesting guests were forever coming and going from Chartwell, unlike at Asthall where Sydney and David loathed entertaining. With her longing for culture, Diana always fixed her attention on the most intellectual visitor in the room. The conversation at dinner often centred on a political theme and, perhaps for the first time, Diana was exposed to casual political references. Edward Stanley, a cousin from David and Clementine's side of the family, was asked by Churchill over dinner if he was a Liberal – the traditional political view in the modern-thinking Stanley family. 'No,' answered Edward. He was, in fact, a Conservative politician; Churchill's question was in jest.

'Why not?' implored Churchill, goading his in-law.

Having served as Secretary of State for War under Lloyd George in 1916, Edward spoke candidly when he informed Churchill that he could not belong to a party led by Lloyd George. Upon which, Churchill launched into an argument glorifying his old friend and former leader, as to convert at least one of his listeners. Diana was one of those listeners; she observed the argument and collected her thoughts, but it would be set aside for a later date. The political tension did not last and Churchill was quick to overlook any acid remarks from an opponent. Always larger than life and filled with bonhomie, he gave an impromptu solo of *Soldiers of the Queen*, beating time with his large, white hand.

Brendan Bracken was another guest who seemed to be a permanent fixture at the Churchill table, much to the annoyance of Clementine who could not tolerate the young man. The Irish-born Bracken spent a delinquent childhood, he often vandalised neighbours' gardens and threw one of his schoolfellows into a canal, and this spirited behaviour, so similar to Randolph's, endeared him to Churchill. In 1923, Bracken organised Churchill's political campaign and accompanying him to the family home, he slept, uninvited, on the sofa in Clementine's drawing room with his shoes on.

Diana, too, was unsure of what to make of Bracken with his thick red hair and black teeth. An American guest echoed Diana's thoughts when he said, 'Everything about the man is phony. Even his hair, which looks like a wig, is his own.' Bracken was said to be the illegitimate son of Churchill, and Randolph and his sister delighted in making teasing remarks about this unspoken subject. Diana Churchill confirmed this when she told Diana, 'There's a rumour that Mr Bracken is papa's *son*.' With a shrill giggle, Randolph added, 'Mummy won't call him Brendan because she's so afraid he might call her Clemmie.'

As always, the visit to Chartwell was never long enough and Diana soon returned to Asthall. She found fault with her daily life; Sydney's running of the house – in contrast to Chartwell with its army of servants – and the company of her eldest sisters could not replace the stimulating conversations she had been privy to. Unlike most aristocratic families, David and Sydney could not afford to employ footmen; they could scarcely afford their small staff as it was. To pay their wages, Sydney kept chickens whose eggs she sold to London restaurants.

The lack of disposable staff presented a problem as the girls grew older. To remedy this, Sydney and David agreed the girls could go out but only if they kept in a group. It was suffocating for Diana, who craved privacy, to venture out with her sisters trailing behind her. As she walked along the main road in the village, Diana daydreamed of a handsome young man stopping his car and proposing they drive together to the ends of the earth. 'If some crazy individual had really suggested carrying me off in this way I am sure I should have gone with him,' she admitted. In hindsight, David was not wrong in ensuring his restless middle daughter was constantly chaperoned.

In 1926, a few months shy of her sixteenth birthday, Diana began to take notice of society and of her place in it. As a girl, and upper class at that, her options were limited. Unlike working-class girls, Diana would not have been encouraged to find employment, regardless of David's threats about their lack of inheritance.

When not at Chartwell, Diana was kept in the dark about most current affairs. At the breakfast table, David went through his normal morning routine of reading the newspaper, and it was through such second-hand tales that she learned of the latest developments. There was no reason why Diana should want to learn of the news, nor would she have been thought of as having a forward-thinking opinion, or, in fact, any opinion at all.

At Chartwell, Diana had received a speedy education and she witnessed the heated political discussions first hand. Clementine thrived on debate, loud arguments and controversy, and all of her life she was actively interested in politics. It was a sharp contrast to Sydney, who supported the Conservative Party, not particularly for their manifesto – if she knew it – but because it was the accepted thing for upper-class women of her generation.

Diana began to see the vacuity of her mother's beliefs and she adopted the habit of slowly chipping away at the opposition – in the form of her parents – until an argument ensued. She was not so foolish as to challenge authority without having solid evidence to argue her case, but her parents seemed incapable of debate; David simply roared, and Sydney became silent, or vague. Diana longed for more and she felt a need to vocalise her views. This was encouraged by Churchill, who invited the 'brats' to sit in on his political debates and, unlike other children of that era, they were not shunned to another room or kept in the dark about current affairs. It was a foreign and exciting world for Diana and she absorbed the differing opinions on the General Strike; a seminal event in twentieth-century English history that had been intensifying for months.

Flexing her newfound knowledge, Diana tried to engage her family in conversation about the strike, but was immediately silenced by her strike-opposing parents. Most of the aristocracy viewed the strike as nothing more than an inconvenience and some went so far to accuse the strikers, who were protesting their working conditions and meagre pay, of being criminals. Many echoed this sentiment, seeing it as nothing more than a hiccup in public services. Nothing much happened beyond the fact that the buses and tubes were driven instead by good-looking undergraduates.[5]

Nancy and Pamela worked shifts at a local canteen serving tea and sandwiches to strike-breaking lorry drivers, and Nancy sought to turn a national emergency into a joke when she dressed up as a lecherous tramp to frighten Pamela. Disheartened by her family's lack of interest in the strike, Diana eagerly accepted an invitation to return to Chartwell, the centre and source of her intellect.

From Chartwell, Diana followed the progress of the strike with great excitement. Tensions mounted and Diana observed the many political debates going back and forth between Churchill and members of the Cabinet. Churchill and the Conservative government were unanimous in their agreement to oppose the strike. The prime minister, Stanley Baldwin, argued that the Trade Union Congress was using it as a political weapon and the most favourable way to retain social reform was through a parliamentary election. After four days of striking, the situation reached a pivotal point. However, there were no newspapers due to the print unions striking, and the public remained completely uninformed. To ease public worry, the government printed its own version of a newspaper, the *British Gazette*, edited by Churchill himself.

It was a common view at the time, at least for those who opposed the Conservative government, that Churchill and other 'militant' cabinet members were hungry for a strike, knowing they had back-up workers to act in severe circumstances. Diana, too, felt it slightly unnerving that the government could swoop in and take over public services, so vital to everyday life, including the printing of a newspaper. She also suspected that this far-reaching control allowed those in power to keep a firm hand over everything that was fed to the mass public.

From the late 1930s and onward, Diana held the belief that Churchill had been a warmonger.[6] She was not yet aware of the rogue political parties stirring behind the scenes and she was oblivious of the appeal of the Communist Party to the working classes, who felt short-changed by the lack of sympathy from the (predominantly upper-class) politicians towards their working conditions.

With an objective stance, Diana pondered her views on the General Strike; she had listened intently to Churchill's argument against it and she learned, from limited resources – newspapers and second-hand facts – of the plight of the miners. After much deliberation, she decided that her sympathies lay with the miners. From the age of 16, Diana developed an anti-Tory stance and declared herself a Lloyd George Liberal.

She returned to Asthall, eager to share her new worldly views. But righting the wrongs of society would have to wait. Diana was about to embark on another milestone in her young life. She was off to Paris for a year.

4

AN AGE WITHOUT A NAME

Paris, caught between the world wars, was bustling with excitement. The epitome of the roaring twenties, the jazz age brought rich American tourists and bohemian writers alike to sample the cosmopolitan delights the city had to offer. At the age of 16, Diana was too young to indulge in the social outlets and too high born to experience the heady lifestyle had she been of age. The reconstruction of the Boulevard Haussmann, damaged by bombs during the First World War, was underway and Paris was once again a vibrant, metropolitan city not yet plunged into austerity by the Great Depression.

David and Sydney brought their children to Paris under less than glamorous circumstances, but, nevertheless, it was viewed as an adventure. David managed to sell Asthall Manor and with the money he received from the sale he set about building his dream home, Swinbrook House. The final phase of building was not yet completed and the family, along with their pet gerbils, decided to economise by taking cheap lodgings in the Villa St Honoré d'Eylau, a small family run hotel. The reality of living in Paris thrilled Diana, and she and her siblings clung to glamour through second-hand tales and the workings of their own overactive imaginations.

The cautionary tale of the young fashion designer, Suzanne Geoffre, did not escape Diana's attention. She was enthralled by the bizarre tabloid stories about Mlle Geoffre, who had approached a surgeon to make her calves thinner. The well-known plastic surgeon, Dr Leopold Levy, agreed to the operation, which went horribly wrong and resulted in the amputation of Mlle Geoffre's leg. The trial between Mlle Geoffre and the plastic surgeon was played out in the press and the judge ruled in favour of the patient, stating that the surgeon should not have performed a dangerous operation in the name of beauty. The topic of beauty would govern Diana's Parisian experience.

Whilst in Paris, Sydney rekindled her friendship with the celebrated artist Paul César Helleu, who, in the years before her marriage, had immortalised her in a painting. Now this admiration transferred to Sydney's children. Smitten by her offspring, his painter's eye appreciated the fine colouring of their blonde hair and blue eyes, with the exception of Nancy, who possessed the dramatic colouring of black hair and green eyes. But it was Diana who charmed Helleu. She, in particular, he likened to a Greek goddess.

If Chartwell had been an education for Diana, then Paris was an awakening. She also became conscious of her effect on French men and their blatant display of pleasure at her beauty. 'Wherever I go I am looked on as the eighth wonder of the world, at last,'[7] she boasted.

In comparison to Diana's youthfulness, Helleu, advancing in his sixth decade, was considered an old man, but his liberal outlook did not let something as trivial as their vast age difference prevent him from admiring her looks. '*Tu es la femme la plus voluptuesse*,'* he often praised her. From a cynical point of view it was hardly an appropriate adornment for Diana who, at 16, stood at the statuesque height of 5ft 10in, with a slim physique to match.

Caught in the limbo between childhood and adulthood, Diana overlooked Helleu's compliments, and her attention was absorbed by his drawing room. She found his collection of Louis XVI furniture, especially the chairs upholstered in white and grey silk, to be aesthetically pleasing. She was curious as to why Helleu hung empty eighteenth-century gilt wooden frames on his walls. His answer was far more peculiar than his action. He advised Diana that if one was not rich enough to possess the pictures one wished for, it was best to have empty frames and use one's imagination. She thought this the height of sophistication. Diana was further elated when Helleu drew her into his confidence, telling her that he admired three things above all else: women, racehorses and sailing boats.

Having come to terms with her middle daughter's advanced intelligence, or perhaps as a distraction to save her from becoming bored, Sydney took the initiative and enrolled Diana in art lessons at the Cours Fénelon. During the customary interview with the headmistress, Sydney was asked of Diana's vaccination history. Diana had never been vaccinated, Sydney confessed – it was one of her deepest aversions along with 'murdered food' (white bread, pasteurised milk and pork). 'Then I regret she cannot come to the Cours Fénelon until you have it done,' the headmistress said.

---

* 'You are the most voluptuous woman.'

'I am sorry,' replied Sydney, unbending in her beliefs. 'She cannot be vaccinated.'

After a long pause, as Diana's fate hung in the balance, the headmistress announced: 'Oh, tant pis.'* Despite the protests and the prior stalemate between Sydney and the headmistress, Diana was eventually accepted.

Ironically, given her restlessness at home, Diana had always been violently opposed to boarding school (such fears were founded on her notion that it would have a 'zoo-like smell'). It was surprising to everyone, not least Diana herself, when she entered the Cours Fénelon art programme and found that she loved it. The ease in which she had settled into her lessons sprang from a bemused curiosity for her fellow pupils. The pupils, mostly from aristocratic French families, came from richer backgrounds than Diana, and she was intrigued by their habit of bringing a governess to sit next to them during lessons, or a footman, who was deposed to the cloakroom to wait amongst the satchels and coats until home time.

Sitting in the classroom of over thirty pupils, Diana would gaze out the window at the Rue de la Pompe, and her habit of daydreaming contributed to her missing vital parts of the lessons. This point was proven when Diana and her classmates, escorted by an elderly governess, Mlle Foucauld, attended Cours Proper, where they were lectured to and questioned by visiting professors from the Sorbonne. When questions were directed at Diana, she desperately scanned the room for Mlle Foucauld, and tilting her ear, she barely heard the elderly lady whispering the correct answer. Although seldom given, the reply, 'Très bien, Mademoiselle Meetfor', was the one she longed to hear.

Diana and her fellow pupils lived for their twenty minute break, given halfway through the school day. As the bell rang, the excitable girls charged down the staircase to the courtyard, interrupted by Mlle Foucauld's exhausted cries, 'Ne dégringolez pas les escaliers!'** It was Mlle Foucauld's mission to turn the boisterous girls into young ladies. After the lessons, Diana walked 100 yards around the corner, to take afternoon tea with Nanny Blor and her siblings at the hotel. This ordinary advancement in being permitted to walk home alone meant the world to Diana, as it was the first time she had been allowed to walk without a chaperone, along a city street.

This freedom was confined to Paris, as Diana learned when the family returned to England to spend the Christmas holidays in London. When David sold Asthall Manor, he garnered enough profit to afford a lease on an elegant, seven-storey townhouse at 26 Rutland Gate. Although both David and Sydney

---

* 'Oh, much worse.'

** 'Do not tumble down the stairs.'

had little tolerance for city life, the girls were delighted by the house's close proximity to Knightsbridge. The eldest girls were allowed to walk to Harrods without a chaperone, but once again, as in the countryside, they were only allowed out in a group. Under normal circumstances the thought would have provoked an argument from Diana about 'life's great unfairness', but instead she bided her time and looked forward to returning to Paris for the new school term.

In the new year of 1927, Diana prepared to travel to Paris, this time without her parents and siblings. Travelling alone in those days was strictly forbidden for a young, unmarried girl of her social class. The idea of sending a member of staff, or worse still paying for a chaperone to accompany Diana, troubled Sydney. Much to her relief, the journey coincided with Winston Churchill's visit to meet Mussolini and he offered to drop Diana off in Paris on his way to Rome.

Randolph accompanied his father and he was thrilled to see Diana again after her long absence from Chartwell. A year had made all the difference and Diana, who was always slightly taller than Randolph, towered over the diminutive boy. Randolph's hope of cutting a dashing figure was further thwarted when he fell victim to acute seasickness, brought on by the rough Channel crossing. 'Poor little boy!' Churchill said when Diana told him of Randolph's plight. She was struck by Churchill's sympathy for his son; nobody pitied her if she was sick on the Channel.

Upon reaching the Gare du Nord, Diana spied two elderly sisters with whom Sydney had made boarding arrangements. She summarised her immediate observations of the elderly sisters, 'One of them is horrid and wears a wig, the other is downtrodden and nice.' Pressed for time before catching his connecting train to Rome, Churchill swiftly entrusted Diana into their care and the three left for her new dwellings at 135 Avenue Victor-Hugo.

The elderly sisters' apartment was not luxurious in any sense of the word, and Diana was alarmed to discover the French taste, which she held in such high esteem, seemed to have been lost on her landladies. If the outside was grim, Diana thought the inside was strictly primitive. She was allocated a bedroom in the basement, its window level with the pavement, with tightly clamped shutters that were never opened during the daytime lest a pedestrian should try to break in. The room was constantly dark, and as Diana lay in bed she could hear the hustle and bustle of footsteps on the pavement and the revolting chorus of men clearing their throats and spitting.

The Dickensian surroundings extended to basic hygiene. Diana was permitted to bathe twice a week in a miniscule tin tub, brought into her bedroom for the occasion, whereupon a maid filled it with a scalding kettle, counteracted by a jug of cold water. The balance was never quite right and the bath to Diana's dismay, was freezing. She wrote a long letter to Sydney, moaning of her discomforts and was sent enough money for an occasional bath at the Villa St Honoré d'Eylau. The elderly ladies thought this very extravagant and an insult to their hospitality. Owing to Diana's displeasure with her living arrangements, a frosty relationship ensued.

Despite the discomfort, Diana found the location useful with its close proximity to the Cours Fénelon, her violin lessons near the Lycée Janson and Helleu's apartment. Diana walked to all three places without a chaperone and the freedom was intoxicating. Emboldened by this freedom, she took the first step towards adulthood and cut her waist length hair into a shingled bob – a popular trend in the late twenties. David affirmed to the Edwardian view of how women should look, preferring women with long hair and their faces free of make-up. Given her father's stance, Diana would have hesitated to cut off her hair had she remained at home. When Nancy first cut her hair, David recoiled in horror, proclaiming that no self-respecting man would want to marry her. Sydney sided with David, and she commented, 'No one would look at you twice now.' Having learned of Diana's rebellion, David teased that her new look was 'a symbol of decadent immorality'.

It had been almost a month since Helleu last set eyes on Diana, and her short hair, he opined, was ghastly, but it did little to diminish her looks. In her spare time, Helleu escorted Diana around Le Louvre and the Château de Versailles, giving her impromptu lessons on paintings, fine art and sculpture. After their day-long excursions, he treated Diana to luncheon where she ordered Sole Dieppoise and Sancerre. Although infatuated by her appearance, his behaviour was always proper. Seizing this moment of high spirits, Helleu asked her to sit for a portrait. There was no question of what her answer would be, for Diana it was the ultimate compliment.

'I pose for endless pictures,' Diana confided in a letter to James Lees-Milne, and Helleu's flattering comments, she claimed, 'never become boring because they are always unexpected.' Helleu sketched and painted Diana several times, and his most favourable piece was a dry-point etching of her head in profile view. The strong lines detailed her ethereal beauty: an attractive jawline, emphasised by her shingled hair, cut as short as a boy's at the back with the sides reaching her ears, formed into soft waves.

The sketch was reproduced in the popular magazine *L'Illustration*, and the prolific recognition turned Diana into a minor celebrity at the Cours Fénelon. The excitement was short-lived and the elderly sisters hastened to plant a dart; 'Helleu?' they hissed at the modern-looking girl sitting before them. 'It is not Helleu to me at all. Frankly I think it is very pre-war.'

Helleu's flattery was never ending and, rather blinded by Diana's beauty, he expected his fellow artists to share his enthusiasm. He brought her to visit his friend, the sculptor Troubetzkoy, who at the time was working on a head of Venizelos, the Greek politician. *'Bonjour, monsieur, la voici la Grèce!'** Helleu jubilantly cried as he pointed to Diana, standing before the sculptor in her plain clothing and her face devoid of makeup. Venizelos, engrossed in his work, cast a lacklustre eye over Diana, before turning away, barely acknowledging her. She felt a fool and thought her exuberant old friend had gone too far. To the sculptor and politician (and many of the grown-ups around her) she was merely going through what the French so lyrically called *'l'âge ingrat'* – the awkward age.

Sensing that her husband's young friend was pining for familiar home comforts, Madame Helleu provided Diana with an inviting atmosphere away from the Avenue Victor-Hugo. After lessons, she would drop in for tea and often stayed to supper, indulging in Madame Helleu's heavenly cuisine of roast veal, boeuf en gelée, îles flottantes and rich black chocolate cake. Helleu loved to see Diana eat and he would happily exclaim: *'Mais prenez, prenez donc!'*** The Helleus' daughter, Paulette, although several years older than Diana, became a critical friend. Paulette found fault with Diana's clumsy homemade clothing and her lack of make-up, still strictly forbidden. She might have attacked Diana's weak spots, but she could not deny her beauty, and that sparked an unspoken rivalry between the artist's daughter and his adolescent muse.

The once friendly letters exchanged between Diana and James Lees-Milne had slowly dwindled to complete silence. After Diana's departure for Paris, Jim became morbidly obsessed with a recent divorcee, Joanie, the daughter of his mother's cousin. Jim sent her love poetry – the typical gesture he would use time and time again with those he admired – and Joanie responded by driving down to Eton to take him to tea. In the New Year of 1926, they eventually began an affair, resulting in Joanie becoming pregnant. However, there is no certainty that Jim fathered the child, for she had so many casual affairs. The baby[8] was stillborn, and he was haunted by guilt, stemming from his view that he had caused a human life, conceived in sin, to perish. Deeply disturbed by the incident, Jim fled England for Grenoble, where he studied a university course in French.

---

*   'Hello, Sir, here is Greece!'

** 'Eat, so eat!'

Jim's thoughts turned to Diana and the memories he held from their happier days in the library at Asthall Manor. The notion of being in love with an unworldly teenager was less troublesome than his love affair with the older Joanie, whose life came to a tragic end when she drowned herself in Monte Carlo.

Filled with a sense of nostalgia, Jim wrote to Diana, playing to her frivolous vanity by addressing her as 'Mona' (after the *Mona Lisa*). Her letter, after a spell of silence 'dropped here today like the gentle dew from heaven. I cannot express my delight but imagine it as being intense ... How I would adore to have a picture of you by M. Helleu.' He implored Diana to send him a memento; a snapshot of her Parisian self so he could see for himself if she had retained her Raphael face. 'You can't imagine what a joy it is to me the thought of having your face with me.'[9]

Diana was becoming accustomed to receiving compliments on her beauty, rather than her brains, and the tokens dispelled in his letters were not a rarity. Jim confessed: 'One can never love a friend too much,' though by now he thought of her as something 'higher than a friend'. As for Diana, she was secretly pleased with his infatuation and had begun to recognise her power over the opposite sex, using it to exploit those who cared about her. Her letters adopted a priggish tone, boasting of her liaisons with French boys, after which, she warned Jim, 'Don't feel jealous.'

It thrilled Diana to evoke feelings of jealousy, to torment the poor love-sick Jim, when she, herself, had been the victim of Nancy's cruel teasing and Paulette Helleu's condescending treatment. Now, it seemed, Diana had the upper hand and she made it clear to Jim that she only confided in him because he was 'so far from England's green and pleasant land, where scandal travels fast'.

Diana's liberal lifestyle in Paris continued and she had become an expert in deceiving the elderly ladies. Although she was permitted to venture out alone during the daytime, Diana was forbidden to go out in the evening without a chaperone. She cared little for their rules and she feigned invitations to sit for Helleu, or cited extra music lessons with her violin instructor. Once out of their supervision, Diana met the young man in question. She juggled several suitors, always escaping with them to the darkness of the cinema, then the height of sophistication for a teenager. She spoke confidently of a trip in a taxi around the Bois de Boulogne with a boy named Charlie (Charles de Breuil), a fairly rich count, extraordinarily handsome, but very vain.

Before Diana had encountered Charlie, she enjoyed a flirtation with a young suitor named Bill Astor, heir to Viscount Astor and his immense fortune. Diana said little of her experiences with Bill, except that she had only flirted with Charlie because French flirting interested her and because it made her think of Bill. At a loss for words, Jim praised her mental fidelity towards the unsuspecting admirer.

Diana dutifully penned chatty letters to her mother, but Sydney was too pre-occupied with the preparations for Nancy and Pamela's parties – they had already come out as debutantes but had failed to become engaged – to give much thought to her younger daughter's daily life. A dull round of lessons, she imagined. Only Diana and her diary knew the truth.

Neither Sydney nor David relished the idea of entertaining and they made a dreary saga of the details, writing to Diana, 'The dance is turning into an immense bore ...' Sydney sent Diana a parcel containing a pair of 'evening knickers' and a dark-blue silk dress with white polka dots. Diana was delighted with the underwear, a sophisticated treat having only just shed the fleece-lined liberty bodice her nanny forced the children to wear. The euphoria dimmed when she tried on the silk dress, only to discover it was too big.

The whirlwind of Diana's social life did not interfere with her schooling, and her end of term report that March spoke glowingly of her '*parfait*' conduct, describing her as '*excellente élève dont nous garderons le meilleur souvenir*'.[*]

The glittering atmosphere was not to last; Helleu fell gravely ill and his death from peritonitis at the end of March was a bitter blow to Diana's self-esteem. The man she worshipped, and who for three months had worshipped her, was dead. 'I shall never see him again ...' her letter ached with melancholy '... never hear his voice saying, "Sweetheart, *comme tu es belle*".'[**]

Shortly before Helleu's death, Diana had called at his flat, hoping to visit her ailing friend. Paulette answered the door. 'May I see him?' She desperately asked.

'Of course *not*.' Paulette brusquely turned her away.

In a sad letter to Jim, Diana wrote, 'Nobody will admire me again as he did.'[***] Jim might have disagreed, but he refrained from telling her otherwise and wrote only to console her.

---

[*]   'An excellent pupil, we will keep the best memories.'

[**]   'Sweetheart, you are beautiful.'

[***] Reflecting on this comment in her old age, Diana said: 'What a horrifying little beast I must have been.'

5

THE UNHAPPY YOUTH

'I have grown a little older, and more intense in my passions of love, sorrow and worship of beauty. To look at, I am the same. Pray for me, to your gods whatever they are. I am very unhappy,' Diana wrote to James Lees-Milne. The melancholic mood was to last. When she returned to England for the Easter holidays, she was further disenchanted by the family's new home, Swinbrook House.

Swinbrook was truly monstrous, inside and out. The building's exterior could have been, according to Diana's younger sister Jessica, anything from a mental institution to a girls' boarding school or an American country club. It was so unlike Sydney to care little about a house and it puzzled the older girls why she had overlooked such an important project. David had a free hand in the design of the house and, unlike Asthall Manor with its Jacobean architecture, Swinbrook was a large, rectangular grey structure with an interior decorated in mock-rustic charm. The drabness of the house was a disappointment for Diana and her sisters, all except Deborah, who loved it.

The greatest insult for Diana was the lack of creative outlets and the privacy that was so freely enjoyed in the library at Asthall. There was no library in Swinbrook, no place where the older children could be alone, and Tom's piano was placed in the drawing room. He hardly ever played, as he did not care to when people barged in and out, slamming doors and carrying on loud conversations with little regard for his musical practice. The only form of entertainment was an indoor squash court, impossible to play in with its bare, windowless walls and deafening echo.

There were no fires in the individual bedrooms and despite the costly installation of central heating, the rooms were always cold. Diana sought refuge in the linen cupboard, huddling next to the heating pipes as she lost herself in a world of literature. Her favourite writers were Lytton Strachey, Bertrand Russell, Aldous Huxley and J.B.S. Haldane, because of their rejection of accepted social standards.

'Go out, darling,' Sydney encouraged her. 'Of course you're cold if you sit indoors reading all day.' Diana had no desire to go out, as she had outgrown the rough and tumble games that her little sisters Unity, Jessica and Deborah still enjoyed. Diana moped around Swinbrook, taking daily walks with Pamela to ease the boredom of life at home. Her independence, she felt, had been stolen from her and the suffering she experienced with the death of Helleu hardened her.

Somewhere beneath this morbid facade, Diana was still a romantic at heart. She was intelligent enough to realise that not all relationships were platonic. Jim's letters from that time, although an escape from the dullness of everyday life, drew her attention to his love for her. In a sophisticated manner, she declared, 'Sex is after all so unimportant in life. Beauty and art are what matter. Older people do not see my point of view.' Diana failed to elaborate on the 'older people', surely a jibe at Jim, who was two years her senior. She did not, however, discourage the correspondence.

In a similar light as Helleu, Jim praised her looks, perhaps hoping to evoke a sense of familiarity, but it did not work. 'I have got dark skin and light hair and eyes which is an unattractive paradox,' she chastised him. In the same sentence, Diana asked if he had seen the various beauties: Mary Thynne, Lettice Lygon and Georgie Curzon, to name a few. Jim's passion could not be quelled, so Diana accepted his gift of books and often shared her critique of his poetry.

Finally, Jim was reunited with Diana in person. The sight of her in the flesh stunned him at first. She was no longer the sweet-natured 14-year-old girl he had mentored in the library at Asthall. The long hair, which he had admired and likened to Botticelli's seaborne *Venus* was gone. Although not outwardly fashionable, she began to alter her looks to appear more grown up in her appearance. This adult version of Diana inspired the same feelings of passion he had felt for Joanie, who wore chic clothes and Parisian scent.

Preoccupied in instigating a romance with Diana, Jim impulsively sent her a poem.[10] Diana's response was not what he had anticipated, and with a critical eye she advised him, 'Read Alice Meynell's short essay on false impressionism called *The Point of Honour*. This is not meant to be rude ...' Taking on an intellectual tone, she confidently told him, 'Byron was a selfish, beautiful genius and not really more selfish than many men and most artists. As to Augusta, she was of the same temperament as I am, and just about as silly.'

Although she was 17 and soon to be coming out as a debutante, Diana was still viewed as a child and, given her status, she was excluded from Nancy and Pamela's social gatherings. The guest list was made up of Nancy's clever and artistic friends, most of whom were high-camp homosexuals who swooped down from Oxford, puzzling Sydney, delighting the little sisters and enraging David. Diana and her sisters would largely surround themselves with 'irresistible' homosexual men all of their adult lives.

During such a gathering, an acquaintance of her older sisters, named Bill (she did not confide if it was Bill Astor), was at Swinbrook for a supper dance. After supper, at about 10 o'clock, Bill slipped away from the party and found himself at Diana's bedroom door. Improperly dressed in only her nightgown, she rushed out to greet him with a kiss on the lips. The entire ordeal, Diana told Jim, lasted about thirty seconds before she pushed Bill away and slammed the door in his face. She was afraid of Sydney's reaction should she get caught, and the severity of her action suddenly struck her with a sense of morality, 'I have quite chucked the Frenchmen, they are nasty, sensual brutes really.' She did not elaborate on whether she was turning her attention towards English men.

Diana may have exerted a liberal attitude towards fleeting flirtations, but she was not so discreet in concealing her liaisons from prying eyes. One afternoon, after sitting at Sydney's desk to write in her diary, she joined Pamela for a walk. During the walk, it dawned on her that she had left the diary not only on Sydney's desk, but also open. The girls raced home, hoping the opened diary had gone unnoticed. It was too late, and by the time Diana reached the house, Sydney had read about not only her sittings with Helleu, but of her unchaperoned evenings with Charlie and the other young men. A row escalated into a bitter exchange of words, with Sydney accusing Diana of being 'wanton' and exclaiming, 'Nobody would ask you to their houses if they knew *half* of what you had done!'

The diary, a piece of sordid literature to Sydney, was swiftly burned and evidence of Diana's shocking trysts no longer existed on paper, except for what she had confessed to Jim. Diana's privacy had been violated, but her punishment was even worse. She was withdrawn from the Cours Fénelon, where she was due to return after the Easter holidays. Diana consumed her meals in uncomfortable and guilty silence, with both parents staring at her as though she had committed a grievous sin.

Diana was furious at the lack of support from her older siblings. Only Pamela had shown a glimmer of sympathy when she tried to save the diary from Sydney's clutches, but that vanished when she reminded Diana of her stupidity in leaving it out in the open. Nancy accused Diana of being 'a bundle of sex with no soul' and

Tom agreed. She was deeply hurt by Tom's betrayal, 'I will never be anything but cold towards him until he owns himself wrong.'

In spite of Sydney and Nancy's accusations, Diana's virtue remained intact. For Jim, plagued by his own borderline sordid affairs with his fellow schoolmates at Eton and his cousin Joanie, it would have mattered little had she compromised herself with another man. For Sydney, the damage was done. With Paris out of the question, Diana, who had briefly enjoyed independence, was demoted to nursery life. She was sent to her great aunt Maude's pretty cottage at Bucks Mill in Devon, along with Nanny Blor, Unity, Jessica and Deborah.

The macabre surroundings of Bucks Mill held no mystique for Diana. The cottage, said to be a built above a smugglers' cave, clung to the edge of a cliff, overlooking a waterfall below. The younger sisters delighted in the thrilling story of their summer lodgings, but Diana was too disgruntled at the practice of bathing once again, as she had done in Paris, in a tin bathtub placed before the kitchen coal range.

Diana's plight was emphasised by her lack of money, no cultural outlets and the bleak and humiliating company of her younger sisters and ageing relatives. Nancy sent Diana gloating letters, boasting of endless dances in London, supper parties, trips to the theatre and meetings with intelligent young men. Diana's daily life was pale in comparison and she referred to the summer of 1927 as 'an age without a name'. She lived for her afternoon walks to the local shop to collect the *Daily Mail*, which was running a serial of *The Story of Ivy* by Marie Belloc Lowndes. Capturing Diana's attention, it was the story of a young, beautiful woman called Ivy – compared in the narrative to George Romney's portrait of Lady Nelson – who married easy-going, laidback idler Jervis Laxton for his money. Having squandered his fortune, she is terrified of a future stricken by poverty. On a whim, Ivy visits a fortune teller who predicts a stranger will enter her life, bringing with him a lot of money. The fortune teller also warns of an ominous event which threatens to blight her forever. Printed in cruelly short extracts, its unpredictable plot kept Diana's mind occupied, though on Sundays the newspaper was not printed and she ached with boredom.

Maude mentioned her nieces to various neighbours, one of whom wrote to Diana. 'Dear Miss Mitford,' the long letter began, its sender was a lady with the macabre name of Mrs Pine Coffin, 'Pray use my valley,' she implored, and Diana graciously accepted her offer. During solitary walks in Mrs Pine Coffin's valley, she sensed her daydreams would render fruitless; nobody would come along in a fast car and carry her off, the thought of which made her lose heart. The suffering and injustice she felt became a life lesson – never again, she vowed, would she be starved of intellect and admiration. An aimless existence was not for her. As the summer drew to a close, Diana was determined more than ever to live at the centre of things.

Diana's letters to James Lees-Milne had fizzled out. Tormented by her lack of communication, Jim turned his affections towards Diana Churchill, whom he had met that summer. The other Diana, 'like a fairy' with her puny frame, pale complexion and red hair, was a haphazard substitute for his original love interest. She was not confident like Diana Mitford; her introverted personality, consumed by spells of depression, worried her parents. Closer to her father, Winston Churchill, who was no stranger to 'the black dog' (as he called his depression), often said of his eldest daughter, 'She is very dear to me.' Regardless of Clementine's silent concerns for Diana, she never exuded any warmth towards her and was constantly making unfair comparisons between her and her extrovert middle daughter, the future actress, Sarah Churchill. Years later, after a series of nervous breakdowns, Diana committed suicide.

In September, Jim was invited to Chartwell and he readily accepted once he learned that Diana would also be staying with her brother Tom. Unlike at Asthall and Swinbrook, where Jim could escape with Diana and Tom, the 'brats' congregated in the drawing room and round the dining table. They listened to Churchill's monologue on the Battle of Jutland as he shifted decanters and wine glasses, in place of the ships, around the table, furiously puffing on his cigar to represent the gun smoke. With Churchill's attention fixed on the children, Randolph seized an opportunity to flatter his beloved cousin. 'Papa,' he mischievously asked his father, 'guess who is older, our Diana or Diana M?'

'Our Diana,' came the reply from Churchill, spoiling Randolph's plan.

'Oh, Papa, nobody else thinks so but you!'

During the stay, Diana was surrounded by her two most ardent admirers and Jim noticed that she outwardly relished being in Randolph's company, despite her frequent protests of his immature behaviour. Jim looked on, feeling deflated.

Diana's attentions were further absorbed by the sheer brilliance and variety of Churchill's guests. The impressionist painter, Walter Sickert, a great friend of the family, was visiting Chartwell. Clementine, in her youth, had asked him who the greatest living painter was. 'My dear child, I am,' he bluntly replied. In his late sixties, Sickert was still a flamboyant character, appearing one day in eccentric clothes and the next in a formal suit with gloves and a cane. Diana was alarmed to see him wearing red socks with his evening clothes and in the daytime an opera hat to take a stroll in the garden. He had already begun work on his portrait of Churchill that would hang in the National Portrait Gallery the following year.

Sickert was preoccupied by artificial light, even on the sunniest of days, and he often painted his subjects in closed off rooms underneath the glare of an industrial strength light bulb. The suffocating heat overwhelmed many of his subjects, notably Sarah Churchill, who fainted from the strain. In an acid moment, Diana reminded Sickert that Helleu did not rely on such props.

Diana was lost to Jim during his visit to Chartwell, for the main guest to really capture her affection was Professor Frederick Lindemann, who taught experimental philosophy at Oxford. Spending hours with Professor Lindemann, he taught Diana to play patience and she thought him a 'real magician, a human ready reckoner of lightning speed'. He was as equally taken with Diana and her radiant smile. They shared many acquaintances in common and she approached him about the various undergraduates they both knew. At the mention of her brother's friend, Brian Howard, he snapped: 'Oh, you can't like him, he's a Jew.' Professor Lindemann loved wealth, found poverty to be the fault of those who were caught in its merciless grip, and his fundamental views matched those of Hitler's Aryan principles – he loathed the working classes and believed in sterilisation for the mentally disabled.

Professor Lindemann gave Diana a beautiful watch made of three types of gold and she was touched by the gesture, for no one had ever given her an expensive present before. Despite his open anti-Semitism and racist views, she was fond of him. Flattery, it seemed, could turn her head and distract her from the ugly elements simmering in the depths of his personality. He dismissed Diana's fondness for homosexual men and berated her further when he addressed homosexuality as 'the very negation of all race survival'.

Diana confessed to Professor Lindemann how bored she was at Swinbrook. 'Why don't you study German?' he suggested. 'Learn German and read Schopanhauer's *Die Welt als Wille und Vorstellung*.' Before they parted, he told her, 'Come and see me next term at Christ Church and tell me how you're getting on with your German.' Diana promised she would. The parting was interrupted by Randolph's candour, 'Oh, she won't be allowed to. Didn't you know? Cousin Sydney has read her diary.'

'Shut up, Randolph,' Diana said, not for the first time, nor the last.

Before she left Chartwell, Diana tried to extinguish Randolph's love for her. He was bruised by her rejection, but he did not obey what he called her 'extraordinarily cruel and callous behaviour'. Randolph asked her, 'Why were you so unkind? Was it because you wished to destroy my love for you?'[11] The words did little to stir Diana's conscience, but it hardly mattered when he informed her that she was unsuccessful, 'for I love you as much as I ever have'. Diana had little time for his devotion and she similarly discouraged Jim. She saw neither Randolph nor Jim in her immediate future.

When Diana returned to Swinbrook she was gratified to notice how pleased David was to see her. Remembering Professor Lindemann's advice, she seized the opportunity and asked, 'May I learn German?'

'Certainly not,' came her father's dismissive reply.

'Oh, Farve, why not? After all, Tom's learning it,' she pleaded. Tom had embarked on an extended trip to Vienna and Munich to study music and to learn German. Adding to her argument, Diana also noted that Nancy had recently completed a term of studying art at the Slade School of Fine Art in London, where she had established herself as a hopeless student and an even worse painter.

'That's different, Tom's a boy,' came the all too familiar, sexist response.

Diana sulked off to the children's drawing room, a place she did not care to be; 'I wanted to go away and never come back.' After the excitement of being feted by the grown-ups at Chartwell, she made up her mind to live for pleasure. There was a small glimmer of hope on the horizon; in the autumn she would be permitted to attend her first ball, the Radcliffe Infirmary Ball in Oxford. As she tried on the homemade ball gown, Diana stared at her reflection in the mirror and wailed: 'I can't go! Everything's wrong!' Her nanny brought her down to earth when she reminded the young beauty, 'Never mind, darling. *Nobody's* going to look at *you.*'

6

COMING OUT

The much anticipated Radcliffe Infirmary Ball did not live up to expectation. Dressed in an unsatisfactory ball gown run up by a parlour maid, Diana lingered on the edge of the dance floor resembling someone in the throes of stage fright. This lack of exuberance from Diana was the result of an overwhelming feeling of disappointment. Surely this could not be the kind of grown-up world she had been aching to join. It was dismal – the men were boring and the entertainment strictly plebeian.

Jaded from the night before, Diana accepted a telephone call from Professor Lindemann. His voice brimmed with eagerness, he (wrongly) predicted that she would be the centre of attention and he playfully asked how many proposals she had received. Diana killed his optimism when she announced, 'None.'

The disappointment was to last. Tom arrived home from Vienna to spend the Christmas holidays at Swinbrook and he dutifully escorted Diana on a round of cheerless hunt balls in the depths of the countryside, which proved as dull as the Radcliffe Infirmary Ball. There was never a chance to leave early, Diana glumly observed, for the ball continued on until the hostess decided that her guests had had enough fun. After the Christmas holidays, Tom left for his usual European adventure, leaving Diana alone to sulk at Swinbrook.

Diana imagined she could live vicariously through Nancy's friends. A procession of lively young men passed through Swinbrook, all possessing the very traits which David found infuriating. The fast pace of the twenties did not mellow his acceptance of the modern young man and Nancy's friends were no exception, although he reluctantly put up with his eldest daughter's ritual of having guests to stay from Saturday to Monday. The merry hordes of young people; artistic, exotic, vain, intelligent and well-travelled, were frivolously dubbed the 'Bright Young Things' by witty gossip columnists.

With astute dedication, Nancy partook in the Bright Young Things' outlandish behaviour but, contrary to popular belief, she did not lead the scene. There were lavish parties in country manors, most notably a circus party hosted by the fashion designer Norman Hartnell and a cowboy party given by William and Harold Acton. As the parties gained popularity, the themes became more bizarre. A second childhood party was thrown, in which ancient nannies were dragged out of retirement to push their overgrown charges in giant prams. Another was an impersonation party, where the guests were ordered to 'come as somebody else, come as your dearest enemy, come as your secret self'. Their bad behaviour continuted when they arranged a lengthy conga line through Selfridges department store, snaking through the various floors and interrupting staff and bemused customers. When they were not causing havoc indoors, the Bright Young Things invaded the busy streets of London to take part in a treasure hunt, conducted by motorcars in and around the city centre.

Diana could be scathing about anything that failed to impress her, and with her by-now-familiar critique, she dismissed the childishly themed parties as 'phony'. With a gimlet eye she observed Nancy's generation, all twenty-somethings caught up in the pathetic throes of 'extreme youth'. For Diana it was an example of how not to behave.

One bright spark appeared just as Diana began to lose hope. In the new year of 1928, James Lees-Milne returned to Swinbrook to stay for the weekend. She hoped to corner Jim for a congenial chat about literature, but the pleasant visit took a turn for the worse when, over dinner, Nancy dominated the conversation. Hoping to shock, Nancy praised an anti-German film she had watched at the cinema. Still harbouring a strong dislike for Germans, David made his usual offensive remark, 'The only good German is a dead German.'

Leaping to the defence of the film and of the German people, Jim stated, 'Anyhow, talking of atrocities, the worst in the whole war were committed by the Australians.'

'Be quiet and don't talk about what you don't understand. Young swine!' David exploded.

Mortified by her father's outburst, Diana broke the heavy silence when she haughtily announced, 'I wish people needn't be so rude to their guests!'[12]

Flexing his authority as master of the household, David trumped the 'unhappy youth' when he ordered Jim from Swinbrook. Frogmarched to the front door, Jim was thrown outside where it was teeming with rain. After several failed attempts to start up his motorcycle, he sneaked back into the house and crept up to bed.

Awaking at six the next morning, Jim bumped into David, stalking the hallway, as he did every morning, wearing his paisley-print robe and drinking tea from a thermos. Anticipating another scene, Jim was pleasantly surprised when David appeared to have forgotten the offensive exchange and greeted him warmly.

The turbulent visit settled into a bittersweet memory for Jim and, although he did not know it at the time, it would be his last visit with Diana at Swinbrook. He rightly sensed that Diana's mind was focused on finding a suitable husband to rescue her from the great boredom of family life. With his 'impecunious and melancholic' nature, Jim knew he was not an ideal candidate, and long after he had departed from her life, Diana remained 'the unattainable object of his desire'.

Diana joined Nancy in the loathing of their parents and of her place in society as a young woman. Although brilliantly witty, well read and popular, Nancy served as a prime example to her younger sister of how not to conduct one's life. With two failed seasons behind her, Nancy made no attempt to find a suitable husband. To the fury of David and Sydney, who could see past the pretence, she attached herself to Hamish St Clair Erskine, the homosexual second son of the Earl of Rosse. Hamish made it clear that he would not marry her, and yet she frolicked around London pretending they were engaged. Failing to form a successful relationship that would lead to marriage, Nancy paved the beginnings of a successful writing career. She wrote part-time, writing chatty articles for her grandfather's magazine, *The Lady*. The payment was small and it barely stretched to cover her living expenses, but she peddled on. She longed to escape Swinbrook and the scrutiny of her parents, but she lacked the financial independence to do so.

In an extreme juxtaposition, Pamela, although she was often briefly engaged, had no desire to dazzle society. She had proven herself useful in managing the family's animals and in helping Sydney to run the house. At least if she failed to find a husband, Diana noted, Pamela could always earn a living. But unlike Diana, Pamela had no ambition to escape the countryside and she seemed content with her lot.

Later, when Diana spoke of freedom, an inquiring journalist asked why she had chosen marriage over a career, and she candidly admitted, that owing to her nature – 'I'm too lazy' – marriage seemed the lesser of two evils. She also added, 'We couldn't imagine that anyone would wish to employ us. For one thing, we did everything badly.' Diana rode every day – badly. She attended tennis parties given by local children, but her sportsmanship was unsatisfactory. Her music lessons were strenuous and dancing classes proved mediocre. Diana wondered if she could type, but that resulted in nothing, for she did not attempt to try. And so, marriage it would have to be.

Hovering on the threshold of adulthood, Diana was all too aware of her father's precarious financial situation. Throughout her childhood, David often told his children that he was ruined, and Diana anxiously wondered where their next loaf of bread would come from. David had lost the bulk of his inheritance trying to farm, and during their years at Asthall he made several ill-advised investments, 'generally the result of talking to some brilliantly clever cove at the Marlborough Club'. The family's fortunes were long spent and although they often joked of their genteel poverty, desperate times were upon them. Faced with no alternative, David began to hold estate sales, selling off the family heirlooms in an attempt to make ends meet. In hindsight, Sydney felt that the building of Swinbrook was the beginning of the end.

One thing was certain, Diana knew either way she would need a firm plan to survive. Her rank in society, the only thing salvageable in the crumbling patrician family, was a firm foundation to start from. Her governess's words reminded her that she was the least important person in the room, but even with that statement, Diana still attracted attention from the opposite sex. Nancy's put-downs sprang from an uncontrollable envy at her younger sister's effortless appeal and Diana was resourceful enough to realise that she could exploit admiration for her own gain. After all, Helleu, Randolph Churchill and James Lees-Milne were proof of that.

On the afternoon of the 8 May 1928, Diana travelled with Sydney to Buckingham Palace for her formal presentation at Court. Photographs of the aristocrats at play were a zoo-like spectacle for the masses, and public events — society weddings and presentations at Court — brought them out in their droves. Curious members of the public lined the Mall, peering through the windows to catch a glimpse of the debutantes before the procession of chauffeur-driven cars passed through the gates of the palace. 'Come and look at this one!' was a familiar cry, especially if the girl was deemed to be very beautiful or extremely ugly — the plain girls were never singled out.

Described as a feverish excitement comparable to that of a girl on her wedding day, the debutante season was 'open sesame' to doors which otherwise might remain eternally closed to the aspirant. But, for a mother in Sydney's position with six daughters, the presentation at Court was predictable, and she braced Diana for the long wait ahead. Books, crossword puzzles and other light, recreational materials were brought along to occupy the drawn-out hours of waiting in the car. Liquids were sparingly consumed that morning, or avoided altogether, for obvious reasons too delicate to mention at the time.

The preparation was rigorous, and before the debutante could be presented at Court, she had to observe strict instructions issued by Buckingham Palace. The rules of dress informed the debutantes that trains were to hang at a regulation 2½ yards from the shoulder and three ostrich feathers (black in the case of a widow) had to be attached to the head, worn slightly to the side. Voluminous crinolines were forbidden, but the dresses did not have to be white (the customary colour), although most were.

The cost of being presented at Court tallied up to a small fortune and Sydney tediously kept a record of the expenditures in her household accounts book. Other costly essentials included shoes, purchased from Dolcis on Oxford Street, which were decent to look at but uncomfortable and tended to pinch after several laps around the dance floor. A wash and set by Phyllis Earle, located on Dover Street, cost 3s 6d, and was reached by the No. 9 bus, getting off at the Ritz. Bus fares were also an expense for Diana, as she did not have the luxury of a private chauffeur. The elbow-length kid gloves, as worn by Nancy and Pamela before her, were given by Sydney along with a strict warning to keep them clean, for they had to be sent up to Scotland by train to be laundered.[13]

As with the dress code, strict rules also applied to the appearance of the motorcar. A 'man on the box' was required to sit next to the chauffeur, but for David and Sydney, who did not employ male household staff, a gatekeeper probably stepped into the part.

The presentation at Court took place in groups, and when it was time for Diana to be presented to the king and queen at the end of the Throne Room, she passed through the State Room, bright with pink and white flowers. Hydrangeas, lilies and Dorothy Perkins roses formed a floral background against the glittering uniforms, Orders and decorations of foreign diplomats and the soft tints of the ladies dresses. The bodyguard of the Honourable Corps of Gentlemen-at-Arms were on duty in the State Room under the captain, the Earl of Plymouth. The King's Bodyguard of Yeoman of the Guard in their scarlet uniforms were also on duty under Captain Lord Desborough.

The Throne Room, in contrast to the beauty of the State Room, was 'filthy, the white walls were so grimy they had turned a shade of dark khaki'.[14] Diana perched on a gilt chair, careful not to crease her dress or become tangled in her train, where she watched the Court's arrival, followed by Their Majesties procession. As the royals walked to the Throne Room, the Irish Guards orchestra struck up the national anthem, and three men in uniform appeared, walking backwards and bowing as the Court entered.

The parade of gowns were a fleeting distraction in the otherwise boring day. Diana observed Queen Mary, who wore an impressive gown of cream and gold lamé, hand embroidered in cut crystal and diamanté, with a train of Irish point lace, lined in gold chiffon with a golden leaf design. She wore a gold crown with the Lesser Star of Africa, her jewels included the Koh-i-Noor, and a blue sash of the Garter and family orders were draped across her gown. The Duchess of York appeared in a white fleur-de-lis gown decorated with diamantés and an embroidered satin train. Disappointment was not far off when Diana noticed that the tiaras worn by the regal ladies were dirty and hardly sparkled, having been kept away in a bank vault – 'nobody had bothered to clean them' – and all of the marvellous jewels looked as though 'they'd been painted in charcoal'. The outfits of choice for the royal men did not hold the same level of interest for Diana, though she agreed they cut a dashing figure in their military costume. King George V wore the uniform of a field marshal, the Prince of Wales that of colonel of the Welsh Guards and Prince George was in naval dress.

By contrast, Sydney was not in the least interested in the spectacle of pomp and grandeur, and she patiently whiled away the hours until they could leave. By now, she was accustomed to the familiar and predictable ritual. Finally, the lengthy wait came to an end and Diana handed a gilt-edged card to the Deputy Lord Chamberlain, who announced her name. Two lackeys spread the train behind her and, ready for the grand entrance, she was accompanied by Sydney. The presentation lasted no longer than a minute and Diana, consumed by nerves and hunger, performed her graceful dip without a mere hint of a wobble.

Having been forbidden the pleasure of food and drink prior to Court, Diana headed to the buffet, where the champagne glasses resembled tooth mugs and the food was limited to Windsor pies. The catering was not carried out by the royal household but was provided by Lyons, the famous teashop chain.

With the reserved swiftness of a curtsey, Diana had symbolically moved from a child to a society woman – for the duration of the season anyway. The stress of perfecting a curtsey was minute compared to the importance of having a successful season, for its success was determined by one thing – a marriage proposal.

Although David and Sydney did not wish to see Diana, or any of their daughters, married at the age of 18 (the ideal age for marriage was considered to be 21), Diana was conscious that receiving a proposal from an eligible young man formally ensured they would be married when she came of age.

A month later, as the debutante season was in full swing, Amelia Earhart made headlines around the world when she achieved the impossible in being the first woman to fly across the Atlantic. The press and public were in a frenzy of excitement when she touched down in England. After the First World War, when women proved to men they could run the country whilst they fought at the Front, the 1920s seemed an age of progress. Even though the death of British suffragette leader Emmeline Pankhurst that same month blighted the celebratory spirit, hope still reigned when women over the age of 21 were finally given the vote.

This progressiveness was lost on Diana as, despite her nonconformist outlook, the only way she could see a life of independence was through marriage. If she was going to follow convention and find a husband, Diana was calculating enough to realise that it ought to be a good husband. She would not be content in a stifling arrangement with little opportunity for fun. It did not occur to her that she could achieve all of those things through her own merit.

7

A DEB'S DELIGHT

The summer of 1928 was dominated by a whirlwind of social engagements, endless supper parties, tea dances and balls. Although Diana was officially out and moving at the centre of things, her new status did not mean freedom. Being unmarried, she still required a chaperone. Diana Churchill was also doing the season and, much to the other Diana's relief, Clementine offered to chaperone her cousin. The family's London base, Rutland Gate, was let to ease David's never-ending financial problems, and the Churchills saved the day when they kindly offered to host Diana at their flat at 11 Downing Street. This, of course, gave Randolph the perfect opportunity to pick up where he had left off.

All of Diana's male friends knew one another, as they had boarded at Eton together and attended Oxford. They were either friends with Nancy or had been schoolmates with Tom, and that also meant they knew Randolph, who wasted no time in using their mutual friends to keep tabs on Diana. 'The poor boy told me that he was so carried away by the radiance of your beauty (my heart goes out to him) ...' Randolph wrote Diana from Eton, having learned of her meeting with a nameless acquaintance at a debutante ball. He recalled Diana's beauty from his memories of her at Chartwell the previous summer, where she looked 'too radiant and beautiful to describe'. He confided to her, much to her exasperation, 'I think I am still within the limits that I am allowed by you' (that of a loving cousin and childhood companion), but he was clever enough to realise that his 'love is one-sided and unreciprocated'. Diana preferred the company of older, worldlier men, for they not only appreciated her beauty, but also served as an intellectual outlet. Randolph, although he worshipped her physical beauty, was no match for her mentally.

The social circle surrounding Diana had grown since Tom's arrival at Swinbrook. It was a relief when he offered to chaperone her at dances, and through her brother she became acquainted with his friend Edward James, the artist and poet, who was also a contemporary of Randolph. It was a small, tight-knit group of young men and James Lees-Milne had been part of this group prior to his impromptu departure from Diana's life.

She was instantly drawn to Edward, whose stutter and uncertainty regarding his sexuality contributed to a lack of confidence, but this hardly mattered to Diana, for she was aware of Tom's brief fling with Jim at Eton. Like Diana, Edward had several older sisters, his mother Evie was described as 'a nightmare' and his father William was distant and dead by the time he was 5 years old. Drawing on his upbringing, brought up fatherless and in the company of dominant women, he was hesitant to pursue the opposite sex. And the traits which Diana had admired in Helleu were also apparent in Edward. They were, perhaps, all the more appealing given he was the right age for her. But unlike her previous admirers, he did not possess any romantic feelings for her, although being a great aesthete he admired her beauty. She adored him, but he made it clear that he wanted a platonic friendship, not love.

Rejection from the opposite sex was an entirely new experience for Diana. The rival for Edward's affection was Tilly Losch, the Austrian-born actress, dancer and choreographer. Although not as beautiful as Diana, Tilly had an advantage in that she was seven years older than Diana, four years older than Edward and experienced with men. Concealing an unhealthy fixation for Tilly, Edward had been following her career, and his obsession deepened when she came to London for her West End debut in Noel Coward's *This Year of Grace*.

Not only was Edward bewitched by Tilly, but Tom and Randolph also fell instantly in love with her. Diana watched the bizarre love triangle unfold and, observing Tilly's treatment of the three men, the beginnings of an intense hatred brewed beneath her aloof exterior. Diana had become an expert in toying with her admirers' feelings, stringing them along and then abandoning them whenever the topic of love entered the equation. Tilly, however, knew how to play men off one another — it made them want her more and, having slept with all three men, she entered into a game of sexual blackmail with the poor, unsuspecting Edward. Unlike Tom and Randolph, Edward's appeal lay in his fortune. And, for the gold-digging Tilly who loathed the idea of love, money made Edward all the more attractive. Diana's resentment of Tilly would later develop into a bitter feud.

On an evening in May, Diana accepted an invitation to a supper party at Carlton House Terrace, hosted by Lady Violet Astor in honour of her debutante daughter, Margaret Mercer-Nairne. As she turned sideways to make polite small talk with the guest seated next to her, Diana met the acquaintance of a tall, handsome young man with bright blue eyes and fair hair. His name was Bryan Guinness.

In person, Diana did not exude overt vanity – as she had done in letters to Jim – but her confidence in social gatherings was beyond her years and she effortlessly conversed with the opposite sex. She had not met Bryan before, though he remembered her from a costume party Nancy had thrown at Swinbrook. At the time, they were not formally introduced, and Bryan had spied the 16-year-old Diana from afar, smiling and silently dancing with his friend, Brian Howard. The image of the teenage beauty stayed with Bryan long after the party ended. Two years had passed since this first sighting, and when he met her in person, Bryan fell in love with her.

Bryan was considered a deb's delight – he was rich, handsome, generous to a fault and, given his background, surprisingly unspoilt. At 22, he was unmarried and had never been engaged, but not for lack of trying. Debutantes saw him as a catch, though with his romantic nature, he could not bring himself to follow the familiar pattern that the men and women of his class adopted. Marriage, to Bryan, was not something he could enter into lightly. He had not fallen in love with anyone before and, as such, he could not take a wife for the sake of bloodlines and inheritance. This sentimentality endeared him all the more to the debutantes who fixed their steely gaze upon him.

Bryan was the eldest child of Lady Evelyn (née Erskine) and Colonel Walter Guinness, the rich Conservative MP for Bury St Edmunds and Minister of Agriculture. The family's wealth came from the family brewery, founded in Dublin in 1759, but brewing did not interest Colonel Guinness in the slightest, as his mind was drawn to scientific matters and philanthropy. When he was not engrossed in his political work, Colonel Guinness set off on a lengthy voyage to the South Sea Islands with one of his many mistresses in tow. Lady Evelyn was unlike her shrewd, serious-minded husband in every way imaginable. Dressed in Paquin, she was petite with pale-blonde hair and a china doll-like beauty, and her quiet, shrill voice resembled a loud whisper. Her interests were focused on an obsession with the chivalric medieval world 'where nature combined with art in a kind of Gothic fantasy land'. And, given the Guinness millions, both Lady Evelyn and Colonel Guinness could indulge in the type of elaborate lifestyle they desired.

The Guinnesses owned two palatial homes in London: 10 Grosvenor Place and Heath House, and both were decorated in Lady Evelyn's idealistic view of the Middle Ages. Grosvenor Place was converted from an ugly Victorian house into a medieval fortress complete with smoke-blackened beams to reflect the pre-chimney days. The Victorian plate glass had been replaced with leaded windows, and two-pronged forks and pewter dishes substituted for china and silver. And, dedicated to authenticity, Lady Evelyn ordered the ceilings to be lowered to reflect the period.

In many ways, Bryan was suited to Diana's tastes; he loved books, music and art, he enjoyed jokes and was a good conversationalist. And he impressed her with his knowledge of the theatre, a world he offered to introduce her to. The more Bryan saw of Diana, the more he fell in love with her. Although she did not feel as strongly as him, she agreed he was handsome and possessed the same gentle nature as Edward James, both of which she found to be attractive attributes.

On a warm evening in July, the Guinnesses held a ball at Grosvenor Place. Before the guests arrived, the housekeeper noticed that two of the young maids, Dorothy Martin and Elizabeth Tipping, both aged 17, were exhausted after a day of preparing the house for the evening's festivities and she sent them upstairs. The maids were curious to catch a glimpse of the guests in their finery, and shirking their orders to go to bed, they climbed over the balustrading round the servants' floor and onto the glass ceiling. The weight of the two girls was too much for the glass ceiling to bear and it shattered, sending them crashing to the marble floor.

Inside the ballroom, Lady Evelyn was entertaining Princess Mary and Viscount Lascelles, the Duke and Duchess of Abercorn, the Duchess of Devonshire and Sir Phillip Sassoon. Bryan's mind was on Diana, who was absent from the ball, and he politely danced with the daughters of his parents' friends. Suddenly, the gaiety halted when a member of staff burst through the doors to alert Lady Evelyn of the incident in the hallway. A footman was immediately dispatched to St George's hospital and two doctors appeared at the scene. Caught up in the frenzy of guests spilling from the ballroom and staff rushing to and fro, Frank, the night watchman fell down the stairs and sprained his ankle.

One of the maids, Dorothy Martin, was pronounced dead, having fractured her skull, the impact killing her immediately. The other maid barely managed to survive by clutching onto a chain from which hung a lamp. She was taken to hospital by ambulance and the party, cloaked in a solemn mood, began to disperse from the ballroom. The marble floor was covered in blood and Bryan was deeply disturbed by the dead body of the young maid and the guests gathering around to watch. The dead body, now a spectacle, struck him with a sense of irony, when only moments before, it was those very guests the maids had risked their lives to see. Bryan fled to Grania's bedroom, where he read aloud from Hugh Walpole's *Jeremy* to distract her from the harrowing scene downstairs.[15]

The tragedy of the night before still haunted Bryan, and to take his mind off the incident, he travelled to the Albert Hall for a matinee performance of *Hiawatha*. As he sat in the back of his chauffeur driven car, he spied two young women, one with black hair and the other with blonde, stepping onto a bus. The sight of the blonde woman convinced him it was Diana, the thought of which lifted his spirits and almost diminished his sadness.

When Bryan reached the Albert Hall, he scanned the auditorium feverishly and was certain he could see Diana's golden hair in the front row of the stalls. As the music struck up, Bryan's suspicions were confirmed when she turned around. It was Diana, and he acknowledged this overwhelming pang of happiness as a sign that she was the girl he was destined to marry.

Diana had only met Bryan a few times, always in the formal atmosphere of a ball or a supper party. They were never alone, except for when they danced, and their conversation remained polite and light-hearted. Despite being certain of his feelings for Diana, Bryan could not gauge whether she felt the same way. But he was determined to find out, and at a ball given by his Uncle Ernest at 17 Grosvenor Place, he invited her to sit outside on the balcony. They missed most of the ball, and as they watched the sun rise over Chapel Street, Bryan found himself in a state of baffled adoration. It later inspired him to write the poem 'Sunrise in Belgrave Square', as a dedication to Diana's cool self-possession: 'You sit politely in your body's box/ I wonder at the wonder hidden there ...'[16] True to form, he was too shy to act on his impulses and, failing to take the initiative with her, the moment was lost.

Bryan left for Holland on a sightseeing tour with close friends, but the few days spent in the picture galleries and country houses could not keep his mind off Diana. His friends teased him about his reputation with beautiful debutantes and he let them think what they liked, for only he knew the true object of his affection. Bryan sent Diana a letter, explaining that he had previously held back from pursuing her because she was 'so terribly young', but he warned her they would have to 'face it together and decide' what to do.

To Bryan's embarrassment, Diana ignored his declaration of love, and when they met in person, he did not mention the contents of his letter, instead he tried to forget he ever sent it. He knew Diana might lose interest in him, and given her beauty and confidence, she would not be without an admirer for long. He decided to put on a show of false bravado and take control of the situation.

Several days after their last meeting, an opportunity presented itself to Bryan when, on 16 July, he and Diana attended a ball at Grosvenor House. He instrumented a way to get Diana outside when he suggested they escape the stuffy ballroom for a breath of fresh air. After what seemed like an eternal stroll down Park Lane until they were safely out of view, Bryan nervously told Diana of his feelings and before she could respond he kissed her. 'Do you – could you – love me enough to marry me?' he stammered.

Diana, truthful in her response, answered, 'I'm very fond of you.'

'But do you love me? You *kissed* me?' he pathetically implored.

She could not imagine the agonies Bryan had suffered and replied, 'A kiss means nothing, I do it without thinking as I'm used to kissing in my family.'

A kiss meant *everything* to Bryan, and in the past he had purposely avoided kissing girls because, in his view, a kiss was sacred. He wrote in his diary of a beautiful Italian girl whom he had met during a three-week tour of Germany. One evening, quite similar to this evening with Diana, they stood on a balcony and it dawned on him that she expected him to kiss her. His heart sank for he could not go through with it until 'true love should some day strike me like a thunderbolt'.

Without acknowledging Diana's rejection, Bryan escorted her back to Grosvenor House and he asked his mother if they could go home. Lady Evelyn did not wish to leave and Bryan was forced to stay for what seemed hours, his tortured soul circling the ballroom in a heartbroken daze.

The next morning, Bryan's misery was interrupted by a note on his breakfast tray. The words, in their neat cursive scrawl, surprised him. Diana had written to confess that she loved him and had agreed to marry him. He replied immediately, 'I still don't know how much you love me, nor really understand what you felt last night.' A flicker of Diana's dual personality revealed itself to Bryan but, nevertheless, he repeated how glad he was at her change of heart. 'I am glad that you are glad. I am glad that I love you. I am altogether glad again.'

Bryan's letter to Diana gave her the upper hand and she was quick to recognise his tunnel vision when he felt closer to obtaining what he desired; in this case, consummating his love through marriage. Absorbed in his passion for Diana, Bryan was blind to her faults and he did not question whether she truly loved him or not. Perhaps he did not wish to hear the truth.

After three months of polite conversation carried out in the grandest ballrooms in London, Diana announced her intention to marry Bryan. 'Oh no,' cried Sydney. 'You are much too young. How old is he?'

'Twenty-two,' Diana told her, confident his age might sway her mother's decision.

'Oh no, darling,' Sydney repeated. 'That's ridiculous. Of course you can ask him to stay if you like, but you must wait two years.'

'*Two years?*'

'Well, one year. You are too young to make up your mind.'

All of her expectations of leaving Swinbrook were dashed in Sydney's final sentence of concealed disapproval. A year seemed like a lifetime to the impatient Diana, and with the certainty of a marriage proposal – it was evident that Bryan would wait for her – she began to calculate the exact strategy it would take to win Sydney over. In her mind, she was already engaged and it was only a matter of time before she could begin living the life she dreamed of.

8

THE ENGAGEMENT

Sydney was neither enthusiastic nor optimistic about Diana and Bryan's longing to become engaged. Diana's young age was not the only element that made her doubt the decision. Sydney felt there would be plenty of time for Diana to find a suitable husband once Nancy and Pamela were settled. She agreed with the age-old custom that daughters ought to marry in order of age. 'You must have one more season in London,' she told Diana. 'So that you can at least meet more people.'

Pleading her case to Sydney, Diana argued that she had met quite enough young and old men to know that Bryan was the one she wished to marry. Sydney could not argue with that, as Diana was the most popular out of her three eldest daughters. In a rare change of heart, for Sydney rarely consented to anything, she permitted Diana to visit Bailiffscourt, the Guinness family's seaside retreat.

Accompanied by her nanny, Diana made the journey to Climping in Sussex to the small farmhouse by the sea, purchased a few years before by Lady Evelyn and Colonel Guinness. Their purchase of the property had saved it from speculators who planned to ruin the entire coast. The house itself was surrounded by mystique and scandal; it had been the home of the notorious Colonel Barker, a woman who had pretended she was a man and under which guise she married a Brighton girl. Diana and her sisters loved the story, having pored over it in the newspapers, and it thrilled her to visit the scene of the crime. However, she was disheartened when she learned the very mention of Colonel Barker's name was taboo – Lady Evelyn did not care to discuss the subject.

The strange tale was not the only thing that intrigued Diana. Lady Evelyn, her two youngest children, Grania and Murtogh, their Willoughby cousins and two nurses lived in an area known as the Huts, in the middle of a cornfield facing out to the sea. As the name suggests, they were authentic huts, made of pitch and pine and set on brick foundations, and smelling of raw wood and sea air. Lady Evelyn, like David, was a builder and she had envisioned a strange house, but in the meantime the family were living in a semi-bohemian state.

Outside the Huts, the flat, treeless landscape gave off an exceptional glare in summer when the bright sunlight hit the cornfields, its rays almost blinding the onlooker. Lady Evelyn took charge of the cornfield and, inspired by the wild flowers growing, she scattered poppy and cornflower seeds amongst them. She had such a passion for wild flowers that she would lean out of the carriage all the way down from Victoria and Arundel, throwing seeds out of the window. 'I'm afraid Walter doesn't quite approve,' she told Diana. Given his post as Minister of Agriculture, this was one eccentricity Colonel Guinness could not endorse.

Diana and Bryan often stole away from her nanny and his family and went for walks through the fields or sat on the beach. On one occasion, everyone loaded into chauffeur-driven cars to go on a picnic and when they had reached their chosen spot on the Downs, the drivers stopped to unpack a huge tea, a frying pan, a pat of butter and eggs. Bryan seized the moment and, bursting with pride, he turned to Lady Evelyn and announced, 'Diana's so clever, mummy, she can cook!'

'I can't really. Only fried eggs. Anybody can do fried eggs,' Diana modestly replied. This modesty was soon dispelled when Lady Evelyn and the children's nurses agreed 'To cook! It was *too* wonderful.'

Although the Guinness children shared a similar camaraderie to Diana's younger sisters, their upbringing was strikingly different. Unlike the Mitford children, who were forced to do lessons in the schoolroom at home, Grania, at the age of 8, was not made to adhere to a traditional curriculum of learning due to her ballet lessons. One of her masters had been the great Massine. Diaghilev and all his dancers had been Diana's childhood heroes and she looked at Grania with a certain level of awe. Murtogh, too, was exceptional in his interests.[17] He never attended the picnics nor did he venture outside much, instead he sought refuge in his room, with the blinds drawn against the sunlight, making toy cinemas. Diana marvelled that Murtogh was not ordered outdoors, as her own father would never have tolerated such a thing, but Lady Evelyn did not dream of depriving her children of their whims.

The visit to Bailiffscourt was a resounding success. 'She's enough to turn anyone's head,' Grania told Bryan. Bryan proudly agreed, and he formed an ally in Lady Evelyn who, won over by Diana's charm, began to take a favourable view of their wish to marry. Sydney and David did not share Lady Evelyn's optimism. Soon after her return to Swinbrook, Diana was promptly sent up to Scotland to be received by the Malcolms of Poltalloch, whose third son, Angus, had fallen in love with her.

Diana's hostess, Lady Malcolm, was reputedly the illegitimate daughter of Prince Louis of Battenberg and Lillie Langtry. Her flamboyance was enough to put Lady Evelyn in the shade; banners hung round the azalea-scented hall in the grand sandstone house on the Mull of Kintyre and bagpipes wailed as the guests dined. Lady Malcolm took an instant shine to Diana; she thought her beautiful, well-mannered and the perfect wife for Angus. Hoping to secure Diana as a daughter-in-law, she encouraged the young people to take evening walks alone in the Scottish hills. Failing to acknowledge the romantic setting or the machinations of her hostess, Diana faithfully corresponded with Bryan, who had ventured to Vienna with Robert Byron to take his mind off her while she was in Scotland.

Bryan responded to Diana's frequent and detailed letters:

> I am green with envy, but not jealousy, I promise you, of Angus. I get really furious when I think of the Clan Malcolm pursuing you, winding smiles around you, stunning you with bagpipe music and then trying to mother and marry you. I suppose one can't blame them for liking you but how dare Lady M be so forward as to propose to you all helpless and alone under her roof.

Bryan had little to worry about, for Diana rebuffed the proposal.

After visiting Poltalloch, Diana stayed with her fellow debutante and friend, Margaret Mercer-Nairne, at Meikleour. Riding through the fertile countryside while the men were working on the moors, Diana spoke of her wish to marry Bryan. Margaret, who thought of nothing except horses and hunting, agreed, 'Yes, marry Bryan, and then you can live in Leicestershire and hunt.' It was the last thing Diana wanted, for she had had enough of country life to last a lifetime. She longed for 'people, an eternity of talk, books, pictures, music and travel' – they were her 'eighteen year old desires'.

When she returned to Swinbrook, Diana told her mother that her mind was made up and that she still wished to marry Bryan. She confided that Lady Evelyn was on their side but, despite her enthusiasm, she could not write to Sydney. 'I couldn't dare,' she had whispered to Diana, when Bryan pressed her to do so. There was only one thing for it. Bryan would have to visit Swinbrook and charm David and Sydney himself.

Diana was eager for Bryan to make a positive impression on her philistine parents, especially her father. She consoled herself with the knowledge that, unlike James Lees-Milne, Bryan lacked a rebellious streak. He would never be outspoken or challenge David's opinions, and she was certain her parents would judge him likeable.

The girls flitted around Swinbrook, waiting for Bryan's arrival. He showed up in plain clothing, a gesture that impressed Sydney, for she disapproved of overt displays of wealth. Furthermore, Bryan was self-conscious about his privileged life and often downplayed his status, opting to dress and to live simply. Naive to such grandeur, Diana never assumed his clothing was plain or bohemian. But his clothing did not represent his romantic and cultured frame of mind, and every time he did or said something 'un-countrified', Diana glowed with pride and pleasure. She viewed him as the 'antithesis of a squire'.

The visit was not without its tense moments, provoked by Bryan's clumsy performance at the breakfast table. He stood, poised at the sideboard, with a plate in one hand, a spoonful of sticky porridge in the other, which he shook violently in an attempt to dislodge it on to his plate, all the time fixing his gaze on Diana as he chatted. David could not tolerate spills of any sort: crumbs on the tablecloth or a spill down the side of the jam jar were enough to cause a furious scene. He thought Bryan a 'clever cove' – quite the compliment from David – and owing to such, he suppressed his annoyance by quietly grinding his false teeth and remaining silent for Diana's sake.

Bryan revelled in the company of the younger children and he enjoyed being part of their lively chatter, the lilting voices of the 'Mockingbird Mitfords' merging into one. Diana loved them, too, but she longed to escape. Swinbrook held no charm for her, and it was that very atmosphere which Bryan most enjoyed, though he pressed her with the plea, 'Do you think we will ever be able to see each other alone? Or will the seminary follow in a crocodile wherever we go?'

When Bryan returned home he was met by an anxious Lady Evelyn, who was eager to hear about his trip to Swinbrook. They went for a walk and Bryan told her it went 'swimmingly' and that he saw no cause for Diana's parents to doubt his intentions. Barely containing her excitement, Lady Evelyn said, 'I can see no point in your waiting, as you are both absolutely sure of your feelings.' His mother warned him that 'people who are in doubt tend to wait for ages', and since he had no doubt, it seemed useless to waste valuable time. She promised to do all she could to convince Colonel Guinness that the marriage should go ahead.

Having returned from his lengthy voyage to 'savage lands', Colonel Guinness's first priority was to have a long discussion with Bryan. He was not as impulsive as Lady Evelyn, and to judge whether his wife's eagerness for the marriage was not merely one of her fancies, he decided that Diana should visit their family home,

Heath House. In doing so, he could make a sound decision based on fact rather than emotion.

They wasted no time in planning their reunion, and as Diana's train pulled into Paddington, she spied Bryan waiting on the platform. He was bursting with excitement, although when she disembarked the train his greeting was rigidly polite; he would not have been so bold as to kiss her in broad daylight or in public. In a gallant effort, Bryan shunned the family chauffeur in favour of driving Diana down to Hampstead himself. They arrived to the bizarre sight of Lady Evelyn wandering along the long and winding path, watering can in hand, sprinkling it with milk. Diana's confusion must have been apparent because Bryan quickly added, 'Mummy's encouraging the moss.'

Everything hinged on this visit and Diana was especially nervous to meet Colonel Guinness, who had been absent during her stay at Bailiffscourt. He used the parliamentary recess as an opportunity to escape on his yacht, away from Lady Evelyn and her idiosyncrasies. Colonel Guinness failed to understand his wife's unique gardening skills, nor did he take any interest in the house – he preferred to talk of politics, people and health. 'What! No vitamins?' he barked when Diana politely refused a slice of raw carrot.

Despite his reserved nature, Diana thought Colonel Guinness was kind, but distant. However, and perhaps most importantly, he threw the young couple a lifeline when he offered to write to David. This small gesture was a momentous relief to Diana and Bryan, but as time went on, Colonel Guinness's attention was spent elsewhere. And, Lady Evelyn, once vocal about the marriage, focused on Christmas shopping, which she started in May. Even though it was still only July, there was, as she warned Diana, only seventy days until the big day.

In the meantime, Bryan spoke of eloping to Gretna Green. This plan soon vanished when he wrote to a parson reputed to be sympathetic to young couples in their position and all they received in a reply was a lecture on self-control. It was as much use as 'shouting halt at the Falls of Niagara', Bryan retaliated. Pondering their uncertain future, he suggested they try another method. 'When you feel most unhappy you must make a point of showing yourself to your father and then you may convince him of how serious we are,' he urged Diana.

Taking this advice, Diana adopted the practice known in the family as 'slowly wearing away'. Day after day, she sat in silence, aloof and withdrawn, her face etched with desperation and misery. Nancy remarked on Diana's sullenness and was met by a defensive – if not witty – remark from one of the younger girls, 'She's thinking of how rich she'll be!'

Remnants of Diana's past were catching up with her. Randolph, although he had been away at Eton and had not entered her thoughts since Bryan's arrival on the scene, was about to intrude on her happiness. The unwelcome news of Bryan and Diana's romance came from Randolph's sister. Diana Churchill had spotted them together at a Harrow and Eton cricket match and she informed her brother that Bryan had been 'much catched' by the object of his boyhood affection. Consumed by rage and jealousy, Randolph was not prepared to allow Bryan to steal Diana before he had a chance to grow up and court her properly. He was always a sore loser and he hatched a plan to separate them before a wedding date was firmly set.

Randolph's first plan of attack was to bombard both Diana and Bryan with letters, explaining how unsuited they were for one another and that marriage would be an 'appalling' mistake. 'You'll hate each other in no time,' he predicted. He also attempted to put Bryan off Diana, warning him that he had known her for many years and that she had been guilty of flirting with other men. She was, Randolph said, possessed by an immoral character. To Diana, Randolph accused Bryan of not being strong enough and that she would do better to wait for him to grow up so they could be together.

Rather than reprimanding Randolph for his meddling ways, Diana laughed it off. This reaction provoked Randolph to write a letter of self-justification. 'You know I never told Bryan anything about you which anyone could possibly resent ... You do not actually see anything WRONG in sin,' he chastised her.[18]

Realising how serious Bryan was about the marriage, and perhaps discovering the restraints that would soon be fixed upon her, Diana asked Bryan if he would mind her going out with other men after they were married. He immediately rejected her request 'because you might think I didn't love you so much if I did'. The couple had been secretly engaged for four months and if Diana had any reservations about continuing with their wedding plans, she did not say.

With a swift change of heart, Colonel Guinness firmly implanted his loyalties towards Bryan and Diana, and a man of his word, he followed through with his plan to write to David. Knowing of David's protectiveness of Diana and the 'damn sewers' who came to Swinbrook, Bryan correctly sensed that any form of contact should come from him.

Bryan wrote to David to arrange a meeting the next time he was in London. David's reply, though amusing, was predictable, 'I never come to London if I can avoid it and as I can avoid it at the moment I am not likely to be there for some time. I understand you are likely to be at Swinbrook within the next fortnight and, if what you want to say will keep till then, well and good.' Sydney's opposition had begun to waver and all that stood in Bryan and Diana's way was David.

A meeting was held at the Marlborough Club and Bryan, consumed by nerves, managed to emote the speech he had memorised. He was not going to let anything stand in the way of marrying Diana. Inside the billiard room, Bryan was left speechless when David, in his no nonsense style, consented to their marriage and an Easter wedding was swiftly agreed upon.

Various elements conspired to sway David's decision. Diana and Bryan's secret engagement was the subject of much gossip amongst their contemporaries and David detested his daughters being the subject of any form of gossip. Pamela's engagement to Oliver 'Togo' Watney had been called off, and the whispers of an impending marriage between Diana and Bryan were becoming louder and would soon catch the attention of the press.

A month later, David and Colonel Guinness discussed the matter at length over the telephone, a rare gesture on David's behalf, for he loathed telephone calls. David confided, 'Don't tell the young people, but between you and me I don't think the end of January or the beginning of February would be altogether impossible.' Bryan was seated next to Lady Evelyn on the sofa, listening in on the conversation. Certain that David had been won over, he raced to his bedroom and dashed off a letter to Diana: 'I think your father is the most kind and considerate and delightful man with far more imagination than any of us, and he hides it under a bushel of ferocity.'[19] In his usual sentimental way, Bryan vowed to love Diana forever and he anticipated a similar response. 'Well, for a long time, anyway,' she nonchalantly replied. The response, by his own admission, shook him to the core.

James Lees-Milne received the news of Diana's engagement with little enthusiasm. It came like a 'cruel blow' which upset his emotional state. Diana tried to console him with a short, but sweet, letter: 'I know you will like him [Bryan] because he is too angelic and not rough and loathes shooting and loves travelling and all the things I love.' Diana was preoccupied with a glamorous, materialistic world and, given Bryan's wealth, it served to make Jim feel worthless. 'When we are married and live in London, you must often come and see us,' she gently coaxed him. He sent Diana a wedding present of books and, apart from a customary thank you note, he did not set eyes on her for the next twenty-five years.

As soon as the engagement appeared in *The Times*, vast amounts of wedding presents were delivered daily to the Guinness's London residence, Grosvenor Place. Upon viewing the presents, Lady Evelyn gave a disapproving moan. 'The glass will be the easiest,' she said as she cast her eye over the endless tokens sent by friends, family and the vaguest of acquaintances. 'It only needs a good kick.' Diana responded with laughter and was quickly brought down to earth when David gently reminded her that people were very kind to send her gifts.

Diana had been spending more time at Grosvenor Place, a Victorian imitation of a French chateau made up of Nos 10 and 11, and as such it had duplicate features on either side of the house. It was quite unlike anything she had experienced, beginning with her arrival, when the front door would automatically open as she approached the steps. This phantom working was carried out by George, the doorman, who sat all day, watching from a tiny window in the porch. He was known for his clumsiness, and the first greeting Lady Evelyn bestowed on her guest was 'Did George knock you down?'

Guided by George, Diana was led along a darkened hall with stripped pine panelling to a lift which she thought resembled a medieval closet. The doors were opened by a nursery maid and tea was laid out in Grania's nursery, the centre of Lady Evelyn's world. So devoted to nursery life, she opted to sleep in one of the night nurseries and, transferring her extravagant tastes onto her children, she ensured it was bright and brimming with toys, books and a collection of sofas covered in chintz.

By contrast, the rest of the house was almost pitch-dark. The downstairs rooms were lined with rough, blackened wood. The furniture, besides refectory tables blackened with age, consisted of dozens of Spanish chairs of various sizes upholstered in dark, hard leather for the back and seat with 'many a rusty nail to catch a stocking here and there in the crumbling wooden frame'. The lamps were made of bent pieces of iron holding faux yellow candles with yellow bulbs of about five watts shaded in thick, old parchment – tallow, not wax, was the note. There were polished pewter plates and dishes crafted by Day, the head chauffeur, who had given up driving to devote his time to making plates because Colonel Guinness liked them so much. Colonel Guinness also enjoyed entertaining over 100 guests at a time, which Lady Evelyn found tiresome, but she did it for his sake. She requested only one thing: there must be more than enough pewter dishes for everyone to fall back on, silver or china would have spoiled the theme.

In spite of the eccentric décor, Diana was more amused and surprised to see a beautiful wooden slide propped on one of the staircases. It belonged to Murtogh, who had admired an exact copy at a funfair and it soon became a popular attraction for those who visited the house. Guests, young and old, rushed up and down the stairs, whizzing down on the slide, watched by Lady Evelyn, who relished the laughter of her guests. Diana was certain of one thing: Grosvenor Place indicated that life, as she knew it, would be very different once she became Mrs Bryan Guinness.

9

A SOCIETY WEDDING

All expectations for an Easter wedding were dashed. Recalling Lady Evelyn's advice that 'people who are in doubt tend to wait for ages', Bryan and Diana agreed that a date should be fixed as soon as possible. Just two months after David and Colonel Guinness conferred, the preparations for a January wedding were underway. Diana did not have to worry about a thing, as with the meticulous planning of her Christmas shopping, Lady Evelyn oversaw the minutest details.

Although they were not of the meddling sort, David and Sydney had one objection to Lady Evelyn's ostentatious plans. Since the age of 11, Diana had denounced Christianity – she leaned towards atheism – and getting married in a church seemed not only a pointless venture, but one which Sydney felt verged on hypocrisy. Siding with Diana, Sydney spoke to Bryan about her concerns. Far from understanding, Bryan found their objection to a church wedding 'most astonishing' and he was troubled by Diana's lack of Christian faith. 'Christian kindness,' he argued, 'was beauty of deed.' And he compared such beauty to the physical attractiveness of Diana – 'the most perfect manifestation' of God's creation. Furthermore, Bryan protested that he wanted to marry Diana in a building 'dedicated to beauty', which he believed to represent 'goodness, which is truth'. There was no alternative. It would have to be a church wedding, otherwise, as Bryan warned, 'it might be the death of my whole family.'

Listening to the plea and seeing no substance in Bryan's argument, David and Sydney decided to go along with his preference for a church wedding. They felt his entire reasoning was histrionic, a reaction influenced by his mother's extravagant ways, which Sydney privately thought were ridiculous. This extravagance manifested itself when St Margaret's Church, Westminster, was chosen, not for its Godly presence, but because of Lady Evelyn's preference for Gothic. Bryan, too, was attracted by its perpendicular architecture. It also happened to be the most stylish venue of the day.

Everything was going according to plan when, the day before the wedding, Jessica and Deborah contracted whooping cough and were ordered to say in bed. Sydney asked if the little girls could leave their sickbeds long enough to take part in the ceremony, but one look at Jessica and Deborah's bright-red faces destroyed any glimmer of hope and Bryan's family protested that the girls were too ill to attend – not everyone understood Sydney's carefree attitude towards illness. It was a bitter disappointment for Diana, who adored her little sisters. 'I could have spared anyone else more easily than them,' she said.

Rutland Gate was once again leased and Lord and Lady Dulverton, to whom Batsford Park had been sold, gave Diana the use of their London house at Wilton Crescent. It was in this unfamiliar house that Diana dressed in her ivory duchesse satin wedding gown, designed by Norman Hartnell. The veil, crafted from the Brussels lace that Lady Evelyn had given her, was attached to a crystal and flower wreath. The elaborate veil and wreath proved irksome and it would test Diana's patience throughout the day. 'Oh Nanny, this is impossible!' she snapped, in a fit of bad temper as she tore off the veil. The veil was only part of the problem, but it represented her suppressed tension bubbling to the surface. The absence of Jessica and Deborah, and Bryan's simpering ways leading up to the wedding day, contributed to her highly strung state. Sensing she was on the verge of tears, Nanny Blor put her arms around Diana and reassured her with an old, familiar phrase: 'Don't worry, darling, nobody's going to be looking at you.' Diana sensed she was hearing those comforting words for the last time.

David was hovering close by, anxiously keeping an eye on the time. Fixated with punctuality, he had been implored by everyone not to get Diana to St Margaret's ahead of schedule. 'We won't get there ahead of the game,' he told her. In a state of nervousness and despair, Diana departed the Dulvertons' house with her veil awry.

Diana's memories of her wedding day were very vague. She recalled walking down the aisle on her father's arm, followed by a flock of eleven bridesmaids, each in tulle Sylphide dresses with a long pearl and crystal cross necklace, a gift from Bryan, draped around their necks. Seeing Bryan and his best man, Michael Rosse, waiting at the altar, she instantly thought how 'neat and handsome' he looked. Her brother Tom managed to engage a trumpeter who filled the church with a triumphant sound when the choir sang Handel's 'Let the Bright Seraphim in Burning Row'. The final recollection of the day, from Diana's point of view, was when the clergyman firmly pressed his hand on her forehead, causing the wreath from the dreaded veil to fall over her eyes. The irritation and discomfort in the final moments of the marriage ceremony was perhaps a symbol for what was yet to come.

In contrast to his bride's irascibility, Bryan remembered the church as being 'gay with flowers and guests'. However, for a fleeting moment, as they stood at the altar, Bryan began to feel something was amiss. The ceremony seemed theatrical, the guests – many of whom he did not know – and the grandeur surrounding what he knew to be of religious significance (Diana cared little for such things) struck him with an unsettling feeling. This feeling of intrusiveness was not unfounded and the strangers inside the church were just as curious as the people waiting outside. The society columns reported every detail. 'The Wedding of the Year', the headlines rang, and photographs of Diana in her finery failed to capture her loveliness. The disenchantment was clear on her face and it obscured any testimonial of her beauty.

Guests, too, voiced their private thoughts on the day. According to their mutual friend, Robert Byron, the wedding itself was 'quite fun', though he noticed that Lady Evelyn seemed 'frankly bored'. Sydney's views were well known; she felt Diana was too young to be in charge of such an enormous fortune – an allowance believed to be £20,000 a year. However, as much as Sydney disapproved of rich people, she understood that in some cases it could not be helped.

As soon as Bryan conquered his feelings of uneasiness, brought on by his overactive imaginings of the guests with their eyes staring at his back, and penetrating his soul as he made his promise to God, he settled into a sense of elation. It was, at that moment, to remain the happiest day of his young life.

Bryan's beautiful teenage bride, once so eager to leave home, felt sullen and irritated by the religious ceremony and his sentimental preferences for hymns and sermons. Perhaps to take her mind off it, Diana silently observed that Michael Rosse resembled Bryan's butler rather than an earl. And she remembered the letters of advice that he dispatched to Bryan which she had read, finding them comical and pompous.

During the wedding reception at Grosvenor House, a group of Bryan's Oxford friends suggested they all meet in Cappadocia later in the year. 'Oh, yes!' Diana jubilantly cried, 'we will. Let's all meet in Cappadocia soon.'

'I don't particularly want to go to Cappadocia,' Bryan mumbled in the whispery voice he used when irritated.

It was the first disagreement of their marriage. A day later they caught the train to Paris to begin their honeymoon and she consoled herself with the assurance that a glamorous life awaited her. The last time Diana undertook such a journey she had been chaperoned by Winston and Randolph Churchill, a child sent hither and thither at the will of the grown-ups. Now she was considered a grown-up, and in the short space of two years she had acquired a wealthy husband, her own maid and access to the Guinness fortune.

One last reminder of her country childhood lingered and, true to form, Sydney had Diana's going away outfit made at Swinbrook. It was a dress of blue printed velvet and a blue cloth coat, its plainness saved by Lady Evelyn's gift of a mink collar and cuffs. It would be the last homemade outfit Diana would wear.

The newlyweds spent the first part of their honeymoon in Paris at Bryan's parents' apartment at 12 Rue de Poitiers, its interior spanning two floors, with large windows overlooking the River Seine. Lacking Lady Evelyn's medieval tastes, the apartment's décor was the embodiment of modern chic. The bedroom had grey satin curtains, a grey satin bed canopy wreathed with three-dimensional pink roses, a wood-burning fire and a daybed strewn with lace cushions. The butler and cook, with little else to do, devoted their time to looking after the couple. But Diana's requests were simple and she asked for one thing: the cook's speciality, a pudding called *tête de chocolat*, which she consumed every day.

In Paris, Diana traded in her trunks of homemade clothing and, encouraged by Bryan, she spent her afternoons shopping at couture houses where she was fitted for custom-made clothing. It was an extravagant indulgence for the girl who once thought the department stores of the *Galeries Lafayette* were beyond her reach. Half-filled with guilt and pleasure, Diana imagined her mother's reaction to a wildly expensive gown made by Louise Boulanger, which she purchased simply because she could afford it. The dress was daring for its time: short, tight, white faille embellished with a blue sash, tied at the back in a large bow so long it almost skimmed the floor.

Wearing her new dress, Diana dazzled Bryan's maternal grandfather, Lord Buchan, when he paid a visit to their Paris apartment. Upon noticing that she towered over his diminutive frame, he turned to his grandson and said, 'Pretty little woman you've married, Bryan.'

Sicily was the next stop on their extensive honeymoon and it provided Diana with her first glimpse of the beautiful Mediterranean, then unspoiled by commercial tourism. The scenery enchanted her with its ruins and temples, reminiscent of her childhood fantasy, where she and James Lees-Milne dreamed of living on a Greek island in perfect seclusion. From her suite at the San Domenico Palace

Hotel in Taormina, Diana wrote a letter to a friend: 'Oh it is so lovely being married. This is a heavenly island, we have been here nearly a week and are going on to Syracuse fairly soon, then Palermo and then perhaps Rome, or Athens or London I am not sure.' Her tone had changed from a besotted young debutante, to that of a worldly, society woman.

10

MRS BRYAN GUINNESS

B ryan's Bar exam loomed nearer and the newlyweds returned to London to the bracing chill of late winter. Colonel Guinness, rich as he was, had made it clear to Bryan that he ought to adopt a profession. Bryan contemplated a career in diplomacy, but the apprehension of exile made him change his mind. When he was younger, his father had presented him with information on a military school for engineering, but Bryan had no interest and he explained: 'I knew my limitations better than he did.' He had no wish to enter the family's brewing business, for he lacked the scientific qualifications to do so. He therefore made up his mind to read for the Bar, though in his heart he would consider himself first and foremost a writer.

Bryan bought his and Diana's marital home at 10 Buckingham Street, a pretty townhouse designed by Lutyens. The rates bill was a staggering £910 per annum, a sum greater than most of their friends' annual incomes. Many young women in Diana's position would have been thrilled with such a house, but she was less than impressed by the home's interior. The furniture was to Lady Evelyn's taste, with refectory tables riddled by wormholes, and although two rooms brimmed with wedding presents, she did not overly care for them. In her absence, Diana's bedroom had been decorated in pink, with a blue brocade bed on a dark-blue velvet dais and fixed to the back were lamps set in silver iron work. Discarding any form of tact, Diana cast a disapproving eye over the garish décor and firmly announced it as 'hideous'.

Parental interference was kept to a minimum, with Colonel Guinness offering Bryan only one piece of advice regarding married life: 'There is nothing so barbarous as for a husband and wife to share a bathroom.' David had a small input, too, when he sent Diana one of his dogs – a gun-shy Labrador named Rubbish, whom she loved.

Before she could settle into married life, Diana had to complete one more initiation into the world of an upper-class marriage. As she had done the year before, Diana travelled to Buckingham Palace, this time with Lady Evelyn, to be presented at Court as the Honourable Mrs Bryan Guinness. The nervousness she had once felt as a young debutante was replaced with a blasé attitude. It was more of an inconvenience to traipse across town to the palace, decked out in the uncomfortable formal wear, standing in the draughty throne room waiting to be paraded before the king and queen. Before her name was called, it suddenly dawned on Diana that she had not practised the tedious manoeuvrings of a curtsey. Lady Evelyn must have read her thoughts, for she leaned into Diana and whispered: 'We ought to have been practising our curtsies all day but I forgot.'

'So did I,' Diana earnestly replied. 'I've been doing household accounts.'

'Household accounts!' Lady Evelyn squealed with horror. 'How *barbarous* of Bryan.'

It seemed a natural chore for Diana, as it was a familiar sight to see Sydney sitting at her writing bureau, filling out her accounts book with great precision. It was ranked with such importance that on the day of Deborah's birth Sydney reached for her accounts book and neatly wrote: 'Chimney swept', completely overlooking the arrival of the baby. Her mother's sensible advice on running a home would have to be abandoned, along with the elegant leather-bound accounts book she had given Diana with her initials printed in gold.

'*Barbarous*,' Lady Evelyn repeated, and she advised Diana to spend *more* money.

In spite of her new wealth, Diana had not been extravagant with Bryan's money. She never thought of Bryan as rich – he 'never seemed like other rich men' – until one day she nonchalantly expressed her wish for a diamond tiara. 'Oh,' he casually replied, 'there is one for you.' It had never occurred to Bryan that Diana would have craved such opulence. And it never crossed Diana's mind that such an expensive item would be at her disposal.

In political circles, the general election of May 1929 was referred to as the 'Flapper Election', due to women over the age of 21 gaining the right to vote. Diana, who had once engaged in political discussions during her summer stay at Chartwell in 1926, abandoned her Liberal sympathies in favour of a materialistic world. This fleeting political awareness hardly mattered when it came to the 1929 general election, as Diana was still too young to vote. Bryan's family, as with her own parents, were staunchly Conservative, and that year Colonel Guinness ran for election.

Diana and Bryan motored down to Colonel Guinness's constituency in Bury St Edmunds. It was a pretty Georgian house and, as with the Parisian apartment, Lady Evelyn went there so little that she had never bothered to renovate it to her Gothic tastes. Diana was suspicious of Colonel Guinness's political career, not because she thought him corrupt, but because she was merely baffled by his circumspect outlook regarding electioneering. He was clever and a good conversationalist, but he was not very good on the platform. The entire business bored him and he often reached for his pocketbook of jokes to punctuate his speeches. Another vice he relied on was alcohol – he confessed to Diana that he drank half a bottle of champagne to get through the entire ordeal of speeches. He kept the champagne in his briefcase and drank it straight from the bottle as he travelled in his chauffeur-driven car. If this was the world of politics, Diana wanted nothing to do with it. Diana was firmly anti-Tory, and loyalty towards her in-laws meant little to her. If she had been of an age to vote, she would not have voted for Colonel Guinness, and in that case she thought it best to abstain from the polls altogether. The Tories were beaten and a new Labour government was formed. With little to do, Colonel Guinness set sail in his yacht earlier than usual.

Still, despite this disregard for politics, Diana found it difficult to escape the subject. Bryan took her to Berlin – Germany had always been a place she wished to visit – and she told Brian Howard of their impending trip. 'You will love Berlin, my dear, it is the gayest town in Europe; in fact, my dear, you'll never have seen anything like it.' Their friend's prediction proved correct. Diana and Bryan were not accustomed to the seedy exploits they witnessed in popular German nightclubs, where men pretended to be women and vice versa. '*Grim*,' she sniped, for that would have been a more appropriate description.

Tom Mitford was also in Berlin, studying law at the university, and when he met with Diana and Bryan his conversation centred on politics. 'There are fights all the time among the students,' he told them. 'Sozis against Nazis. The other day one lot threw the other lot out of a window.'

'Out of a *window*?' came Diana's astonished reply.

'Well, not a very high window. But sometimes they do kill each other,' Tom added. It was the first time Diana had heard the expression 'Nazi'. She asked him which side he was on. Tom thought for a moment and concluded it was the Germans' own affair, but if he was German he would be inclined to be a Nazi.

'Would you?' asked Bryan, perhaps in disbelief.

'Yes; no question.' Tom confirmed. He justified his decision with: 'It will be either the Nazis or the Communists.'

For the majority of the upper classes so keen to preserve their wealth, Communism posed more of a threat.

Germany had been an awakening for Diana; the strange nightclubs, the violent political upheaval and Bryan's indifference to it all made her question the world around her. She was unnerved by Tom's explanation of the Nazi Party, then considered a band of thugs, but she longed to know more. Diana's naivety was unravelling to reveal a hardened view on the world. Bryan was still caught up in sentiment and beauty and it did not occur to him that his young wife was mentally advanced beyond his capabilities. To Bryan, she was still the epitome of sweetness.

Taking advantage of her gilded life, Diana embraced her social position and she made new acquaintances as she entered the world of opera and theatre. Bryan, who was usually quite anti-social, approved of her enthusiasm for the arts, for he, too, was a keen theatregoer and belonged to various clubs for Sunday performances. Recalling happy memories from her childhood, Diana remembered trips to watch Shakespeare at Stratford-upon-Avon and the *Matinée Classique* in Paris. Since her marriage, she realised she had overindulged: 'It is extraordinary how boring a boring play can be, how draughty the theatre in which it is performed can seem, how unending the intervals.' After exhausting the traditional and modern plays and the musical comedies, Diana used the theatre to gain entry into a new social circle.

During an outing to the opera with Bryan – who preferred to watch the performance and not mingle – Diana was introduced to Emerald, Lady Cunard, the American-born socialite who, in her youth, had fabricated an entirely new persona for herself. Changing her name from Maud to Emerald (because she liked them) and surrounding herself with the arts, she became a master at cultivating a materialistic lifestyle. As usual, her box was filled with interesting artists and fellow socialites, amongst them Diana's hero from her youth, Lytton Strachey.

Hoping to establish common ground with Emerald, who was old enough to be her mother, Diana approached her and timidly asked, 'You knew Helleu, didn't you?'

'*Helleu*?' Emerald snapped in her mid-Atlantic accent. 'Of course I knew Helleu. *Everybody* knew Helleu!'

The remark had disturbed her and Diana learned that Emerald loathed to be reminded of dead friends, it was only the living she cared about. Bearing no grudge against Diana, Emerald invited everyone back to her home at Grosvenor Square, otherwise known by her foes as the wasps' nest.

Supper tables were laid out in the upstairs drawing room where the Marie Laurencin pictures hung. And fanning the spark of conversation in a way that was rare in London, Emerald encouraged her guests to converse freely, rather than limiting them to their neighbouring guest. She often pitted her guests against one another for her own amusement and to start a raucous discussion. Bryan skirted around the current of animated chatter, wishing he were at Buckingham Street alone with Diana. Suddenly, as she was apt to do, Emerald interrupted the lively scene, and announced: 'Come along, Mr Strachey, I want you to sit next to Diana Cooper.'

'I'd rather sit next to the other Diana,' Strachey gallantly replied.

Lytton Strachey, who was approaching his fifth decade, seemed older than his years. Diana warmed to this thin, gently mannered man who spoke in a high pitched voice. This admiration was founded on feelings of awe, as she had worshipped him for years, having read his books which thrived on nonconformist ideals.

Strachey was a founding member of the elite, intellectual Bloomsbury Group, and intimidated by his intelligence, Diana feared Strachey would become bored with her. To her relief, they 'flew together like iron filings and magnet' and conversed easily about a vast range of subjects until the early hours of the morning. Strachey liked to teach, and she was eager to learn. This unabashed admiration from Diana shone, and although outwardly shy, he was prone to compliments. Above all else, her extreme youth seemed to please him.

But Diana's initial feelings of unease had not been unfounded. In a letter to his fellow Bloomsbury, Roger Senhouse, Strachey spoke of his reluctance towards her, whom he confided was 'probably too young to provide any real sustenance'.

11

HE-EVELYN

T he frivolity of the upper classes during the interwar era encouraged the society columns to create new stars, who achieved notoriety through merely being the offspring of the aristocracy. Diana's celebrity was in ascent; a dizzying element for a girl who had spent her childhood as the scapegoat for sibling teases and vitriolic putdowns. Now she had what all young debutantes desired: independence achieved through a brilliant marriage, masses of stylish clothes, a house in a desirable location of London, dazzling friends and a rich, adoring husband. Despite the materialistic distractions, Diana was soon to discover she was not as completely free as she had once thought.

Influenced by leading society magazines, namely *The Tatler and The Bystander*, Diana began to throw lavish parties at Buckingham Street. Along with a reluctant Bryan, she hosted a tropical themed party on board the *Friendship*, a riverboat permanently moored at Charing Cross Pier. It brought together the prominent figures of the Bright Young Things and fellow aristocrats, who fancied themselves to be bohemian; the latter appealing more to Bryan, than his impressionable wife. Resenting this media association with the foolishness of the Bright Young Things, Bryan failed to see how their friends compared to the attention seeking ways of this youthful set which the author Evelyn Waugh so gleefully satirised.[20]

Nancy was a great friend of Evelyn Waugh and his wife, also named Evelyn, and to avoid confusion they went by the monikers of 'He-Evelyn' and 'She-Evelyn'. Knowing of He-Evelyn's desire to witness this set first hand, Nancy invited the Waughs to Diana's tropical party. Out of place in the gaiety of the *Friendship*, He-Evelyn silently observed the misbehaving guests dressed in Zulu costumes and sarongs, as ordinary commuters scurried along the embankment to catch the last train home.

The Waughs existed on the fringes of Diana and Bryan's inner circle; He-Evelyn knew Bryan from Oxford and She-Evelyn was a close friend of Nancy, who was staying at their five-room flat at 17A Canonbury Square. He-Evelyn liked people because they amused him or he was fond of them. Sometimes he sought their company because of some oddity which delighted the novelist in him, but he confined his true friendship to a very narrow circle. This very narrow circle would soon include Diana, of whom he had read so much in the pages of magazines, and owing to such whimsical reports of beauty and privilege, He-Evelyn had already made up his mind to dislike her.

But to Nancy's horror, the years spent in the library of Asthall were being regressed when Diana unintentionally snared her eldest sibling's guests. Nancy had known He-Evelyn for years,[21] though one look at her younger, glamorous sister and it seemed years of loyal friendship stood for nothing. As with Tom's friends all those years ago, he became smitten with Diana.

Two days after the feted tropical party, the Waughs' marriage ended due to She-Evelyn's affair with John Heygate. They gave up the flat at Canonbury Square and Diana offered Nancy a room at Buckingham Street. He-Evelyn came to visit Nancy but it was an excuse to see Diana, the latest object of his boundless curiosity.

When they weren't entertaining in London, Diana and Bryan spent most of their weekends at his parents' house, Poole Place, on the edge of the sea at Bailiffscourt. Jessica and Deborah often travelled down with their nanny. It was a family affair, with Lady Evelyn in the Huts with Grania and Murtogh. Bryan threw himself into the juvenile antics of the children, especially the two Mitford girls, and he became their most treasured playmate.

The sea coast and wholesome atmosphere failed to amuse Diana, and her critical eye was distracted by the odd architectural structure of Poole Place, which she announced as 'frankly hideous'. The landscape's appearance had severely changed since her first visit to Bailiffscourt the year before; the fields were no longer barren and forest trees were planted to form a barrier against the ferocious sea wind. She teasingly talked of building a tower constructed of steel and glass, where she could admire a silent view. Perhaps it was a jibe at the noise and intrusion of family life, with children and their nannies charging in and out of the huts, raising their voices and insisting on Bryan joining in on their games. He, in turn, would coax Diana to make an effort, too.

The tower of steel and glass was a joke, but Colonel Guinness and Lady Evelyn did not understand this form of 'Mitford teasing'. They believed Diana wanted to spoil the landscape they had been so keen to preserve when they purchased Bailiffscourt. Pondering the unintended insult from his daughter-in-law, Colonel Guinness offered to buy Bryan a country house of his own, but Bryan objected, claiming Poole Place was as good as any. It was only when Colonel Guinness said it was unwise for families to live on top of one another, as 'it could lead to disagreements', that Bryan realised his father was embittered by Diana's joke.

If Diana's extreme youthfulness presented in her an unguarded moment of immaturity, her generosity more than made up for her juvenile streak. Her newest friend, Evelyn Waugh – who no longer required the title He-Evelyn given the abandonment of She-Evelyn – was consumed by the break-up of his marriage. His depressed demeanour, exacerbated by the need to stay at his parents' house in Hampstead, was proving to be a distraction to his writing. So, Diana offered him the solitude of Poole Place as an ideal retreat to finish his manuscript. Waugh had accomplished his goal of obtaining inside knowledge on how this illusive inner circle interacted and, now with his ideas intact, he needed to form the plot of his novel, *Vile Bodies*.

Warned by Diana of its 'ugliness', Waugh set forth to Poole Place in late autumn, undeterred by the freezing coastal winds and the noisy ferocity of the English Channel. Poole Place fascinated Waugh and he was equally intrigued by the work going on in the nearby fields, where Lady Evelyn was constructing her medieval vision. She wanted gnarled trees for the newly built house to nestle in and they were bought and transferred from afar, carefully replanted in the best soil, bound together in straightjackets of thick straw and tied down with great cables and pegs. The architect, Mr Phillips, obeying Lady Evelyn's strict orders, imported squirrels and field mice to give the new trees a touch of authenticity. Eccentricity tickled Waugh and the sight of armies of men, lorries and cranes required for the trees was no exception.

When Diana and Bryan motored down to Poole Place to visit Waugh, he insisted on being driven over to Bramber to see the museum made by a 'disgusting clergyman' who had killed and stuffed tiny animals, modelling them into a variety of bizarre poses, such as a kitten pushing a guinea pig in a pram. Always a lover of animals, it made Diana feel sick, but Waugh enjoyed the grotesque spectacle. There was sometimes menace in his brilliant eyes.[22]

The friendship with Diana and Bryan happened before Waugh's conversion to Catholicism, an act which baffled those closest to him. He must have spoken to Diana about his interest in religion, for she once remarked to a friend: 'Evelyn prays for me.' The phrase struck a chord of ridiculousness, prompting the friend to scoff: 'God doesn't listen to Evelyn.' At this point in their friendship, Waugh could see no fault in Diana and if she was prone to a waspish remark he did not take it to heart.

Nancy vied for Waugh's attention and, frustrated by his lack of interest in her, she wrote to him using age-old tactics to draw his attention towards her. She whined about her farcical love life and tried to engage him by speaking of her minor literary success. When she boasted of a small cheque, Waugh offhandedly told her to invest it in new clothes – by dressing better she might attract a rich man. Nothing else mattered, he only had eyes for Diana.

12

CONFINEMENT

As summer began, Diana said goodbye to the last attachment to her childhood. Rubbish, the dog David had given her, mysteriously vanished from Poole Place, having torn away from the maid who was holding him. Two days later, when the police returned Rubbish, he was suffering from deep and painful gashes. Diana lay by his bed, imploring him not to die, but her desperate pleas could not save Rubbish. His frail body was ravaged by a recent attack of seizures and she made the humane decision to euthanise the dog. To make up for Rubbish's death, Bryan presented her with a large Irish wolfhound named Pilgrim. The dog required constant attention, feasting on raw meat cut into small pieces and hand-fed to him by Diana. Although fond of dogs, she resented Pilgrim's time-consuming ways.

There were more pressing matters to contend with. That June, Diana discovered she was expecting a baby. Not yet 20, she responded to the pregnancy without much enthusiasm, and the thought of a confinement, before and after the birth, did not thrill her. Bryan was ecstatic, he longed for a child of his own, and wanting to revel in his happiness, he asked Diana to keep the news a secret.

In August, Diana and Bryan went to stay at his father's house, Knockmaroon, on the edge of Phoenix Park in Dublin. 'We are happy here,' he recorded in his diary.[23] They were content staying indoors, looking at the River Liffey and watching the cattle grazing in the meadows. This scene of quiet domesticity made Bryan suddenly feel as if he were travelling through life in 'a sensation of immense speed'. The prospect of becoming a father made him acutely aware of his own mortality and the 'insane rate at which I was travelling to my death', but all morbid thoughts left his mind when he glanced over at Diana 'sitting on the sofa secretly expecting our first child'.

Gone were the lively parties, often lasting all night, and Diana and Bryan filled their evenings with trips to Dublin's Abbey Theatre. Regardless of any situation, she could always find things to make her laugh. Whilst attending *John Ferguson*, a play by John Ervine, a disgruntled man suddenly awoke from his daydream and yelled: 'That's not Irish, that's an *Ulster* word!' He charged from the theatre, stamping on Diana's toes as he left.

Having attended the theatre almost every night, Bryan and Diana became acquainted with the actors, but he refused to relent to her longings to join them for late suppers after their performances. They promptly returned home to Knockmaroon and Diana was early to bed for the sake of the baby. He remembered in his diary how he had scattered rose petals around her golden head as she slept and, seeing her eyelids flutter and her head turn over, he departed just as she started to wake.

When they returned to England, Bryan's thoughts turned to his growing family, and he took Colonel Guinness up on his generous offer to buy the couple a country house of their own. Diana and Bryan were drawn to Wiltshire, influenced by friends who lived there and the happy memories of his days at Oxford. Close proximity to London was important for both Bryan and Diana, due to his career as a barrister and her longing for the lively social activities that only London could provide.

The house agents John D. Wood drew Bryan's attention to Biddesden, an eighteenth-century country house, which charmed Bryan and reminded him of his own childhood spent at Bury St Edmunds. For Bryan, the house was a 'gateway to happiness', even if Diana openly reminded him of her loathing of the countryside, having just escaped it. But disappointment was not far off when Bryan discovered that Biddesden was priced too high and he hated to ask Colonel Guinness if he could increase his budget.

Putting Biddesden out of his mind, he and Diana travelled to Paris. Combined with the cheerful company of Evelyn Waugh and Nancy, Diana also hoped the beauty of the location would compensate for her lengthy confinement.

Waugh confessed to feeling shattered by the unexpected ending of his relatively short marriage and, far from sympathetic, Diana admitted that he showed no signs of heartbreak. He cavorted around the Rue de Poitiers in high spirits, enchanting Diana with witty stories and doing all he could to keep her entertained. Inside the flat, she relaxed in the quiet splendour of watching Bryan, Waugh and Nancy work on their manuscripts. Waugh was struggling to meet his deadline for his travel book, *Labels*, Bryan was composing *Singing out of Tune* (inspired by the failed marriage of the Waughs) and Nancy worked on her first novel, *Highland Fling*.

In the fifth month of her pregnancy, Diana was overcome with fatigue and she spent most of her time in bed reading their manuscripts and dispensing her critique, whether it was required or not. When she felt lonely, Bryan, Waugh and Nancy moved their writing stations into her bedroom. But it was hardly an ideal setting, as demonstrated by Bryan when he shook his pen so violently that the ink spattered the delicate silk curtains.

During fleeting bursts of energy, Diana and Waugh went on short walks, drives to the countryside and trips to the cinema. Behind Waugh's exuberance, he concealed a deepening love that had been growing since Diana fascinated him at the tropical party. Ever a trusting friend, Bryan did not think it strange when Waugh adopted the odd practice of lying in bed next to Diana during her afternoon naps. Diana, on her behalf, thought his attentiveness was strictly platonic. She was touched when Waugh worried about the birth of the baby, hers being the first pregnancy he had observed. 'I don't know what to say about the imminence of Baby G. Dear Diana it seems all wrong that you should ever have to be at all ill or have a pain.'[24]

Returning to London, the close relationship with Waugh continued. Diana and Bryan treated him to a birthday luncheon at the Ritz, but as her pregnancy advanced, her social life wilted. With Bryan occupied with his career as a barrister, Diana and Waugh grew closer and he now had her undivided attention.

It was an unusual set-up for its time, but her condition made it somewhat acceptable for them to spend so much time alone. Diana had a table installed in her bedroom and she and Waugh enjoyed private, though miniscule, supper parties. They went to luncheons in Hampstead at Waugh's parents' house and took silly little trips to the zoo. Even though Diana could not abide living things imprisoned in a cage, she still managed to erupt into peals of childish laughter at the monkeys. All too often, Diana grew bored with the confines of Buckingham Street and she called on Waugh to accompany her on some 'carriage exercise' in her chauffeur-driven Daimler.

Some years later, Waugh drew on this unique experience when he wrote *Work Suspended*. The narrator falls in love with Lucy, the pregnant wife of his friend who spent her days 'lying in bed in a chaos of newspapers, letters and manicure tools'. It was an age suited to parody and Waugh's imagination smouldered with all sorts of silly manifestations. Still, Waugh peddled on with *Vile Bodies*, finishing it in time to present its dedication to Diana and Bryan on Christmas morning: 'To BG and DG' it read. In return, Diana and Bryan gave Waugh a gold pocket watch.

The following month, Waugh, still full of admiration for Diana, presented the Guinnesses with the complete manuscript of *Vile Bodies*,[25] bound in leather with its title stamped in gold. But having discovered that his young friend was quite unlike the protagonist of his novel, Waugh wrote to Diana: 'I am now convinced that *Vile Bodies* is very vulgar and I am sorry for dedicating it to you but I will write many more exalted works and dedicate them to you.' The fictional portrayal of Diana played on his mind and he wrote to his friend Dig Yorke: 'She seems the one encouraging figure in this generation – particularly now she is pregnant – a great vat of potentiality like the vats I saw at their brewery.'

Waugh's eagerness to dedicate his future writings to Diana seemed optimistic. Before the birth of her baby, Waugh was making plans to stay in Dublin to complete his latest manuscript, a biography of Jonathan Swift (it was never written). He encouraged Diana to recuperate from the birth at Knockmaroon, where they 'could have fun'. Diana agreed and she looked forward to the revival of her social life.

Christmas was a flamboyant affair, held at Grosvenor Place, where the guests were treated to an abundance of food. First came the traditional food, and on each plate there were three or four tiny parcels, as well as elaborate crackers. Afterwards, the guests were ushered to the drawing room, given a pair of scissors and directed to the presents which were piled up in groups along the walls and in the corners. Viewing the spectacle beyond her wildest imagination, Diana understood why Lady Evelyn began her Christmas preparations months in advance. It was an alien experience for Diana, whose family Christmases consisted of the same ritual each year: a family dinner followed by a fancy-dress party and a photograph snapped using the self-timer.

Over the festive season, Diana's elderly grandmother, Lady Clementine, visited Buckingham Street to enquire about the baby. 'When do you expect the baby?' she asked.

'In the beginning of March,' Diana said. 'In fact it might be born on the thirteenth.' (13 March was David's birthday, Lady Clementine's less favoured son.)

'Oh, I hope not!' cried the old lady, and with a sympathetic tone she added, 'poor darling Dowdy! Always so unlucky!'

Unlucky was a poor adjective to bestow on Diana. As 1929 came to a close, and still only 19, she looked forward to the birth of her first child and the subsequent relaunch of her social life. She could not have anticipated the personal and social upheavals the thirties would bring, nor could she have predicted the exceptional change in her own her destiny.

13

A GILDED LIFE

On 16 March 1930, Jonathan Bryan Guinness was born. Diana was filled with happiness when she looked down at her newborn baby sleeping in his elaborately trimmed cot. The feeling elated her, and in spite of the pain she had endured and Sydney's pessimistic statement that 'all babies are ugly', Diana thought her son was 'perfect'. Bryan fussed by her bedside and treated her with the utmost care. She had given him what he always longed for and he fell even more deeply in love with her. He spared no expense and lavished her with an enormous painting, the 'Unveiling of Cookham War Memorial' by Stanley Spencer.

A nanny would have to be engaged. Diana had known no different, she had been cared for by a nanny until her marriage to Bryan, and it never occurred to her that she would look after the baby herself. Nanny Higgs had come by good recommendation from the Churchill family, she had been the eldest children's nanny and doted on Diana: 'What a character!' she often said. Though Diana Churchill, like her cousin Diana, was now grown up.

Although Nanny Higgs became a close friend to Diana, she was strict about her duties and interaction between mother and baby was kept to a minimum. Nanny's day off was the occasion Diana looked forward to most, it was the only opportunity she had to push her baby son in his pram – a novelty she anticipated every week. In between, she had to make do with walking Pilgrim the dog.

Before Jonathan's birth, Diana had purchased dozens of pretty frocks from the children's retailer, Wendy, owned by Bryan's aunt. No one objected to Diana dressing her baby son in girls' clothing and Bryan was too ecstatic to care about the smaller details. The nursemaid's patience was tested daily when she changed the baby several times a day into his pretty dresses adorned with numerous tiny pearl buttons. Even the nightgowns were made from the finest lace and linen, and hungry Jonathan detested this morning ritual of dressing which delayed his feeding and he would cry until red in the face.

Planning the christening, Diana wanted to carry on with her unusual approach to clothing and dress Jonathan in long, black lace trousers. If only for the sake of formality, Bryan convinced her to go with a traditional gown. The christening was indeed a formal affair, conducted on a lavish scale, with the society columns printing stories and photographs of Bryan glowing with pride and his young wife, not yet 20, gazing adoringly at the baby's chubby face scowling from beneath the lace bonnet. Squashed to the back of the group photos were Randolph Churchill and Evelyn Waugh, the appointed godfathers, each festering an intense dislike for one another – a dislike they both carried until the end of their days.

In early summer, London's society events were in full swing and with youthful gaiety Diana launched herself back on the scene. Bryan had reservations about parties, balls, tea at the Ritz and endless trips to the theatre once again consuming their lives. Waugh, too, disapproved of her eagerness to indulge in such frivolity and it caused friction between the two. Like Bryan, he preferred to have Diana all to himself, to sit in a quiet corner where they could talk, but Diana, by her own admission, was 'pleasure loving'. Waugh's jealousy transferred to Bryan, who was not happy when Diana began passing over his luncheon invitations in favour of her husband, with whom she dined at the Savoy Grill during his afternoon break from his barrister duties at the Temple.

The once close friends were reunited on Diana's 20th birthday that June, when Waugh presented her with a charming Briggs umbrella. However, inspired by his feelings of resentfulness, he recorded in his diary that Diana broke the umbrella the following day – an untrue account, as she cherished it for years until it was stolen. Two weeks later, at a supper party given at Buckingham Street, Waugh continued with his unusual behaviour. He instigated a fight with Randolph in the servants' hall, resulting in both men punching one another until the brawl was broken up.

Diary entries written by Waugh detail the breakdown of his friendship with Diana and reveal the bitterness which blighted their meetings:

D and I quarrelled at luncheon.
D and I quarrelled at dinner.
Quarrelled with D again and left.

Four days after recording the last event in his diary, Waugh avoided Diana at Cecil Beaton's cocktail party. It pained her when he did not lapse into their old, familiar rapport and he simply bid her goodnight and left. Diana must have featured heavily on his mind, for later that evening, Waugh sent a letter to Buckingham Street. His bad behaviour, he wrote, was due to his unease with himself and the parting words, 'don't bother to answer', left Diana with little doubt as to how she should proceed. Waugh's petty behaviour enforced Diana's firm belief that 'in friendship there must be neither possessiveness nor jealousy. Either would wreck it.'

Thirty-six years later, a month before his death on 10 April 1966, Waugh offered Diana some closure when he wrote to her, shouldering the blame for the ending of their friendship. He broke it off out of 'pure jealousy' provoked by an infatuation with her. She had shown him kindness and empathy during a turbulent time in his life and this inspired him to see Diana in a romantic light. She had become the 'unobtainable object' of his desires and, even though a sexual relationship was off limits, he wanted her all to himself as an 'especial confidante and comrade'. That, Waugh told her, was 'the sad and sordid truth'. Except for his letter, they never spoke again.

14

AN INTERVAL IN FRIENDSHIPS

Diana pined for Evelyn Waugh and she pondered how to get him back. Her former friend's attention was consumed by his new celebrity status; *Vile Bodies* had been a major success and Waugh was in demand at parties and in fashionable salons in London. He also directed his affection towards the Bright Young Thing, Baby Jungmann, who, alongside her sister Zita, had many admirers.

Despite Waugh's abandonment, Diana was not bitter and she recalled her fondness for his company when she said: 'Wherever Evelyn was he made it exceptional – brilliant company! His malicious wit, his quickness on the uptake ... he was an incredibly clever man who saw the fun in everything and made life wonderful.' With this in mind, she sent another invitation to Waugh, once again inviting him to join her and Bryan at Knockmaroon, but, as he had done before, he declined the invitation.

Through Waugh, Diana and Bryan had become friendly with the artist Henry Lamb and his wife, Lady Pansy. At Bryan's insistence, Diana extended an invitation for the Lambs to visit Knockmaroon and, in Waugh's place, she invited Lytton Strachey, who delighted her when he accepted. But unbeknownst to her, Strachey had once been infatuated with Lamb, whom he had initiated into the Bloomsbury set. Lamb was aware of Strachey's feelings and, as soon as he embraced him, he was rebuffed. 'Absolutely out of the question, impossible!' the artist was reported to have shouted at Strachey. To ease the tension, Lamb decided they must discuss the matter and, although he admitted his 'brutality', Strachey kept up the pretence of the past flirtation and teased, 'You knew I was a dangerous character.'

As much as Diana admired Strachey, he was not an easy guest and she rather wished he had imitated Waugh and stayed at home. From the moment Strachey departed England, his visit had begun on a sour note. He was an uneasy traveller and he felt imprisoned in his uncomfortable cabin as the ferry battled across the Irish Sea. There was no car to greet him on the quayside and, 'owing to the incompetence of the idle rich', he was forced to catch a rickety train to Dublin. He then took a taxi, hoping to get to Knockmaroon, but it ended up lost. When Strachey finally arrived at Knockmaroon he was in no mood for Diana's rigorous social calendar, and by her own admission she was too self-absorbed to afford her weary friend much empathy.

Trips to the Abbey Theatre were more than Strachey could bear. He had tolerated quite enough of 'Irish actors pretending to be Irish people' and he refused to go to any more plays. 'Oh do,' Diana implored him. But her plea fell on deaf ears, for Strachey had retreated behind his beard and spectacles and could not be reached. It was a relief to him when a bout of illness swept through Knockmaroon and many guests, including Bryan, came down with a nasty dose of the cold. Bryan was the significant victim, and with him out of action Diana was at a loss to entertain lavishly.

Strachey was delighted by this bad fortune and in a positive mood he wrote a letter to his companion, the artist Dora Carrington: 'Diana remains very dashing and superb' – in spite of the plague which had stricken her guests. He was also tickled to discover that she, too, liked monkey puzzles. 'So I suppose you adore her,' he teased Carrington.[26] Ironically, the calamitous trip was oddly refreshing and he began to write his first piece of literature in months; an essay on Froude, which he later read aloud to Diana and his guests.

Towards the end of their stay at Knockmaroon, Lamb painted a life-sized portrait of Bryan, Diana, Jonathan and Pilgrim. It was a prophetic piece, with Diana looking one way and Bryan looking the other. In a poem *The Composition by Henry Lamb*,[27] inspired by the painting, Bryan described Diana as sitting up 'in wonderment, and listens, watching like a startled doe, to see what next will come ...' With the exception of small disagreements, Bryan had no indication that his lovely young wife was less than enchanted by her gilded life.

As the seasons changed, a dark shadow of grief was cast upon the lives of the carefree Bright Young Things. Days after the gaiety of Guy Fawkes Night, Diana Skeffington – the daughter of Viscount Massereene and his wife, Jean Ainsworth – perished from typhoid at the age of 21. This Diana was a dazzling star on the Mayfair social scene and her striking dark looks were rumoured to have caught the eye of Edward, the Prince of Wales. A few days later, a further blow was delivered when Meriel Lyttleton, daughter of Lord Cobham, had succumbed to meningitis at the age of 19. And, then, Evelyn Colyer, one of 'The Babes' who had played at Wimbledon in 1923, died in childbirth.

With little happening on the social scene, Diana and Bryan left for an opulent trip on board the Orient Express for an excursion to Venice, Greece and Constantinople. The trip was unremarkable and, having proclaimed Constantinople as a 'dying city full of filth and beggars', Diana was relieved when they boarded the luxurious train for the journey home.

15

THE BLOOMSBURY SET

The unpleasant experience of Knockmaroon did little to diminish Lytton Strachey's admiration for Diana. The burgeoning friendship was soon revived when she and Bryan accepted an invitation to Ham Spray, Strachey's country home near Berkshire, which he shared with Dora Carrington. It was the apotheosis of a typical Bloomsbury arrangement, with Carrington's husband, Ralph Partridge, also residing with his mistress, Frances Marshall. Despite Strachey's praise for Diana's charming personality, Ralph and Frances found her blank gaze and affected speech irksome and they privately nicknamed her 'Dotty Di'.

Diana had never experienced a living arrangement so blatantly unconventional. Carrington seemed content to devote her to life to Strachey and, undeterred by his homosexuality, she viewed their relationship as an unofficial marriage. As she had told James Lees-Milne, Diana held enough contempt towards monogamy to embrace an open mind as far as extra-marital affairs were concerned. But this was quite different to her grasp on what she knew and what she understood. Standing next to Strachey in the window of his library, Diana spied Roger Senhouse crossing the lawn. 'Almost *too* charming, don't you think?' Strachey inquired in a tone that made Diana realise that Roger was his beloved. Where did Carrington fit in? Diana wondered.

At Knockmaroon, Diana had voiced her keenness to meet Carrington, a request that troubled Strachey. He envisioned Carrington, small and shy, peering through her pale, thick fringe at the statuesque Diana. He need not have worried, for Diana declared: 'I loved her at first sight!' To Diana, Carrington resembled a real life Beatrix Potter character in her unfashionable cotton dresses. Her pale skin was sunburnt from her avid interest in gardening and her hands were worn from toiling in the soil 'working for her beloved Lytton'. Carrington's entire persona seemed so simplistic, and Diana could not have imagined the complexities that plagued her.

The Bloomsbury set were everything the teenage Diana once held in esteem. Hidden away in the linen closet at Swinbrook, she had pored over their writings, admired their art and read their essays on aesthetic criticism. Regardless of their mutual admiration for one another and the passionate affairs within their exclusive circle, Diana found the Bloomsbury set far more 'reserved and chilly than most people'. This disenchantment towards her heroes filtered through to their quirks, which she found ridiculous – they refrained from offering a farewell parting, for it offended a Bloomsbury to say goodbye or goodnight. They looked up to Strachey as their perennial master, adopting his speech pattern of emphasising one or two words in a conversation and punctuating their responses with his characteristic, 'Oh indeed'. They were nothing more than his disciples. Diana also critiqued their style, declaring their clothes dowdy – a stark contrast to their brilliant ideals. She privately decided they were middle class and, therefore, they were dull.

Before Diana and Bryan left Ham Spray, Carrington cooked a rabbit pie for supper. The meal went against Sydney's Mosaic dietary rules – an extensive list ranging from shellfish to 'the dirty pig' – and, as Diana discovered, her mother and Moses were correct. Later in the evening, she fell violently ill and Bryan summoned the doctor, who diagnosed her as suffering from food poisoning. An odd diagnoses, for nobody else fell ill. He injected Diana with a strong sedative and when she awoke the party had left, all except Carrington, who remained her faithful nursemaid. When she recovered, she worried about the impression she had left on Strachey; she feared the disastrous beginning at Knockmaroon and her illness had conspired to portray her in an unfavourable light.

As a consolation for interrupting the weekend party at Ham Spray, Diana invited Strachey to dinner at Buckingham Street. It was a calculated approach, for Diana was certain she could restore Strachey's confidence in her by introducing him to Harold Acton, whom she 'revered as well as loved'. But Strachey was not impressed: 'A rather dreary dinner,' he confided to Carrington.

The dreariness soon turned into dread when Diana suggested they all attend a party given by 'Ma and Pa Redesdale' at Rutland Gate. Strachey felt intimidated by David and Sydney. Perhaps the inconvenience of having their home overrun by their offspring's pleasure-loving friends presented them as standoffish. Nancy and her fictitious fiancé, Hamish St Claire Erskine, were in attendance. Strachey had previously met her at Knockmaroon and found her amusing, but his opinion of her suitor was less than flattering – 'A tart,' he wrote to Carrington.[28] Surprisingly, he found the mood of the party quite informal, 'like a choice flower bed – each tulip standing separately, elegant and gay ... Tom Mit[ford] was undoubtedly the beau, the fine fleur of the ball.' The high point of the party, for Strachey, was his introduction to Tom, and his romantic nature was quite 'shattered by his charm and beauty'.

When Diana and Bryan were not travelling or visiting friends in the countryside, she found herself alone throughout the day. It was a freedom she had become used to, and Bryan's presence around the home and in her company began to feel intrusive and irritating. She had established a carefree routine of trips to art galleries, afternoon shopping sprees and taking tea at the Ritz. Following Bryan's announcement of his intention to quit the Bar, her exhilarating spell of independence dangled precariously before her. When Diana questioned his motives, she learned of the discouraging and fateful exchange that had taken place:

'I'm afraid you'll never get any briefs,' a fellow barrister told Bryan.

'Why not?' asked Bryan.

'Well, because when there's a brief going for one of us the clerk always gives it to me. He says Mr Guinness doesn't need the three guineas.'

It was a jolt of reality for Bryan, who had little interest in commercial law, and he came up with a variety of feeble excuses to address his disinterest in his chosen profession. One excuse was that his wig gave him headaches. So, without a backward glance, he quit the Bar. Bryan longed to spend his every waking moment with Diana, and he viewed the Bar as something that stood in the way of him fulfilling this ambition.

Far from being thrilled at his announcement, she viewed it as another upheaval in her life. And, after Christmas, Diana had another unwelcome discovery. She was pregnant again. Bryan was ecstatic, and, to compensate for her negative response, she put his mind at ease and agreed that a second child was, indeed, a much wanted addition to their family. 'But,' as she hastened to add, 'just not then.'[29]

16

THE HAPPY FOURSOME

A s Diana's pregnancy advanced, she busied herself with the renovation of their new country house, Biddesden. Although since her marriage she had become accustomed to living in beautiful and comfortable surroundings, she could not muster the same levels of enthusiasm as Bryan. Owing to the arrival of the baby and feeling exasperated by its disruption in her life, Diana put on a placid front and tried in vain to enjoy the summer. But the heat, combined with the impending confinement, weighed heavily on her mood. Bryan wanted to postpone his trip to Europe, but Diana urged him to go. In truth, she longed for the respite, as since giving up the Bar his constant attention had become unbearable.

With Bryan gone, Diana luxuriated in the joy of the new house; the furniture, paintings and décor were all selected by her. Though, in the evenings, Diana felt an uneasy presence filling the room. A superstitious undertone loomed over Biddesden, a familiar relic from her childhood at Asthall Manor, where it was believed a poltergeist had forced David to sell the property. This ghostly apparition was in the form of a vast painting of General Webb on his battle charger. The portrait came with the house and if it was moved General Webb's ghost was said to ride up and down the staircase, making the house uninhabitable until it was put back where it belonged.

Diana, who had not forgotten her vision at the age of 6 in the garden of Batsford Park, wondered if there was an ounce of truth in the tale. The haunting played on her mind as she lay in her four-poster bed adorned with oyster satin curtains and lined with Prince of Wales feathers. Her eyes fixed on the five long windows looking out at the darkened view, she was too afraid to sleep because she was convinced she heard footsteps on the stones outside. Lytton Strachey eventually cured Diana of her night terrors. 'I had hoped,' he said, as he raised both hands to display astonishment, 'that the age of reason had dawned.' She pondered Strachey's remark and on the surface she agreed with him, but inside she remained unconvinced.

Pamela Mitford visited from Swinbrook and her presence at Biddesden allayed Bryan's concerns at leaving Diana behind on his European trip. Self-taught in the art of running a house, and with a knowledge of animals and the land, Pamela seemed the perfect person to manage the 200-acre farm at Biddesden. If her evenings were free she dined with Diana, and she became friendly with the set who visited the house. Out of the diverse group of artists and aristocrats, it was the poet John Betjeman who gravitated towards Pamela. Theirs was a placid friendship away from the chaotic chatter of Diana and Bryan's friends, but Betjeman mistook Pamela's kindness for love and he proposed. 'I rather turned him down,' she said.

Betjeman charmed Diana and, having made no attempt to conceal that his father was in trade, his writer's imagination relayed to her the descriptions of his family to such an extent that she wanted to know what they were really like. An opportunity presented itself, when among Diana's wedding presents was an onyx cigarette box made by Betjeman & Sons. Taking a screwdriver, she removed one of its hinges and went along to 36 Pentonville Road, asking if it was possible to have it repaired. The clerk to whom she spoke said he would fetch 'Mr Ernest': Betjeman's father, Ernest, appeared and treated Diana with the utmost courtesy, thinking her just another upper-class customer. After going along with the charade, she slithered away, feeling ashamed for having spied on Betjeman's family.

Having spent a considerable amount of time at Biddesden, the haunting of General Webb was also felt by Pamela, who claimed she had encountered his ghost one evening when Diana and Bryan had gone up to London. Given her status as farm manager – miraculously during an agricultural slump she managed to turn over a small profit – Pamela had been allotted the small cottage on the grounds of Biddesden as her home. While the cottage was being renovated, she stayed in the main house, sleeping in a bedroom above a two storey-high hall overlooking the driveway.

At two o'clock in the morning, after the household staff had retired to their quarters, Pamela let the dogs out for a run. On the lawn, they became startled and bolted into the house, emitting piercing howls. Although shaken from the shrill, unexpected noise, she left Diana's dog downstairs and took Bryan's dachshund upstairs with her. It was in her bedroom that Pamela became aware of an unseen presence. She felt it watching her and hovering over her from behind the bed. She stayed awake until morning, relating her experience when she said: 'The ghost never left me. I lay rigid, with the dog shivering in its basket. It was the other side of the room, but it shook so much you could feel the vibrations through the floorboards.'[30]

John Betjeman also experienced a terrifying incident at Biddesden, when one night he dreamt that he was handed a card with wide black edges and on it his name and a date were engraved. He knew it was the date of his death. Throughout the years, several guests verified the haunting of General Webb, and those disturbed by its manifestation never stayed at Biddesden again.

Ham Spray, a mere 12 miles away from Biddesden, allowed Carrington to motor over at a moment's notice. Diana imagined she knew Carrington intimately, but she soon discovered this to be an illusion. Shy, sweet Carrington had concealed from Diana the fact that she maintained a number of lovers, but regardless of her promiscuity, Strachey remained the star of her life. Flattery, Diana learned, was a powerful weapon which Carrington used with an unusual skill. With the constant storm of jealously that prevailed at Ham Spray, she was able to remain calm despite the currents of bitterness.

'The Happy Foursome', was, in truth, anything but happy. With her comings and goings from London, Diana was largely sheltered from the more sordid elements which lurked beneath the surface at Ham Spray. She learned that Carrington had only agreed to marry her husband a decade earlier to keep the *ménage à trois* together. Strachey even accompanied them on their honeymoon to Venice.

Shortly after the marriage, Carrington met Bernard 'Beakus' Penrose and began an affair with him but, as always, her love for Strachey prevented her from committing to Penrose. When she became pregnant with Penrose's child, Carrington aborted the pregnancy and ended the affair.

Further pulled into the murkiness of Carrington's secret life, one of her great friends Phyllis de Janzé, with whom she attended the Slade School, had begun to confide in Diana. Collecting men as though they were charms, she had abandoned her French husband for a succession of lovers. Referring to her bedroom as 'the office', Phyllis entertained the men at her small house on Chapel Street. But more than anything, Phyllis sought a rich protector to relieve her of her genteel poverty.

In comparison to her contemporaries, Diana lived a life they could only dream of, but when drawing on her experiences against Carrington and Phyllis, she began to feel as though she hadn't lived at all. She was further impressed by Phyllis's perseverance; her beauty and charm eventually won her the admiration of a very rich man.

It seemed to Diana that if Phyllis, a mere shadow in her life, could confide in her, then so could Carrington. As Carrington failed to divulge her secrets, Diana merely assumed she had none to tell. Still, a small voice warned her that all was not as it seemed. Brushing doubt aside, she focused on the attributes which had attracted her to Carrington in the first place. Above all else, Diana valued non-conformity, and there was no denying that Carrington embraced this attitude in her private life, as well as in her artistry. As a token of their friendship, Carrington gave Diana and Bryan many pieces of her artwork; flower pictures modelled out of crumpled silver paper and a rococo fantasy of shells, mounted on a wooden board taken from a sewing machine.

It was nothing short of a tragedy, Diana thought, that Carrington placed Strachey and his needs before her own and, as such, a painting would go unfinished or a fleeting creative idea might be abandoned altogether. She was like a bird singing, all too easily interrupted.[31]

17

LIFE AND DEATH

Without the intimacy of her friendship with Evelyn Waugh, Diana was more active during her second pregnancy. As September approached, Diana and Bryan departed Biddesden for Buckingham Street, where she awaited the birth of her baby. She went to the theatre almost every night and one of the plays which captured her attention was *The Front Page*. So engrossed with the play, Diana decided to ignore the twinges of labour so that she could stay for the final act. In the early hours of the next morning, on 8 September 1931, she gave birth to a second son.

'Clever' was the chosen adjective bestowed on Diana after the birth – 'Aren't you *clever*?' her friends remarked when they learned she had produced another healthy son. She made no secret of her frustration – not that she minded the baby, Diana loved her babies – it was the confinement that bored her. Furthermore, she was increasingly irritated by Bryan's incessant fawning over her. He imagined Diana would have more children, as soon as possible. Wouldn't she like a daughter? He, and others, questioned.

For Diana, the answer was no. Given her statuesque height of 5ft 10in and Bryan's towering frame, she realised any daughters that might be born to her would have to rely on their physical attractiveness to advance in life. Height, Diana realised, could also be a hindrance should they lack in the looks department. Her mind drew on Unity's imposing physique and, as such, Diana knew they would be at a pathetic disadvantage.

Lytton Strachey was the first of Diana's friends to arrive, making it clear that he came to see *her* and not the baby. 'Take the baby to your room,' she ordered the monthly nurse, 'Mr Strachey can't bear newborn babies.' Diana remembered his grimace upon seeing a photograph in *The Tatler* of her holding baby Jonathan in her arms.

The nurse obliged and then disobeyed her orders when she interrupted Diana and Strachey mid-conversation. She carried the baby into the room, for she could not believe any visitor would not want to see him. The baby held no charm for Strachey and, noticing its mop of dark hair, with forced enthusiasm he said, 'What long hair!'

'Oh,' said the nurse, sensing his disdain. 'That will come off.'

With a mischievous shriek, Strachey lowered his voice to a confiding tone and asked, 'Is it a wig?'

The baby was named Desmond Walter Guinness, but Diana did not care for the name and she confessed to Strachey: 'I don't know why I have called him Desmond, only Bryan wanted such queer names he read in a book of them like for example Diggery. I thought it sounds like the comic man in Shakespeare, perhaps a gravedigger.' The name symbolised more than a compromise, it was a battle of wills. With each passing day, Bryan's constant attention grated on her and she could not fathom the logic behind his possessiveness. Love, to Bryan, meant being with the person you loved most and the more you loved them, the more you wanted to be together. Diana soon began to have outbursts of rage at Bryan, often chiding him and insulting his goodness.

After such quarrels, Diana felt compelled to grovel for his forgiveness. The guilt of hurting someone as sweet natured as Bryan distressed her, though, in the back of her mind, she felt an urge to fight against his overbearing expressions of love. An ironic stance given Diana's past affinity with lonely young men and her natural way of making them feel comforted and understood, yet she could not stand Bryan needing her so fiercely. As passive as he was to her moods, Bryan sensed the severity of Diana's restlessness, displayed through his poem, *Love's Isolation*:[32]

I see into your sight ...
But oh, I cannot find
A way into the light.

Since their days in the nursery, Diana and her sisters were experts at hiding their true feelings from prying eyes. The shop front, as they referred to it, was often mistaken for vagueness: 'a fault of our upbringing that it should be considered unthinkable to admit to weakness, misery or despair.' The shop front deceived her closest friends, including Bryan, who soon put aside his doubts and decided that whatever stirrings of discontent Diana may have felt were due to the upheaval of the new baby.

At the age of 21, Diana had experienced a full life. It was an age when her contemporaries were only just getting married, and her experiences had already eclipsed her eldest sisters, Nancy and Pamela, who were yet to marry. Bryan felt his sole purpose was to make Diana happy, and with her restlessness stirring at the back of his mind, he strived even harder to evoke the happiness from their first months of marriage. However, it seemed only Bryan could see glimmers of her true self behind the shop front. When Diana reunited with Carrington, she sensed nothing of her young friend's sorrow and praised her physical appearance, noting that Diana 'looked lovely in a curious bottle green jersey with a white frill around her neck'.[33]

Diana's unhappiness coincided with Strachey's long and painful illness that struck him that winter. The happy foursome at Ham Spray had all but disintegrated. Gone were the days of endless laughter, rowdy supper parties and intellectual chatter. Strachey had been the hero of Diana's youth. He was a pivotal influence on her maturity between the conspicuous ages of 19 and 21, and it seemed ironic that his final exit wavered over her own private turmoil. She watched her friend fade from a mysterious illness that had quickly ravaged him. Later the post-mortem concluded the cause of Strachey's suffering was stomach cancer; a growth blocked the intestine and perforated the colon, though at the time it remained undiagnosed.

'I have very little faith in there being any happiness for human beings on this earth,' Carrington wrote to Strachey, three months before his death. As if she could foresee the misery of her life without him, she attempted suicide by locking herself in the garage with the car's engine running. Rescued in time by Ralph Partridge, Carrington recovered to nurse her beloved Strachey for a few days before his untimely death at the age of 51.

In the aftermath of Strachey's death Carrington went through the motions of living, and she continued to visit Biddesden, as had been her routine for the past year. It was no longer the cheerful, 'May we come over?' telephone call which Diana looked forward to, but a vague, solemn figure consumed by grief. Carrington gave Diana an eighteenth-century waistcoat Strachey had bought years before. 'We could never think of anyone worthy of it because it was so beautiful,' she told Diana. Silk embroidered with little flowers, pink and blue, Carrington advised Diana to have it altered. 'I'd like to think of you wearing it,' she said.

Diana was absent during Carrington's last visit to Biddesden, where she seemed bright and cheerful, a complete contrast to her prior morbidity. On that particular visit, she asked to borrow Bryan's gun. 'What do you want the gun for?' someone inquired.

'To shoot rabbits,' Carrington replied.

'But there aren't any rabbits.'

At that moment a rabbit darted across the lawn. 'Look!' she shrieked, winning the petty argument. In that final statement her fate was sealed. After her guests had left for London, Carrington shot herself.

Immediately after the deaths of Carrington and Strachey, Diana claimed her life was 'useless and empty'. She sought comfort in her friend, the sculptor and fellow Bloomsbury, Tommy Tomlin. They began to take long walks through London and spoke of nothing except their deceased friends. Tommy knew suffering; he was gripped by bouts of depression, an unpredictable and menacing force which blighted his creativity. Diana felt useless at consoling him, for she was still caught up in her own personal grief.

During one of their outings, Tommy suddenly paused, as though frozen, and turned to Diana. His ashen face and colourless eyes penetrated her soul and, without warning, he announced: 'Everything in the whole world is terrible but there is one good thing ... Hitler has lost grounds in the German elections.'

18

THE AGE OF REASON

In 1932, Diana and Bryan moved from their first marital home on Buckingham Street to a vast, four-storeyed townhouse in Cheyne Walk, overlooking the Thames. The house itself was tinged by sadness. It had once belonged to the artist Rex Whistler and, prior to the Guinnesses moving in, the Earl of Dudley and his late wife Lady Rosemary, who was killed in a plane crash two years before. It was also in this house that the Dudleys resided with their 7-year-old son Jeremy before he was killed on the Embankment whilst on an outing with his nurse.

Despite the tragedies suffered by its previous occupants, Cheyne Walk was a revelation for Diana as a society hostess and as a platform for expressing her exquisite taste in interior design. The panelled drawing room spanned the entire first floor, with long windows overlooking the Thames at the front and the garden from the back. Bryan gave her a free hand with the décor and she adorned the rooms with fine art. No expense was spared, even a small Aubusson carpet was installed in the children's nursery. 'So good for them to see pretty things when they're crawling about,' she trilled.

Artists scrambled to paint Diana's portrait, and among the first to be commissioned at Cheyne Walk was Augustus John. She did not favour him in the same light as Henry Lamb, thinking him elderly with bloodshot eyes (he was only in his fifties), but Bryan was fond of him and his family. Frequent confrontations between the couple were not uncommon and to avoid another disagreement she went along to John's squalid studio at Mallord Street. Diana further appeased Bryan when she accepted John's invitation to stay at Fryern Court. 'Pubs and 'shove ha'penny' are not among the entertainments I enjoy,' she bemoaned.

John Banting asked to paint Diana's portrait, resulting in a huge head and shoulders study on a canvas measuring 6ft by 4ft. She never cared for the portrait, but felt compelled to keep it. Bryan bought it because Banting was poor and desperately needed the money.

An impression of the young Mrs Guinness lingered in the higher ranks of society and she caught the attention of C.B. Cochran, who had ambitions of producing *The Winter's Tale* on the London stage. He had only one leading lady in mind: the Hon. Diana Guinness. There was no evidence that Diana possessed any acting talent and she certainly did not harbour a dream of becoming an actress. For Cochran, it was simply a matter of marketing. By casting Diana in the role of Perdita, he would use her physical good looks and socialite reputation to launch her as a new star to the theatregoing public.

Theoretically, there was nothing in Diana's domestic life standing in the way; her two sons were in the nursery and Bryan was fond of the theatre. Dr Rudolph Krommer, an acquaintance of Diana's, not unlike Helleu whom she kept around for his generous flattery of her, went to Cochran and talked him out of it.[34] The project was abandoned and he hunted for another leading lady. For a short time Diana was bitter about the rejection, but she soon got over it.

Diana's attention was absorbed in the planning of a spectacular ball for 300 guests, young and old, rich and poor. They descended on the garden at Cheyne Walk, its trees lit from beneath with garden lanterns. Every detail was considered: a Russian orchestra played in the drawing room for those who wished to stay indoors and supper was served in the two dining rooms with maids wearing green and white floral dresses. On the warm night, Diana was a vision in a pale-grey dress of chiffon and tulle, adorning her frame with all of the diamonds she could lay her hands on. Dazzling in her tiara of ruby and diamonds, she left no doubt of her position as a leading society hostess. 'I feel as if I had been raised from the dead,' Robert Byron said in praise of her energy and execution of the ball.

Two memories stood out for Diana: manoeuvring an intoxicated Augustus John out of the house and into a taxi, and the clumsy position of Winston Churchill as he leaned against the tall painting of Stanley Spencer's *Unveiling Cookham War Memorial* which hung on the staircase, its position having to be defended by Eddie Marsh against Churchill's hefty frame.

Lack of personal possessions had become a familiar complaint throughout Diana's childhood. There were so many children that even Diana's clothes were not her own: 'I was just their tenant on their way down from Pam to Unity.' Perhaps for this reason, she was given the nursery bird, a goldfinch named Dicky. Conversing about what they possessed, she confidently announced: 'Well, Dicky's mine, he must be very valuable.' At that impressionable age, Diana associated personal belongings with monetary value, regardless of how insignificant a thing might be.

As she aged, Diana realised the cruelty of keeping a living thing in a cage, 'it would put heaven in a rage'. To her delight, at the age of 7, Diana was given an object she had desired since she first visited Batsford Park. On display in the business room was a figurine of a Japanese goldfish made from pink jade, which had belonged to her grandfather, Bertie. 'You must take great care of it,' her father warned. It was irreplaceable, a memento of Bertie's time spent abroad, and Diana kept it in her possession throughout the day. At night, she placed it on a table close to her bed so when she awoke, it would be the first thing she saw. After great care and consideration the inevitable happened: Diana dropped the figurine on to the stone floor and it smashed. 'You've broken the goldfish,' David said in grave tones. She had been trusted with something special – a rarity in every sense – and she had succeeded in destroying it.

The enviable world in which she moved – summer balls, supper parties and trips to the theatre – were a minor distraction for Diana for, apart from her time on the social scene, she felt a deepening void in her life. Carrington and Strachey crept to the forefront of her mind, and she could no longer distract herself from her sorrowful feelings. Her life seemed empty and her position in the world, pointless.

For some time, Diana had been kicking against the privilege which her life as Mrs Guinness afforded her and she sought a deeper meaning to her existence. The economic depression of the early thirties concerned Diana enough to bring up the topic when the opportunity presented itself, only to be humoured by Bryan and put off by Colonel Guinness.[*] The latter's reasoning was that Diana, with her beauty, youth and position, had no cause to meddle in what was viewed as the government's problem – male and upper class, at that. But society around her was changing radically and she found it to be a contrast of extremes – in January of 1932, the Archbishop of Canterbury had forbidden church remarriages of divorcees. Although Diana herself was not directly affected by this law, she resented its patriarchal, religious restraint.[35]

To those who were privy to Diana's intimate thoughts and views, it seemed her frame of mind ran from one extreme to the other. 'Dotty Di', the unkind

---

[*]   With the Conservatives being voted out during the 1929 elections, Colonel Guinness opted not to stand for re-election in 1931 and upon his retirement was given a hereditary peerage, the 1st Baron Moyne of Bury St Edmunds. For consistency he will be referred to as Colonel Guinness throughout.

nickname bestowed on her by Frances Marshall and Ralph Partridge at Ham Spray seemed fitting. She was a social butterfly, at home in fashionable salons and yet her thoughts wandered to the economic depression. This level of inconsistency did little to convince anyone that Diana was serious about social matters.

A year ago, when she had turned 21, Diana gained the right to vote, but she did not use it. Had there been a Lloyd George Liberal in her constituency she would have voted for him but, alas, there was not. The Tories still held the majority and the 'absurd figure' of Ramsay MacDonald leading the country as prime minister was, she felt, unworthy of her vote.[36]

In summer 1932, registered unemployment statics totalled 3.5 million. Hit hardest by economic problems were the industrial and mining areas of the north. The distressed areas, as they were called – slums – contained millions of Britons surviving on a meagre dole payment. Ramsay MacDonald and his Labour government failed to solve the problem. 'Could it be beyond the wit of a man to manage the economy of a powerful and rich country which owned a quarter of the globe in such a way that its citizens could eat their fill and live in decent circumstances?' Diana questioned. A question for which she found no answer.

It caused Diana to resent her station in life: not the monetary privilege, but the ability to move through life relatively unscathed. 'For the rich, however, life went on much as before the crisis,' she bitterly recounted. Invitations to parties and balls, concerts, operas and plays, travels abroad, country house visits, hunting, shooting and horseracing was still their priority.

Diana often told a tale, recounted from the early days of her marriage to Bryan. He led her through the woods at Versailles, where they became more and more lost. Adamant he knew the way, Bryan insisted on leading Diana deeper and deeper into the woods, until she abandoned all hope of finding a way out. Exhausted, Diana trailed behind him as he scanned every corner for an exit, all the while keeping up an optimistic pretence. She eventually gave up and sat under a tree, refusing to move until Bryan went to find a taxi. Diana had lost faith in him and even though he tried to convince her otherwise, she knew it was a lost cause.

Opinionated and observant, Diana needed someone to guide her to the answers she sought. Bryan, as far as she could tell, was not suitable for the task in hand. She sought a strong protector and this was partly why she could not reciprocate the romantic love so freely dispensed by James Lees-Milne and Randolph Churchill, and now Bryan. The fates heeded her call and as she blindly tried to make sense of the world around her, a man entered her life who offered to lead the way. As the young and confused often do, she put all of her trust in him.

19

THE MAN, MOSLEY

As with all of her admirers, Sir Oswald Mosley first caught sight of Diana from afar when she attended a ball given by the Duchess of Rutland at Sir Phillip Sassoon's house in Park Lane. This impression of Diana, with her 'starry blue eyes, golden hair and ineffable expression of a gothic Madonna' stayed in Mosley's mind long after this first, fleeting glimpse. 'You were sitting with Billy Ormsby-Gore,' he told her when they were formally introduced at Barbara St John Hutchinson's 21st birthday party. Although the Mosleys and Guinnesses moved in similar circles, Diana could not recall seeing or meeting him. Her perfect tunnel vision overlooked Mosley on those prior occasions, and up until then she had no reason to make his acquaintance, she was content with her artistic friends.

A deeper malice lurked in Mosley – 'his eyes were as dark and as cold as a shark' – but it was lost on Diana who, on their first meeting, found him dull. She was further disappointed by Mosley's after-dinner speech which centred on politics. Cimmie Mosley, Diana decided, cut a frumpish figure, quick to defend her husband's politics and overly sensitive to those who opposed them. Overall, Mosley left an indifferent impression on Diana.

Bryan often urged Diana to share her intimate thoughts on whether she found a particular man attractive or not. Since Diana did not show signs of enthusiasm for Mosley, Bryan did not bother to question her. Though, by this stage in their marriage, Diana was prone to berate Bryan for prying and all too often it escalated into a fight.

Meeting Diana in person intensified Mosley's memories of her. He thought her 'tall and slim, with huge blue eyes, beautiful legs and small, graceful hands and feet', and her physical presence was spectacular but waspish. When Mosley questioned Diana about her politics, she snapped, 'Lloyd George Liberal.'

With Mosley absent from parliament that summer, he and Cimmie found themselves more sociable than ever and it was inevitable they would cross paths with the Guinnesses. Diana began to warm to Mosley and his political conversation, and modesty did not prevail when he told Diana he was certain he could solve the unemployment crisis. 'Lucid, logical, forceful and persuasive,' she wrote of Mosley's charisma, and he soon convinced her, as he had thousands of others, to believe in his ideology. 'From that moment we met everywhere, and I listened to him talk,' Diana said of the several meetings which followed.

In many ways, Mosley possessed everything Bryan lacked – he had experience with women and a strong sense of self-assurance. This level of arrogance charmed Diana and manifested a level of trust. She believed in Mosley and was confident he had all of the answers, and sensible ones, too. He spoke of real issues, whereas Bryan was lost in his books, plays and poetry. Mosley's age also appealed to Diana: he was fourteen years her senior and she was attracted to older, worldlier men. For someone who admired experience and knowledge above all else, it seemed Bryan was too young for her.

Oswald Ernald Mosley adored women; when he was a young boy his parents had separated and he was brought up by his mother, Katharine Maud Edwards-Heathcote, and his paternal grandfather, with whom he and his father shared their namesake. But among family and friends, he was affectionately nicknamed 'Tom'. Growing up in the depths of the Staffordshire countryside was a tough, rural life, where he was exposed to the cruelties of nature and the torture of defenceless animals. Due to his philandering ways in London and the spending of the family's fortune on booze and whores, Mosley's father had been exiled from the family seat, Rolleston Hall. Before departing his son's life, an early lesson of his brutality lingered. He ordered a boxful of two dozen rats and set his hounds on the rodents, while his small son looked on. It was a harrowing lesson, but one Mosley took to heart – to survive, one had to exert brutality, there was no room for cowardice if one were to thrive.

With no interest in academia, Mosley's experience at Winchester College was mediocre. He ignored his lessons and dodged the passes of homosexual school-mates (he had little tolerance for such things), but he excelled at fencing and boxing. He had been taught by his grandfather and father to exploit 'the good clean English fist', and this was a tactic he would use throughout his life.

In 1914, months before the outbreak of the First World War, Mosley entered the Royal Military College at Sandhurst, and was expelled five months later for a riotous act of retaliation against a fellow student. During the war, he was commissioned into the 16th The Queen's Lancers and fought on the Western Front. He then transferred to the Royal Flying Corps, but crashed his plane while demonstrating in front of his mother and sister. The injury left him with a permanent limp, but he defied medical orders and returned to the trenches before he was fully recovered. Consequently, he passed out from the pain at the Battle of Loos. Mosley spent the remainder of the war at desk jobs in the Ministry of Munitions and the Foreign Office.

At the age of 21, with no university education or practical experience, Mosley decided to go into politics as a Conservative MP. He was passionately anti-war and this view motivated his political career. His title and family background (directly descended from the Baronets of Ancoats) and his war service stood for something in politics, then dominated by the elite.

Mosley was a desirable politician, and local Conservative and Labour Associations preferred him in several constituencies. He became the youngest member of the House of Commons to take his seat, and soon distinguished himself as a confident orator and political player. Conflict arose when Mosley disagreed with the Conservatives over Irish Policy when he opposed the use of the Black & Tans to suppress the Irish. The Liberal *Westminster Gazette* admired his stance and praised him for having 'human sympathies, courage and brains'.

During his crusade in politics, Mosley met and married Lady Cynthia Curzon, known as Cimmie. The whispers about Mosley's roguish reputation were enough for her father, Lord Curzon, to be wary of his credentials as a suitable husband. Curzon suspected Mosley of being motivated by social advancement: politically (he was a respected politician who had served as the Viceroy of India) and financially (Cimmie's late mother, the American heiress Mary Leiter, had left her three daughters a substantial trust fund). Curzon's instincts proved correct, though short-lived. He died five years later, during which time Mosley had begun affairs with Cimmie's sisters, Lady Irene Curzon and Lady Alexandra 'Baba' Metcalfe, as well as Curzon's widow, Grace.

In 1924, Mosley abandoned the Conservatives 'who mistrusted brilliance' in favour of the Labour Party, who had just formed a government. It was a daring move on Mosley's behalf and it spawned his infamous phrase: 'Vote Labour, sleep Tory.' Cimmie supported Mosley's new ideology and she, too, became vocal in left-wing politics, once remarking: 'Titles are a bit of a joke. I cannot get rid of my title, though I don't think much of it.' It was a literal statement that further infuriated her father when Mosley made light of her comment and referred to her in an official letter as 'the wife'.

Livid at his son endorsing any form of socialism, Mosley's estranged father spoke freely to the press:

> My son has not done a decent day's work in his life. He has money from the Mosley family and money from his wife ... My son was born with a golden spoon in his mouth, he was brought up on the fat of the land ... I am sorry, exceedingly sorry, that my son has joined the Socialist Party.[37]

Mosley joined the Independent Labour Party and allied himself with the left. The party soon dissolved and he used his time out of parliament to develop a new economic policy that continued to form the basis of his economic beliefs until the end of his political career.

When Labour won the 1929 general election, Mosley was certain that Ramsay MacDonald would appoint him to one of the great offices of state. He was disappointed and embittered when MacDonald gave him the lowly post of Chancellor of the Duchy of Lancaster, where he was responsible for solving the unemployment problem. Mosley's ideals proved too radical for the Labour Party and many of his proposals were blocked by the Cabinet. Cimmie encouraged his plans, and with her support he devised the document that he called the 'Mosley Memorandum'.

The 'Mosley Memorandum' appealed for high tariffs to protect British industries from international finance, state nationalisation, suggestions for early retirement pensions to free up jobs for the younger generation, a publicly funded road building scheme to provide jobs for the unemployed and a programme of public works to solve unemployment. He also proposed that the government should form a small inner-Cabinet modelled on Lloyd George's 1917 War Cabinet, where they would 'possess almost military powers' to fight against unemployment.

The 'Mosley Memorandum' was rejected by the Cabinet and in May 1930 Mosley resigned from his ministerial position and left the Labour Party. His sensational exit mattered supremely to himself and his half a dozen followers, but very little to the party itself. Ambition still motivated his political beliefs and in 'an amazing act of arrogance' Mosley formed his own party, the New Party.

Having gained a disappointing third-class degree from Oxford in the summer of 1931, James Lees-Milne felt adrift with no real prospects and no hope for the future. A welcome distraction presented itself to Jim when the sister of his recently widowed Aunt Dorothy asked him to help with the campaign for her son's political party. Her name was Maud, the adoring mother of Sir Oswald Mosley. 'Aunt' Maud took Jim under her wing and his job predominantly consisted of 'going from house to house in the backstreets begging for votes from impoverished and bemused citizens, usually wives in soap suds up to their elbows with babies clutching their pitiable skirts'.[38]

Witnessing Mosley in action had inspired Jim to summarise his early attempt at leadership: 'He was a man of overwhelming egotism ... He brooked no argument, would accept no advice. He was overbearing and overconfident.'[39] The entire campaign and party was 'a political abortion'. The final result of the 1931 election delivered the inevitable news that the New Party and Mosley had lost their previously held seats and had failed to win any new ones.

Later in the year, Mosley travelled to Rome to study the movements of the Italian fascist leader Benito Mussolini, 'a man who had brought order out of chaos in Italy'. Observing Mussolini's brand of fascism left little doubt in Mosley's mind that Britain could prosper from a similar regime. From this idea, Mosley founded the British Union of Fascists.

20

THE DEMON KING

While the dictators Stalin, Mussolini and Hitler were emerging in Europe, Sir Oswald Mosley was in transition. Through Toryism, socialism and fascism, he had run the gamut of political ideologies. Diana loathed Toryism, and she viewed socialism as a facade which concealed Ramsay MacDonald's incompetence as prime minister of a Labour government. Fascism, she surmised, 'had all the answers and sensible ones, too'.

Having witnessed Churchill in action during the General Strike of 1926, Diana was intrigued by the political debates taking place at Chartwell on how to deal with the striking miners – all very heavy-handedly, she thought. At this point in her political views, and up until she first met Mosley, Diana maintained that she was a Lloyd George Liberal. Under the influence of Mosley, this liberal ideology soon wore off. Lloyd George, Mosley explained, had no sense of the dramatic (Mosley was a talented orator) and furthermore, he felt no twinge of responsibility. His statement was backed up when Mosley reminded Diana that Lloyd George was one of the co-signatories of the Treaty of Versailles. This information would become relevant during Diana's future visits to Germany, where she witnessed first-hand how unfair the Treaty of Versailles was to the country – a view shared by many at the time.

Mosley's blatant disregard for both the Conservative Party and the Labour Party, having served as an MP for both, appealed to Diana's nonconformist nature. Having been privy to the policies of both parties, she agreed that Mosley heading his own political party, the British Union of Fascists, was a logical response to Britain's economic crisis. Diana admired originality and gumption and, to her, Mosley possessed both.

Still troubled by the poverty gripping the working classes, Diana's thoughts were focused on Ramsay MacDonald's inability to stabilise the economy and to provide British workers with a decent wage or 'meagre dole' to live off. Mosley vowed to use himself on the disposal of hereditary wealth, beginning with an investigation into the lives of those who had contributed nothing for the good of the country. In essence, Mosley was appealing to the working classes who felt victimised by the government and he promised to rid society of the bone idle – to him this meant immigrants. It was a short-sighted statement on Mosley's behalf, for most of the bone idle belonged to his own class.

Diana was besotted by Mosley's life experience, as he was different from her cultured and artistic friends, whom she had begun to view as shallow. His appeal lay in being 'the best of companions; he had every gift, being handsome, generous, intelligent and full of wonderful gaiety and *joie de vivre*'. He appeared to her as 'the cleverest, most balanced and most honest of English politicians'.[40]

Critical of Mosley's swashbuckling looks, James Lees-Milne thought him more likely to 'appeal to Mayfair flappers than to sway indigent workers in the potteries'. And drawing on his experience as campaigner for the calamitous New Party, Jim summarised Mosley's charisma: 'His eyes flashed fire, dilated and contracted like a mesmerist's. His voice rose and fell in hypnotic cadences. He was madly in love with his own words ...'[41]

Mosley and Diana met frequently. They took walks in London parks, dined together at fashionable restaurants – the Ritz, the Devonshire or Boulestin – and each social invitation presented Mosley with the opportunity to talk of politics. As soon as he had convinced her of his ideals, he veered on to the subject of personal matters. Diana learned of Mosley's participation in the war, something he used to affirm his respectability in society. And, appealing to her naivety, he emphasised that when she was still in the nursery, he had been to the front line, where he witnessed the devastation of war first-hand.

Proof of Mosley's experiences convinced Diana that he knew what he was talking about and that he must be right. Bryan, aside from their travels and artistic friends, had experienced very little. Bryan chose to live vicariously through the characters he wrote about in his (then unpublished) novels, and his use of poetry to express his feelings could hardly compare to Mosley and the real world.

As he had done with numerous young women before, Mosley slowly reeled Diana in with his tales, and then his charm. Diana was so enthralled with him that she cared little of concealing her growing infatuation. And she hardly spared a thought for Bryan when she accepted Mosley's offer to visit his flat at 22A Ebury Street. 'That bloody, damnable, cursed Ebury [Street] how often does she come there?' In a rare outburst of jealousy, Cimmie had bombarded Mosley. She was usually so tolerant of his indiscretions; he often had affairs with beautiful, young society women.

In the beginning there was nothing unique about Mosley's involvement with Diana, whose profile had grown in stature in the three years that she had been married. With her beauty and reputation as a society hostess, Diana was seen as a catch. To those a generation above her, in the same circle as Mosley and Cimmie, the liaison was viewed as nothing more than pleasure seeking in what had surely become a dull, upper-class marriage. When Cimmie discovered Mosley's infidelity – as she always did – he consoled her with the explanation that none of the women had meant anything to him.

In her autobiography, Diana glossed over the complexities of their affair and those who were hurt in the process of their infidelity. It was not as clean-cut as she believed. That summer, Cimmie was pregnant with her third child and was forced to spend three months in bed due to illness. She tried to convince herself that Diana was one of her husband's 'sillies', but behind the flippancy Cimmie was aware that Diana was different. Until Diana, Mosley had never fallen in love with any of them. 'If you had said you would like to take Diana out for the day Sunday, I would have known where I was. Oh, darling, darling, don't let it be like that. I will truly understand if you give me a chance. But I am so kept in the dark.'[42]

As though to make up for keeping Cimmie 'in the dark', Mosley sat her down and confessed each and every affair to her. About three dozen in their thirteen years of marriage. He did not confess his liaisons with her two sisters and step-mother. That, he decided, would have been too cruel.

Bryan was a patient man, but he was not a fool. In the beginning of the affair between Diana and Mosley, Bryan had generously opened Cheyne Walk to Cela Keppel, who was doing the season for a second time. Cela was Diana's friend, but she had grown fond of Bryan during the three years in which she had known him. Cela found it uncomfortable when Diana returned to the marital home, giddy with praise for Mosley and confiding the intimate details of their affair. 'Isn't the Leader wonderful?' she implored Cela to agree with her. Mosley, by then, had adopted the title of 'Leader'. Unsure of how to respond to Diana's conversation of her lunchtime liaisons with Mosley and of his 'marvellous lovemaking' in comparison to Bryan and 'his inexperienced advances', Cela remained silent.

Bryan thought Mosley arrogant and 'a self-worshipping atheist'. Prior to Diana's growing obsession with the 'Leader', Bryan remained blind to any signs of her ruthless streak. He did not sense the same ruthlessness when she rejected his marriage proposal, leaving him heartbroken, only to reconsider the following day.

Bryan tried to muster enough courage to forbid Diana from lunching with Mosley. But she used his traditional views to belittle him and with a cruel laugh she said: 'Who'd ever heard of such a thing?' She was drawing on the custom, so fashionable at the time, for husbands and wives to lunch separately.

Unable to confront Diana in person, Bryan decided there was only one thing for it. He wrote Diana a letter, painfully expressing his concerns should she carry on with Mosley. He could not bring himself to accuse her of being unfaithful, but the thought lurked in his mind. He begged her to consider their marriage, the children and the devastation it would cause.

Loyal friends who sided with Bryan tried to distract Diana from such meetings with Mosley. 'You can't – you mustn't see him. Come and lunch with me instead,' they begged her, to no avail. Diana echoed the same sentiments she had once told the crestfallen James Lees-Milne — monogamy was pointless and unrealistic. Nothing could deter her, even when Mosley confessed to breaking off his affairs with Paula Casa Maury and Georgia Sitwell, both of whom were her friends, and both of whom were sleeping with him while he openly pursued her.

Rather than doubting her decision to continue on with Mosley, Diana admired his honesty. She was in love with the Leader and it seemed Bryan would have to take on the role of an understanding husband if he was to remain in her life. 'If you're going to mind infidelity, you better call it a day as far as marriage goes. Because who has *ever* remained faithful?' she was apt to say.

21

TURMOIL

As the summer of 1932 drew to a close, Bryan felt as though he might have a breakthrough with Diana. When the season ended, the smart and fashionable set departed London for Venice. At the end of August, Diana and Bryan left for Europe with their friends Barbara Hutchinson and Victor Rothschild, who were engaged to be married. The foursome motored through the south of France en route to Venice, stopping at Saintes Maries de la Mer. Prior to leaving London, Diana and Mosley conspired to meet up in Arles, as he too was motoring down.

Cimmie, who had recently given birth to her third child, was suffering from kidney trouble. Deeming the motor journey too uncomfortable, Cimmie, her children and lady's maid, Andree, travelled by train. Mosley calculated this would delay Cimmie's arrival, thus giving him a day or two with Diana. In their desperation at being parted for ten days, Mosley and Diana did not consider any obstacles that could have thwarted their plan.

In Avignon, whilst staying at the Jules César, Diana developed diphtheria. A sympathetic doctor permitted her to remain in the comfort of the hotel room rather than moving her to the clinical isolation of a hospital. For Diana it was a major crisis, not because of her illness, which kept her bed bound, but because she was terrified a letter might arrive at the hotel from Mosley and be opened by Bryan. The placid, easy-going trip quickly became a comedy of errors. After exhausting all of her options, Diana decided to take Barbara and Victor into her confidence, whereupon she explained the delicate situation to them. They did not condone her betrayal of Bryan, but to save further anguish they managed to send a telegram to Mosley in Arles, telling him to meet Diana in Venice.

Nine days later, she made a full recovery and they set forth for Venice. Giddy at the prospect of reuniting with Mosley, Diana was in a most congenial mood. Bryan appreciated her high spirits, but he could not have realised what lay behind this veil of happiness.

Venice, a playground for the wealthy, attracted sophisticated travellers in their droves. As soon as the Guinnesses arrived at their hotel, Diana wasted no time in becoming reacquainted with her old friends from the London social scene. Tom Mitford was there, staying at Malcontenta with Baroness d'Erlanger, whose guests included the scandalous courtesan Doris Castlerosse and, most importantly, the Mosleys. The scene unfolded before Bryan's eyes; it was not the quiet holiday he had anticipated and, before long, Diana had invited everyone to join them on the Lido.

Shadowing Diana was Randolph Churchill who, since becoming Jonathan's godfather, had firmly re-established himself as part of her scene. The tiresome behaviour from his youth had not subsided and this disregard for others was also apparent at a party at Cheyne Walk, prior to Venice, where Nancy claimed Randolph 'tried to rape' her. 'It was very funny,' she wrote to Mark Ogilvie-Grant, imploring him to keep it a secret.[43]

Bryan sulked under a cloud of misery; he disliked raucous crowds at best. Joining him in this feeling of misery was Cimmie, who was still plagued by bouts of ill health. Randolph, as always, was making a nuisance of himself by playing pranks on the unsuspecting Brendan Bracken, once poking fun at his dubious paternity by calling him 'my brother'. A fight escalated, with Bracken chasing Randolph down the Lido, and an American tourist, echoing Bryan's exasperation, exclaimed: 'Fun is fun, but that Randolph Churchill goes too far!'

The crowd quickly packed up for a late afternoon of sightseeing. The rigorous tour brought them to St Mark's Square, where they overheard a flighty American girl asking her friend: 'Is this Florence or Venice?' 'Consult your itinerary,' was the reply. 'If it's Monday, it's Florence, if it's Tuesday it's Venice ...' The throng of tourists, standing elbow to elbow, peering at their tour guides and snapping photographs provided Diana and Mosley with the perfect cover.

They were forever plotting an escape, waiting for an opportunity to steal away, hiding down narrow alleyways and sneaking into a gondola to ferry them to a tiny, nondescript hotel for an illicit afternoon. Appearing hours later, they conjured up a feeble excuse, but no one was deceived. When the entire group had quite enough of tourist attractions and decided to spend their afternoons on the Lido, it became impossible for Diana and Mosley to leave. They were desperate to be alone, and over lunch Mosley leant across to his friend Robert Boothy and told him: 'Bob, I shall need your room tonight between midnight and 4 a.m.'

Boothy was astonished at Mosley's request and he was certain Bryan and Cimmie, who were sitting within earshot, had overheard. 'But Tom, where shall I sleep?' he jokingly responded.

'On the beach,' he answered. It was not a joke. Mosley was serious and Boothy spent the night sleeping on a recliner in a beach hut.

Selfishly caught up in his and Diana's happiness, Mosley lacked sympathy for Cimmie, who spent the remainder of the holiday in excruciating pain from her illness and in tears from his betrayal. For Bryan, it was not only a realisation that he had failed to prevent Diana from 'running off with the demon king', but tangible evidence that his wife was in love with another man. Humiliation and scorn raged through him, but in spite of Diana's behaviour, he still loved her.

The splendour of Venice and Mosley's agreeable company contributed to Diana's euphoric mood. Not even the realities of Biddesden could taint her happiness. And, to ease the guilt she had once felt, Diana told herself that Bryan finally understood the situation with Mosley. This, she hoped, might relieve her from upsetting him more than she needed to. To prove her point and to demonstrate her commitment to Mosley, Diana refrained from the physical aspect of their marriage. As far as Bryan was concerned, Diana might as well have withdrawn her love.

Bryan could not accept that his marriage had taken the discourse of an aristocratic union. He became passive aggressive and adopted the semi-whispering voice which Diana loathed. 'Prison' was her exact term for Biddesden and her marriage. Endless questions prevailed when Diana left the room or made a phone call: 'Who were you with?', 'Where are you going?', 'What are you doing?' he repeatedly asked. She could feel his eyes obsessively following her as she moved around the room, prompting her to react with a snide remark. A remark so cruel it caused Pamela, who had been spending her evenings with them, to gasp with horror. Pamela echoed the thoughts of those who knew the couple: 'He worshipped her, and she walked all over him.'[44]

The tense atmosphere of Biddesden was relieved by Diana's delight in being reunited with Jonathan and Desmond. She was a good and thoughtful mother, not even Bryan could deny that. He clung to the image of Diana tending to the children on their brief visits from the nursery. This image of faux domesticity gave Bryan a glimmer of hope that, in some way, Diana was still attainable to him.

22

COURTING SCANDAL

Cimmie was loyal to Mosley in marriage and in politics, and she oversaw the tedious details of his political propaganda. She designed flags bearing the newly designed fascist emblem and chose the music for the party's anthem. It was far-fetched, but Cimmie managed to convince Mosley that the tune of Sousa's 'Stars and Stripes Forever' could be used, with original words by their friend Robert Sitwell.

With great fanfare, Mosley launched the British Union of Fascists (BUF) at its headquarters in Great George Street. A fortnight later, the BUF's first public demonstration took place in Trafalgar Square. With his tanned complexion set off by a white shirt and dark suit, Mosley made quite an impression as he posed on a plinth at the bottom of Nelson's column. He was surrounded by a protective barrier of eight bodyguards, all wearing black shirts – the trademark of their (future) uniform and origin of their nickname, the 'Blackshirts'.

Taking the daring and symbolic step, Diana began to attend Mosley's political meetings. Accompanied by Doris Castlerosse – who cared little about her questionable reputation – the two beautiful women sat amongst the crowd of upper-class supporters and working-class militants, both equally spellbound by Mosley's speeches. Mosley played to the gallery, cutting an impressive figure in his full fascist regalia of black shirt, breeches and jackboots, flanked by his bodyguards as he took to the stage. 'All the swagger and vanity to Mrs Bryan Guinness and Doris Castlerosse,' Irene Curzon recorded in her diary.

Irene, the eldest of the three Curzon sisters, was the self-appointed matriarch of the family, when upon the death of their father, Lord Curzon, in 1925, she became a baroness in her own right, inheriting the barony of Ravensdale.* A striking woman, with black hair and dark eyes, Irene emphasised her exotic looks by dressing in a 'flamboyant, colourful, hit and miss style'. Although she wallowed in luxury, Irene was not as superficial as the aristocratic set who were intrigued by Mosley's BUF. She donated large sums of her personal wealth to the founding of youth clubs in the impoverished East End of London. Dedicating three nights a week to this, Irene played down her wealth and travelled on the tube to the clubs. Aside from the clubs' frequent outings, once a year she took the children on holidays around the British Isles and abroad. To the boys and girls of the East End, Irene became a cherished friend.

The youngest Curzon sister, Baba, 'confident in her own impeccable chic', was equally enthralled with Mosley, each sister having slept with him during his marriage to Cimmie. Unlike Irene, whose affair with Mosley was brief, Baba had an ongoing relationship with him and viewed Diana as a rival for his affections.

Even though she did not compete with Diana, Irene still felt an uneasiness about her presence in Mosley's life. She was extremely protective of Cimmie and, since becoming aware of the affair and the unhappiness it had caused her sister, feelings of hatred for Diana simmered beneath her jolly exterior. 'How that battered washed-out woman could have produced those six hooligan girls I do not know,' she said of Sydney and her spirited daughters.

In 1932, the same year the BUF was founded, Mosley had a historic debate with Jimmy Maxton, the leader of the Independent Labour Party. It was held at the Friends House in Euston Road with David Lloyd George in the chair. The hall was policed by Mosley's Blackshirts, and Redshirts from Maxton's party. All of Mayfair turned out to watch the encounter and the audience was impressed by the brilliant and profound exposition of fascism, still unfamiliar to a majority of Britons at that time. Maxton called himself the average working man, opposing Mosley's social rank and position.

Lloyd George interjected on the debate and told the audience: 'If you have complete dictatorship, or a socialist policy in its entity then the king himself must go or

---

* Irene was created a life peer in 1958 for her tireless work for youth clubs. Taking her seat in the House of Lords, Irene spoke of the importance of youth work in the East End, and argued on behalf of female prostitutes – a subject she knew well from her charity work. Shocking, and impressing, the men with her typical bawdy language, she informed the House: 'They will charge a fiver, your Lordships will forgive me for being so sordid and vulgar, for a long spell and £1 for a quick bash.'

else remain as a puppet, as he is in Italy.' Many argued that fascism and Nazism grew in Italy and Germany out of chaos, but as the horror of a revolution was not yet upon Britain, they could not see it spreading without the whip of national bankruptcy.

Mosley agreed that revolution was not an issue, although he reminded the audience that the unemployment crisis was spreading, as it had done in Germany before Hitler came to power. Mosley reassured those who opposed a dictatorship that he would only bring fascism to England by constitutional methods and honest elections.

In a sense, Diana already had reason to believe in Mosley's ideology. The political hero from her youth, Lloyd George, had given Mosley an endorsement when he declared that his extension of fascism was far more attractive and sensible than Labour's socialism: 'I have never heard in a short time a case put with such brilliant oratory as Sir Oswald has done.'

At the end of October, Diana and Bryan threw a costume ball at Biddesden and, fresh from the political stage, Mosley and Cimmie featured prominently on the guest list. Keeping within the lavishness of Diana's parties, many guests consulted the theatrical costume designer, Oliver Messel, to make their costumes. Cimmie came as a shepherdess, Mosley opted for all black – BUF colours – and Diana, draped in a white gown, appeared as a Greek goddess.

Familiar friends from the early days of Buckingham Street and acquaintances from Ham Spray spilled through the doors of Biddesden to view the spectacle of Diana and Mosley for themselves. The affair had become common knowledge in their circle. Rosamond Lehmann, intimate with the Bloomsbury set, recalled: 'Diana was in a Grecian dress looking greatly beautiful but sinister, which I always thought she was with that huge white face.'

If sinister was a quiet observation, it certainly played out in Diana and Mosley's treatment of Bryan. They danced all night as though 'magnetised together' and Diana cared little of scorn; the guests observed her joyous expression, laughing with her mouth wide open, in the arms of Mosley. Bryan stood off to the side, silent and 'looking like a shattered white rabbit'.

Bryan's presence did nothing to suppress Diana's glowing admiration of Mosley. Prior to the ball, Bryan tried to exert authority and had forbidden Diana from seeing Mosley. A great argument escalated and she defiantly warned him that she had a right to choose her friends. Rebelling against Bryan, she told her guests of Mosley's greatness – 'like having a crush on a film star' – and this greatly played to his ego.

Mosley, drunk on political power, was throwing his weight around, knowing that Bryan wanted to intervene but did not have the nerve to stop him. Drawing on his customary method of using 'the good clean English fist' to settle a dispute, and knowing Bryan would never challenge him to a physical fight, Mosley believed this gave him the right to carry Diana off as his prize. He had won. Diana must have caught the horrified expression on Henry Lamb's face, who felt protective of Bryan, for she coyly added: 'You're thinking what a frightful bounder he is ...'

During supper, Diana and Mosley vanished from the table, having gone upstairs, only appearing hours later when the guests were leaving. Unlike Venice, she made no effort to invent a feeble excuse for her lengthy disappearance. Cimmie, a decade older than Diana, had begun to lose her looks as the reoccurring bouts of illness following the birth of her last child began to take its toll. Her recent weight gain and frumpy costume did nothing to dispel the guests' pitiful looks in her direction. The pity humiliated Bryan, further fuelled by his powerlessness in stopping Diana from seeing Mosley.

That same evening Mosley and Diana committed themselves to one another, and when she spoke of her decision to leave Bryan, Mosley encouraged it. The excitement was incredible, like Mosley she had decided to stake her life as he was doing, on something she believed in – him. The following morning she told Cela Keppel: 'I'm in love with the Leader and I want to leave Bryan.'

Mosley firmly believed he had the right to have two wives, a state of affairs which he tried to rationalise to Cimmie. His unfaithfulness and the pain it caused her could be eased if she could accept his desire to appoint a full-time mistress. He tried to convince her they could have a 'lovely life together' if only she could accept his 'frolicsome ways'.

Diana fitted the bill – she was eager, enthusiastic and supportive. His proposition to Diana was clear: yes, he loved her, but he would never divorce Cimmie for her. Cimmie, he explained, was too respected by his political cronies, and to divorce the mother of his children would cause great scandal and reflect badly on the BUF. Something he did not need given the lack of success with the New Party.

Accepting Mosley's conditions, Diana had secondary reasons for leaving Bryan. Marriage, she had found, did not agree with her free-thinking ways. Despite Bryan remaining faithful to her and his financial generosity, he oppressed her with his possessiveness, and their differing ideals exasperated her. Diana thought she had been in love with him, and in the first year of their marriage she had been very happy, but four years later she found he had only appealed to her because she needed to escape from home.

Although she did not regret any of it, Diana knew she could not continue to be with Bryan. She could not go on hurting him, chastising him and eventually succeeding in breaking his gentle spirit. It would be a betrayal to herself, and she was certain that one day Bryan would find the sort of wife he needed.[45] Weighing up her options, she took her own personal happiness into account.

Before Diana told Bryan of her decision to leave him, she broke the news to her closest friends. 'Youthfully arrogant,' Georgia Sitwell berated Diana over tea at the Ritz. She ought to have known, after all, as she reminded her friend, Mosley had abandoned her as soon as he met Diana. Aside from Diana's treatment of Bryan, they were horrified at Mosley's manipulation of her. He had persuaded this inexperienced, infatuated young woman to throw away her entire life in order to make herself more available to him. As much as they tried, her friends could not make her see sense. 'Advice is given by the unworldly. Perhaps worldly people know from experience that it is never taken,' she said.

At the end of November, Diana approached Bryan with the words he had been dreading. It was not a rash decision, for Diana had waited a month before breaking the news to him. Despite her friends' best efforts to persuade her otherwise, she could not bear to hurt Bryan any longer. It had taken only a few minutes to dissolve their life together. To argue the case would have proved pointless, for behind the brief parting, Bryan sensed her uncompromising determination.

23

A CLEAN BREAK

B ryan fled to Switzerland for three weeks, and before his departure he warned Diana that Mosley was forbidden to visit Cheyne Walk. He need not have worried; during his absence, she hardly saw Mosley. His devotion to building up the BUF eclipsed any attention he might have spared for Diana, who had given up so much for him. This limbo in which Bryan had left her did not sway her decision to become Mosley's full-time mistress, and she patiently awaited his return to broach the subject of divorce.

As Diana learned, the divorce would be the least of her worries; the scandal of her actions had erupted through London society. Adele Astaire, modern in her views, confided to Nancy: 'I don't mind people going off and fucking but I do object to all this free love!'[46]

To Nancy, Diana's life seemed the epitome of glamour. Unmarried, approaching 30 and surviving on a meagre allowance from her father and the small sums which she accumulated from her writing, it was not difficult for Nancy to feel envious of her younger sister's life of luxury; a life which Diana seemed intent on throwing away on a whim. The golden cage that Diana complained about did not seem so awful to an outsider looking in. Nancy was one of the few on Diana's side, but her jealousy of Diana was well known, and could there have been an element of spite in the advice she so freely dispensed?

'It would be so awful later to feel that I had been, even in a tiny way, instrumental in messing up your life,' Nancy wrote to Diana. Grateful for Nancy's support, Diana's judgement was obscured and she assured her eldest sister: 'Darling you are my one ally.' Regardless of Bryan's swift exit and Mosley's absence, Nancy sensed the eerie calmness would soon erupt into an explosive scene. Nancy retreated from Cheyne Walk, out of the firing line to the safety and isolation of Swinbrook House, offering Diana the vague excuse: 'I should stay here at present.'

Writing to Diana, Nancy stuck to her role of older sister soliciting advice, whether it was wanted or not: 'You are so young to begin getting in wrong with the world, if that's what is going to happen.' Nancy discussed the situation with their brother Tom, who warned that Diana's 'social position will be nil' if she continued on with her plan to divorce Bryan. 'Whatever happens I shall always be on your side as you know,' Nancy told her. 'And so will anybody who cares for you and perhaps the rest really don't matter.'

Personal feelings hardly mattered when it came to protecting the family name. David and Sydney were furious with Diana and they had forbidden Jessica and Deborah from visiting her. It was a bitter blow for Diana, who loved her little sisters, and she could tolerate just about anyone's disapproval except her brother's, and Tom strongly disapproved. He was fond of Bryan and thought that for a temporary infatuation Diana was ruining her life and would live to regret it.

Addressing the situation with Mosley, Diana adopted a new tactic. Believing David and Sydney would understand her philosophy, she told her furious parents that Mosley had never been faithful to Cimmie. His wife would think nothing of it. What was meant as a consolation hardly seemed appealing to David and Sydney, when she added: 'I was just another girl he fancied.'[47] They hastened to remind their daughter that she was not just 'another girl', she was a married woman. Diana understood the permanency of what she was about to do — 'I looked forward to a long life alone' — though most sceptics predicted it would last a year, at the most. She naively believed she could continue on as before, seeing her friends and socialising.

'I believe you have a much worse time in store for you than you imagine,' Nancy warned Diana. The anger which David and Sydney had felt, gradually gave way to authority. Given her young age, her two young children and her lack of personal wealth (Bryan was her only source of income), her parents, Tom, Randolph Churchill and Colonel Guinness banded together with the hope of bullying Diana into changing her mind.

If anyone could have understood how Diana felt it would have been her mother. Two years after her marriage to David, Sydney fell out of love with him and considered running away with another man. She packed her bag and was on the verge of leaving when her conscience was pricked by the sight of Nancy, then a baby, up in the nursery. Perhaps she realised the scandal that would have followed and she knew her position in society, as a woman without means to an income, was nil. Abandoning this fancy, Sydney stayed with her husband and soon had a second baby and then another, until she had seven children.

Diana knew if she were to stay with Bryan, the same fate of producing more children would feature in the near future. By succumbing to what everybody else wanted for her, a type of prison Diana thought, she risked incarcerating herself in the role society had chosen for her. 'It was not surprising that my parents reacted angrily to my rather wild decision to leave Bryan and attach myself to Mosley. I was twenty-two, happily married with two baby boys and a husband the whole family had become fond of.'[48]

It was a small victory and a testament to her character that Diana did not relent. When Colonel Guinness returned from one of his lengthy voyages, he was horrified by the situation. Once fond of Diana, he abandoned his past feelings towards her in favour of Bryan, whose dignity and wealth he sought to preserve. The familiar topic of hypocrisy did not arise when Colonel Guinness observed the matter in hand. He was no stranger to infidelity, often departing on one of his cruises with a mistress in tow. His most notable mistress, Vera, Lady Broughton, was the unhappy first wife of Jock Broughton, the disgraced member of Kenya's Happy Valley set, who would later stand trial for the murder of the Earl of Erroll in 1941. And, although unofficially confirmed, Colonel Guinness was also rumoured to be the potential father of the actor Alec Guinness, whose mother had 'slept with the entire crew on Lord Moyne's yacht'.

In terms of his own indiscretions, Colonel Guinness found there was no comparison to Diana; she was openly cavorting with Mosley and any hint of scandal in the family was enough for everyone to close rank. Diana did not care what her father-in-law thought and Bryan's wealth, with the prospect of a permanent income through alimony, did not sway her decision.

Failing to influence Diana, Colonel Guinness and David agreed to target the source of her reckless behaviour and visited Mosley at his flat on Ebury Street. This supposed scene was exaggerated by Nancy for her own comical purposes, and she portrayed Mosley as the ultimate villain, 'dead white and armed with knuckle dusters'. Both men repeated the same plea: 'You must stop this. You are ruining a young marriage, with young children, and this is awful. She's only twenty-two, how can you do such a thing? You must give your word you will not see her any more ...'

'Diana must be allowed to do what she wants,' argued Mosley.

With his patience wearing thin, David interjected: 'Are you prepared to give up Diana now?' It was more of a command than a question.

'No,' Mosley responded.

'Then,' said Colonel Guinness, 'we shall put detectives on you.'

'Very well,' replied Mosley, undeterred by the threat.

Divorce at that time required one of the partners to take responsibility as the named guilty party. Colonel Guinness was determined to prevent a divorce – he knew Bryan would shoulder the blame – and Diana was determined not to *be* divorced and refused to give 'a particle of evidence'.

David unwittingly sullied his daughter's reputation further when he told Colonel Guinness: 'I suppose you know that my daughter is laying in a store of furs and diamonds against the time when she is divorced.' He had been the victim of a Mitford tease. The truth was that Diana said to one of her sisters: 'I hate country shoes and had better get some while I'm rich.' And so Colonel Guinness, who was willing to restore familial relations with Diana once the idea of a divorce and Mosley were abandoned, suddenly turned violently against her.

True to his word, Colonel Guinness did set the detectives on Diana – 'a great army' of them at his own expense. He hoped to gain enough damning evidence against her to use in a future divorce hearing. She found it all 'extremely amusing … It is rather heavenly to feel that they are around – no pick-pockets can approach.'

Mosley escaped relatively unscathed. Cimmie was still suffering from bouts of illness and, distracted by her propaganda duties for the BUF, she managed to remain in the dark where the advancements on Diana were concerned. By the end of 1932, the BUF claimed 50,000 members and had the financial and propaganda support of Lord Rothermere's *Daily Mail:* 'Hurrah for the Blackshirts', the newspaper's headline screamed. Proud of Mosley's success with the party, Cimmie also fooled herself and her husband into thinking her health was on the mend. Feeling wretched, she opted to overlook the burden of pain and used her feminine wiles to win him back. She took great care in selecting her new winter wardrobe, which she bought from Paris. But it was still not enough to oust Diana.

Bryan went to Switzerland with the Mitfords on their annual holiday, leaving Diana alone at Cheyne Walk with her children and staff to celebrate Christmas. Hoping to maintain a cordial relationship with her daughter-in-law, Lady Evelyn invited Diana to the Grosvenor Place Christmas party. Declining the invitation, Diana used Colonel Guinness's hiring of the detectives to make a joke at her in-law's expense: 'It is such a big house to surround so thought it more friendly to save half a dozen men and stay at home.'

She did not stay at home and, in a startling turn of events, Diana received an invitation to the Mosleys' New Year's Eve fancy-dress party. It was a family affair with Irene, Baba and her husband, Fruity Metcalfe, and their three children in attendance, having spent the festive season with Cimmie and Mosley.

The Mosley/Metcalfe Christmas was a disaster on all fronts, with Baba and Fruity bickering since their arrival – he disapproved of Baba's private lunches with Mosley and she accused her husband of being unreasonable.

It was unknown why Cimmie had invited Diana into the family circle. Many believed her tactic lay in her old custom of inviting Mosley's mistresses so she could observe their interaction with her husband and to see how they fitted in with his inner circle, thus creating an intimidating environment for them. Having grown up in a family where the nurturing of self-esteem was not a priority, Diana was not always aware when she was being mistreated and she had become indifferent to criticism. 'I was perfectly accustomed to snubs – they were the normal thing; it was admiration that astonished,' she said. Without incessant fawning or encouragement, the seed of individuality germinated in Diana, and without an ounce of self-consciousness she exerted her personality. Jessica commented on her siblings, her reasoning applying to Diana's all too baffling actions: 'My family was its own nationality. Each of us needed an interpreter.'

The unapologetic presence of Diana at Cimmie's New Year's Eve party did not inspire her harshest critics to interpret the reasoning behind her attendance. Irene and Baba continued to curse Diana's existence, more so than ever when they noticed the pain Cimmie was going through over 'Diana Guinness bitching up her life'.[49] They firmly believed that Diana wanted 'to bolt with Mosley', why else would she 'nail her colours to the mast' and leave Bryan to venture into the unknown?

Diana accepted Mosley's decision to remain with his wife and children. She left Bryan because she wanted to be free from her own marriage; she did not expect to become the second Lady Mosley. Knowing of Mosley's unfaithfulness to Cimmie, Diana did not think she would cause Cimmie any more anguish than Mosley's other liaisons. She repeated her familiar phrase: 'What difference would it make?' Years later, when mutual friends told her of Cimmie's plight, Diana agreed that nothing would have made her give up Mosley, but had she been aware of Cimmie's pain, she would have perhaps altered the course of her actions.

Before Bryan's Swiss holiday, Diana managed to discuss financial matters with him. Bryan offered her a 'tiny' alimony of £2,000 per year, but David, who was acting as her trustee, was advised by Tom 'to stand out for more'. Diana planned for Jonathan and Desmond to live with her, and Bryan did not fight her decision. Given the heartbreak she had already caused him, Diana never refused Bryan access to their children. She also arranged to take with her Nanny Higgs, her lady's maid, a manservant, a housemaid and their cook, Mrs Mack, who had been with them since their Buckingham Street days. Mrs Mack preferred Diana over Bryan, and was all too willing to follow her to the new house and, given her mistress's reduced living arrangements, to accept a lower wage.

As the New Year beckoned, Diana prepared to leave Cheyne Walk and her marriage. But, in an ironic turn of events, Bryan decided to leave Diana. With Colonel Guinness making her life difficult, she chose to remain at Cheyne Walk, thus forcing Bryan to leave her. 'The onus will be on HIM,' she wrote to Nancy. The unhappiness of remaining in their marital home was too much and Bryan moved into his parents' house at Grosvenor Place.

With Bryan out of the picture there seemed little reason why Diana could not continue living at Cheyne Walk. But, with the detectives camping on the pavement outside the house hoping to catch evidence of Mosley's visits, she realised it was time to find her own premises.

24

SOCIAL PARIAH

The location of Diana's new townhouse at 2 Eaton Square was largely inspired by its close proximity to Ebury Street. In her new role as devoted mistress, Diana realised she would have to adapt to Mosley's schedule and living close by allowed him to drop in unannounced between his political and family engagements.

The Great Depression contributed to a slump in rental properties in the affluent areas of London and, owing to such economic despair, Diana negotiated a token rent of £300 per year. The house, having remained vacant for some time, had become dilapidated. On conditions presented to her from the Grosvenor estate, Diana agreed to repair the house herself, for which she was given a grant. As such, the move was delayed by a month or two.

Bryan remained at his parents' house at Grosvenor Place and, sorry for the inconvenience she had caused him, Diana offered to find him a flat. Tom Mitford recommended Swan Court, where he kept a bachelor flat. Touched by her gesture, Bryan took the opportunity to send her a note, awkward in its tone, confessing: 'I do love you for it. I mean, I would if you wanted me to.' She did not want him to and she ignored his note. Taking a formal approach, Bryan had his secretary, Miss Moore, write Diana a letter regarding Cheyne Walk and the servants:

Dear Mrs Guinness, would you mind seeing the servants yourself about the dissolution of Cheyne Walk and consequent future arrangements? They are so hurt that it has come through me and not through their mistress. We all want the road to be as smooth as we can make it and it would help very considerably if you would do this.

Bryan added, 'The servants are resenting your going away so much.' From under the watchful eye of his father, Bryan also wrote a letter to Diana to protest her lunching with Mosley at the Ritz. 'I cannot consent to your associating with Mosley, either at Cheyne Walk or anywhere else. I do not mean that I shall send a policeman to fling him out but I cannot in any way condone your meeting him.' He broke his stern tone to add: 'Love from Bryan.'

Once the house at Eaton Square was ready, Bryan sold Cheyne Walk, giving Diana all of the furniture from it – it had been more to her taste, anyway. He preferred to live modestly and the flat at Swan Court suited his needs, though he still kept Biddesden. So far the transition for Diana had been relatively painless.

Mosley gave her a car, which she kept at a nearby garage for 9s a week. It was an incentive for her to form her own life; he was still worried that she might become a demanding element in his. And, sensing she might feel lonely in her new house with a small staff and only her two children for company, Diana invited Nancy to move into the spare bedroom at Eaton Square, or the 'Eatonry' as her sisters nicknamed it.

Struggling to adapt to this new situation which had been sprung upon him, and without much of a say in anything, Bryan compared the loss of Diana to 'having a limb amputated'. Jonathan and Desmond spent alternate fortnights with each parent, and when Bryan had the children he often invited Diana to join them for tea. If he had anything harsh to say about her conduct, he kept it to himself.

Not everyone was so gallant. The news of Diana publicly establishing herself as Mosley's mistress spread through London society, and Irene responded venomously when 'the whole of London' quizzed her and Baba for gossip about the affair. Abandoning discretion, Irene let her feelings be known: Diana was a 'blithering cow faced fool insanely dithering recklessly trying to ruin Cim's life'.[50]

With false bravado, Bryan, who was in bed with flu, wrote to Diana from Swan Court: 'It is very bad for us to think of each other. We must stop it.' He admitted to weeping over their break-up: 'All the dye will be washed out of my eiderdown if I go on like this.' Their wedding anniversary was coming up and he wondered if she, too, would 'shed a tear'. He added that his novel, Singing out of Tune, which he began writing in Paris during her confinement, would soon be published. The plot centred on a couple who separate, and he begged her to dismiss anyone who asked if it was inspired by their marriage.

The thoughts which Bryan warned her not to have were one-sided. However, Diana agreed that they should remain friends and, hearing that he had the flu, she paid a cordial visit to Swan Court. Still confined to his bed and feeling wretched, Bryan made an effort to be cheerful for her sake, but she misread his magnanimous mood as making an effort to move on. After her departure, Bryan wrote a letter to her, pouring out his feelings, hoping to convince Diana to return to him. 'Don't you find that I am the one you will miss most? Are you sure – are you really sure that the circle of our love is complete ... are you positive that you love Tom* [Mosley] more than me?' For Diana, the answer was yes. She read on, his tone remained the same, pleading with her to return. 'Which of us would you most want to breathe in your ear if you were dying? I have this strong feeling that we both belong to one another, that we are bound by our mutually broken virginity.' He begged, 'Ask yourself the question night and day.'[51]

Bryan's letter failed to nudge her conscience to do the right thing by him and by her reputation. Verifying that his sentimental feelings would always infuriate her – the letter had that very effect, it pushed Diana in the opposite direction. More than ever, it strengthened her longing for a clean break.

---

* Mosley's boyhood nickname remained with him throughout his adult life. Not wanting to get him mixed up with Tom Mitford, Diana never referred to him as such. She chose the private nickname 'Kit' for him.

25

THE DEVIL AND
THE DEEP BLUE SEA

An undercurrent of tension was brewing between Mosley and Cimmie. Wavering between hysterical outbursts and passive aggressiveness, she told Mosley: 'I schooled myself the whole week never to even mention her [Diana] in case I should say something I regret.' Having suffered from the humiliation of her husband's public betrayal for a year, Cimmie could ignore it no longer.

Escaping the tension at home, Mosley fled to the Eatonry, where he was greeted by Diana's unwelcome news: Bryan had finally consented to a divorce. The prospect of the once unobtainable divorce had allowed Mosley to dodge his responsibility towards committing to her. For Cimmie, it hovered over their marriage. She realised that if a young woman such as Diana, in an enviable position, could throw her entire life away she would stop at nothing in stealing another woman's husband. Mosley dreaded the news of the divorce reaching Cimmie and his lack of enthusiasm prompted Diana to react furiously. Having escaped his wife's wrath, he was not prepared to tolerate a petty squabble with his mistress.

With the unfinished business of their argument playing on her mind, Cimmie spent a sleepless night awaiting Mosley's return. In his absence, she felt guilty about the bitter words they had exchanged and, accepting the blame for the situation, she wrote him a letter: 'I want to apologise for last night but I was feeling already pretty rotten and that made me I suppose silly.' Feeling 'pretty rotten' was an understatement. During her last pregnancy, Cimmie had suffered from kidney trouble – an ailment not helped by a series of infections, and also afflicting her was a curvature of the spine, leading her to believe the lower-back pain was due to its inflammation. Her mental health was also in a delicate condition, given the stress and misery she had endured with Mosley and Diana.

That same evening, after the argument had taken place and Mosley had fled, Cimmie's appendix burst. She was rushed to the London Clinic, where she was diagnosed with acute appendicitis. At only 34, she appeared to be healthy and strong and under normal circumstances an appendectomy should have posed no threat. Assured that Cimmie was recovering nicely, Mosley seized the opportunity to escape from her bedside to spend the night with Diana. In her post-operative state Cimmie developed peritonitis and in an age before antibiotics it proved untreatable. On the morning of 16 May, Cimmie whispered to Mosley: 'I am going. Goodbye, my Buffy.' Later that evening, she was dead.

A bitter feud intensified over Cimmie's deathbed. Tensions between Irene and Baba seemed beyond repair when she realised the depth of her younger sister's 'unnecessarily provocative' obsession with Mosley. To demonstrate her disapproval, Irene, who at the age of 37 had become engaged to Captain Miles Graham, had previously written to invite Cimmie to the quiet wedding, asking her to keep the news from Baba. But the timing of the letter was ill-judged. Cimmie, too weak to read the letter, had discarded it to her bedside table, well within view of Baba. Baba retaliated by refusing Irene entry into their sister's room, forcing her to sit outside with Mosley's mother and Cimmie's maid. It further wounded Irene when it was Baba whom Mosley first turned to – 'the one bright spot in a losing fight' – provoking Irene to react with jealousy. 'If I had not kissed him on the stairs he would have passed me by!' she fumed.

Despite Mosley's philandering ways, he deeply loved Cimmie and, realising that his conduct in some way had contributed to her death, he lapsed into a state of turmoil. Captain Miles Graham thought him genuine and he asked the maid where Mosley kept his guns. Mosley kept a pistol under his pillow and its pair in the top drawer of his chest of drawers. He swiftly removed both.

With Mosley and Baba united in their grief and, perhaps, their guilt, Irene, who had knelt at the foot of Cimmie's coffin and promised she would never fail her, decided to take care of the practical matters. She arranged to have the three Mosley children and their nanny collected from their family home. 'I was nervously worried at the dim future of all those children and the babe and wished to God they were my own. Tom is such an undependable quantity,' Irene recorded in her diary. And Mosley did not protest when Irene appointed herself as the children's surrogate mother.

Despite their animosity, Irene and Baba managed to agree on one thing – Diana was responsible for Cimmie's death. Vivien Mosley, who was 12 at the time of

Aged 14, Diana had bewitched James Lees-Milne, and long after they parted ways, she remained the 'unattainable object of his desire'. (Courtesy of Beinecke Rare Book and Manuscript Library, Yale University)

The Queen and her Court. *Left to right*: Ralph Jarvis, Randolph Churchill, Diana, Tom Mitford, Diana Churchill and James Lees-Milne, 1927. (Courtesy of Beinecke Rare Book and Manuscript Library, Yale University)

The unhappy youth: James Lees-Milne stands next to Pamela and Nancy. (Courtesy of Beinecke Rare Book and Manuscript Library, Yale University)

THE CAMERA LOOKS AT YOUNG SOCIETY.

THE HON. MRS. BRYAN GUINNESS   *Lenare*

Diana often graced the pages of society magazines. Pictured here at the age of 18, the portrait captures her youthful optimism. (Private collection)

Batsford Park enchanted Diana. (Courtesy of Debbie Catling)

Asthall Manor was bought with the profit garnered from the sale of Batsford Park. Diana loved the library and the children's private quarters, known as 'The Cloisters'. (Courtesy of Debbie Catling)

Left: Swinbrook House was a poor substitute for Asthall. (Courtesy of Debbie Catling)
Right: Rutland Gate was the family's London base. (Photographed by Sholom Ellenberg, reproduced by kind permission of Meems Ellenberg)

Diana and Bryan leave St Margaret's, Westminster, following their marriage. (Courtesy of Stephen Kennedy)

Diana and Lady Adelaide 'Dig' Bidddulph at Forthampton Court at a meet of the Ledbury Hunt, 1929. (Private collection)

Diana leaves a post-operative appointment with Dr Gillies, 1935. (Courtesy of Stephen Kennedy)

Irene lived a varied life and often mixed high society with the artistic world – as seen here photographed with Charles Chaplin during a visit to Hollywood in 1926. (Courtesy of Stephen Kennedy)

Clockwise from right: Dazed by Nazism, Unity always wore her Swastika pin. (Courtesy of Stephen Kennedy); In this study by Paul Tanqueray, Diana was noted as having ash-blonde hair and china-blue eyes. (Private collection); Deborah and Lord Andrew Cavendish, photographed in 1939. (Private Collection)

The HON. DEBORAH MITFORD and LORD ANDREW CAVENDISH.

THE HON. LADY MOSLEY

Cannons of Hollywood, Dover Street

Diana's ethereal beauty continued to be celebrated long after she disgraced society. (Private collection)

The Mosleys after their release from prison. (Private collection)

Cimmie's death, believed Diana had 'destroyed' her mother: 'Peritonitis is what killed her ... but with Diana there, she didn't want to live.'

When the opportunity presented itself, Mosley stole away to the nearest private telephone to inform Diana of Cimmie's death. Later in the evening, he escaped to the Eatonry to deliver the news she had been dreading. They could not see one another for some time and despite him reassuring her 'it will be all right' Diana knew in her heart it wouldn't.

The divorce proceedings occupied Diana, and Bryan — sweet and loyal until the end — agreed to set up false evidence to make it appear as though he had spent the night in Brighton with a prostitute. The prospect of her much longed for freedom could not elevate Diana's mood and, sick with worry, she was momentarily relieved when Mosley made a brief appearance at the Eatonry. 'Well, have you jumped your little hurdle yet?' he teased her.

The comment triggered a rare confrontational response from Diana and she turned on Mosley, attacking him: 'It isn't a hurdle, you are talking of my whole life!' It had been six weeks since his last visit and Mosley spun his usual web of lies: citing the children's grief and Irene and Baba's disapproval as the reason for his absence. Diana, far from unreasonable where his children were concerned, accepted his answer. It could not have been further from the truth. Baba offered to move into Savehay Farm — the Mosley family home — to help Irene care for the children. Although she had little patience for her own children let alone somebody else's, it provided a flimsy cover-up to disguise her affair with Mosley, something they had both instigated.

Diana's instincts told her different and, as much as she tried to ignore Baba's presence and how Mosley felt about his sister-in-law, she could not ignore the facts. Trying to overlook any unpleasantness, Diana reminded herself that Baba was a surrogate Cimmie and, as such, was really no threat at all.[52] Mosley carried on with his deceitful ways and he assured Irene and Baba that his involvement with Diana was strictly platonic. He was only going through the motions, he told them, of dining with Diana and paying calls to the Eatonry, as it would have been cruel to abruptly end their relationship. This excuse was good enough for Baba, who believed him. Irene, however, was far from convinced.

The three devoted a shrine to Cimmie, and her personal gardener, Norah Lindsay, motored down to Savehay to meet with Baba and Mosley. They walked in the woods and discussed the plans for her memorial garden. Lindsay found Mosley 'quite calm but looked all the time as if he had been condemned ... poor unhappy man'. As though to compensate for the poor treatment of his wife when she had been alive, Mosley commissioned a pink sarcophagus by Lutyens and a marble tombstone bearing the words: 'Cynthia Mosley, My Beloved.' Loyal friends reported every detail to Diana and she listened, pale and withdrawn, and fearful for her future. She learned that the funeral had been an intimate affair with only Mosley, his mother, Irene and Baba in attendance. Later that day, a memorial service took place at St Margaret's, Westminster, for extended family and friends. The only mourners in black were members of the BUF, and Cimmie's loved ones were asked to refrain from wearing traditional mourning colours. As always, all eyes were on Mosley.

Baba and Irene forgave one another of their previous rift to focus on one thing – their hatred of Diana. And Mosley's formidable mother, known as Ma, participated in trying to sway Mosley's attention from Diana. She told him of the apparent whispers circulating around London that Diana was boasting she would marry him. His mother further warned him that those who knew of Diana confirmed she was 'a most determined minx and talked freely to everyone'.[53] Mosley, in his role of bereaved widower, rebuffed this rumour and he defended Diana's character, claiming she was 'dignified and sweet and would never chatter loosely like that'. Hearing Mosley's gallant defence of Diana, Ma wept and said he was 'so marvellous to his children that perhaps Cim had died to save his soul'. Irene scoffed at such a notion.

Suspecting Mosley of dishonesty, Baba flew at him, hysterically begging him to give up Diana. Irene tried to persuade him that it was 'hurtful to the memory of Cimmie'. A master of deceit, Mosley successfully convinced Irene and Baba that his affair with Diana was over. Believing this to be true, and observing how involved Baba was in Mosley's life, Irene prayed 'this obsession will utterly oust Diana'. Certain the 'trouble-maker' Diana had been erased from their lives, Irene broke off her engagement with Captain Miles Graham, sold her house, dismissed her staff, euthanised her old dog Winks and embarked on a cruise of the South Sea Islands. Having regained her strength, she returned home to rescue the Mosley children from 'whatever new high jinks their father might advance on'.

One of the dreaded 'high jinks' was still in the form of Diana. Sneaking around the corner from Ebury Street, Mosley visited the Eatonry once it was dark. He told Diana of the situation with Baba, how grief had consumed her and the irrationality of her feelings. Diana listened to his monologue, though not entirely deceived. It was simpler than Mosley had let on. Baba was useful to him, serving as a go-between for him and her other lover, Count Dino Grandi, Mussolini's ambassador to London, and the dubious role earned her the nickname 'Baba Blackshirt'.

Leaving that small fact out, Mosley convinced Diana that it would be best if he and Baba went on a motoring holiday to France. He reassured her it was platonic and that his children would also be joining them. This was, in fact, a lie. Irene had agreed to take the two eldest children on holiday to the Canary Islands, while baby Micky remained at home with his nanny. Far from understanding, Diana was furious but little could be done to change Mosley's mind. With both women convinced that each had been romantically eradicated from his life, Mosley set off for the Continent, with one of his mistresses in tow.

In spite of the family drama surrounding Diana's wish for a divorce, the actual hearing was brief and without ceremony. Summoned to the witness stand, Diana stood before the judge and in her typical reticent manner she conveyed the false evidence. Explaining the marriage to Bryan was a happy one until the birth of their second child in 1931, she confessed that 'differences arose and there were quarrels'. The previous March, she explained, Bryan presented her with a letter stating that he had spent the night with Miss Isobel Field at a Brighton hotel. Validating this charade, a paid witness from the hotel was called to provide further evidence. It did not trouble the atheist Diana to lie under oath, but for Bryan the entire set-up proved distressing. A decree nisi was finally granted to Diana by Lord Merrivale, on the grounds of misconduct on Bryan's behalf.

Keeping to her word that she wanted nothing more than her freedom, Diana repeatedly refused the large sums of money, which, given the false evidence of Bryan in the role of adulterer, was rightfully hers. She also refused the marriage settlement offered to her from Lady Evelyn and Colonel Guinness. It baffled the solicitor and he warned her: 'You are signing away millions.' With her integrity intact, Diana returned the Guinness tiaras, brooches and kept only the presents Bryan had bought her since their marriage – a three-strand cultured pearl necklace, large Victorian paste earrings and a bracelet of diamonds and cabochon rubies. Regardless of the hurt and betrayal Bryan had suffered, it was not the end of his feelings for Diana, and he sought to ensure her security should Mosley abandon her. He convinced Diana to accept £2,500 a year and insisted the income would be hers for life, even if she remarried.

Life was unbearable for Bryan and, longing to escape the prying eyes of his contemporaries in London, he retreated to Biddesden with Jonathan and Desmond. He tried to concentrate on writing his novels and aimed to write 1,000 words per day, but he seldom achieved it. He also busied himself by acting as a non-executive director of the brewery, looking in on it during his visits to Ireland, and he read the weekly notes Colonel Guinness sent him with little interest. Reflecting on this miserable time, Bryan aptly described himself as a rolling stone: 'I gathered no moss, made no notes, recorded no conversations.'

Diana was equally unhappy and, largely cut off from society, she found her engagement book becoming increasingly vacant. Many hated her because of the divorce. Sympathies lay with Bryan, and their old friends Henry and Lady Pansy York told him that Diana had had an affair with Randolph Churchill. The old guard shunned her and, to the young debutantes, shop-soiled Mrs Guinness was a cautionary tale. Still, Diana had a few friends who remained loyal and she enjoyed trips to the cinema with Henry York, attended concerts with her brother Tom and continued to receive supper invitations from Emerald Cunard, who had given her the amusing nickname 'Golden Corn'.

Emerald was extremely modern in her outlook, and her visual intelligence and love of the arts elevated her into an altogether higher category from the general run-of-the-mill, snobbish hostess. Furthermore, she provided a light-hearted environment for Diana, who was amused by her rare lapses of Americanisms. One day, Emerald invited Diana over to the house she rented while her own home was being repainted and, giving Diana a tour, she complained in her shrill voice: 'There are no faucets near the basin.'

'Faucets, Emerald. What are faucets?' Diana teased.

'*Faucets*,' Emerald became furious. 'Everybody knows what a faucet is. It's American for tap!' This short-tempered response was similar to when Diana asked Emerald if she had known Helleu. Diana sensed that, not only did Emerald detest being reminded of her dead friends, she also disliked being reminded of her origins.

During this interval in her dwindling social calendar, Diana had grown close to her younger sister Unity, who disobeyed David and Sydney's rules to visit her at the Eatonry. Twice a week, the sisters went to the Women's League of Health and Beauty, but these various outings, along with Unity's company, could not distract Diana, and all too often she found her mind and her suspicions wandering to Mosley and Baba, who were in France. Longing to escape London, and with her children staying at Biddesden with Bryan, Diana decided to take a holiday.

The location of the holiday was inspired by an impromptu social visit that spring. Bryan's cousin's wife, Mrs Richard Guinness, had invited Diana to meet 'a very interesting German' and when she arrived she found this interesting German playing the piano. 'He is a personal friend of Hitler,' said the other Mrs Guinness. 'He plays the piano for him when he is exhausted after a great speech. He is David to Hitler's Saul.' The man in question was Ernst 'Putzi' Hanfstaengl, Hitler's press secretary.

Diana's first recollection of Nazism was from 1931, when she and Bryan had visited Tom Mitford in Berlin. She recalled the violence in the streets, the graffiti and the silent terror sweeping Berlin. Tom's remark of hypothetically siding with the Nazis was brought back to Diana. Since that visit, anything regarding Nazism was related to her through newspaper reports and gossip, and she innocently asked Hanfstaengl about the Jews. 'Oh the Jews, the Jews, that's all one ever hears in London, what about the Jews!' Hanfstaengl shouted. 'People here have no idea of what the Jewish problem has been in Germany since the war. Why not think once of the ninety-nine percent of the population, of the six million unemployed,' he informed the stunned guests. 'Hitler will build a great and prosperous Germany for the Germans. If the Jews don't like it they can get out. They have relations and money all over the world. Let them leave Germany to us Germans.' Adopting a friendly tone, he turned to the guests and added: 'You must all come to Germany ... you will see with your own eyes what lies are being told about us in your newspapers.'

Prior to her evening with Hanfstaengl, it had not crossed Diana's mind to holiday in Germany and, remembering her trip with Bryan blighted by the salacious nightclubs, she was not in a hurry to return. With Mosley in France and her once-good friends in Venice, there seemed no reason for Diana to stay in London. Not wanting to travel alone, she extended an invitation to Unity and together they left on a trip that would change the course of their lives forever.

26

DETOUR

Since her early teens, Diana longed to experience the idealistic image she had formed of Germany, portrayed to her through Tom's musical tastes, her grandfather's books and Professor Lindemann's advice that to ease her adolescent boredom she ought to learn German. It was a culture, he warned, too advanced for the frivolous, modern world. Upon reaching Munich, the impression of Germany embedded in Diana's memory from her last visit had changed dramatically.

The rigid schedule of sightseeing around Bavaria delighted Diana. Baroque churches, castles and trips to the opera were a world away from the sleazy Berlin nightclubs that were the catalyst of her experience only two years previously. Bavaria was also the heartland of the Nazi movement, a familiar term which existed in the foreground of her mind following her meeting with Putzi Hanfstaengl.

The Jewish question, too, was never far from Diana's thoughts. Since the end of the First World War the influx of Jews to the East End of London did little to convince a vast number of Britons that Jews were good for the economy. They viewed the Jews as opportunists, accusing them of moving in on businesses whilst British men were off at war. Xenophobia was rife among the ruling classes; the British Empire lay in lands beyond Europe and in its position of Imperial ruler it looked down on foreigners. They were indecent, dishonest and louche. 'Abroad' was 'unutterably bloody' and for the Victorians, the generation above Diana, the Continent was a 'place of banishment or refuge' and shrouded in secrets – it was not the sort of lifestyle a decent person would enter into willingly.

With her love of art and culture, Diana had somehow risen above such prejudice, yet the outlook she would soon adopt mirrored the view of her paternal grandfather, Bertie Redesdale. Diana had only known Bertie for the first six years of her life, during which he was a distant, elderly figure in mourning for his dead son and often bedridden from bouts of illness. In his younger days, Bertie had established himself as a landowner, diplomat, writer, collector and lover of all things exotic. This fondness for culture did not pass on to his son David, but skipped a generation and attached itself to his granddaughters.

Another ancestor with similarity to Diana was Bertie's mother, Lady Georgina, who was a bolter. She scandalised society – much as Diana had done in leaving Bryan – when she abandoned her husband Henry Mitford to live with Francis Molyneux, whom she later married. Divorce was a social taboo in those days and Lady Georgina was alienated from her children, lest she inflict her wicked sense of immorality onto them, too. Some say Francis Molyneux fathered her children and not Henry Mitford, but nobody in the family knew for certain and, presumably, nobody cared.

A glittering diplomatic career awaited Bertie when he entered the Foreign Office in 1858, where he was appointed Third Secretary of the British Embassy in St Petersburg. It was during his service in the Diplomatic Corps in Peking that he met the Japanologist Ernest Satow and in 1871 his novel, *Tales of Old Japan*, was published. The publication was credited for introducing classical Japanese tales such as *The Forty-Seven Ronin* to the Western public. Bertie also edited and wrote lengthy introductions for two of Houston Stewart Chamberlain's books, *Immanuel Kant: A Study and Comparison with Goethe, Leonardo da Vinci, Bruno, Plato and Descartes* and, most notably, *Foundations of the Nineteenth Century*, published in Germany in 1899 to great success.

Foundations of the Nineteenth Century was a love letter to the superiority of the Teutonic people. It emphasised Chamberlain's sole view that a racially pure German race should rule the world. Chamberlain was openly racist and a rampant anti-Semite. He made no apologies for his views and argued his case for a racially pure Germany by wrapping the text up with scientific, philosophic and culturally based arguments, all of which were founded from his own unstable beliefs. Given its theme, it was ironic that Bertie opted to praise the Jews in his introduction for Chamberlain's book. He wrote: 'The charities of the great cities of Europe would be in a sad plight were the support of the Jews to be withdrawn ... Politically too they have rendered great services ...' – the latter part was believed to be a reference to Bertie's hero, Benjamin Disraeli.

This striking parallel between Bertie Redesdale and Diana could have been argued from a predestination point of view. Bertie, a well-travelled man and admirer of Eastern culture, contradicted himself when he befriended

Chamberlain. Much like his granddaughter Diana would do in her relationship with Mosley, Bertie risked his respectable reputation amongst the aesthetes to support a view that racial origins determined almost everything – a bizarre stance, given that Bertie had fathered two children with a geisha.

Through his connection with Chamberlain, Bertie became acquainted with Siegfried Wagner, and this introduction to German opera at Bayreuth was described by him in quasi-religious terms. It validated a view that had been agreed by many respectable English scholars of the time, that the German people were, indeed, a superior race. Mosley, too, had a small but significant connection to this argument on racial origins. It was believed that Mosley was one of the initiates of the Children of the Sun – a Dionysian cult comprised of children of Britain's Roundtable elite. Among the initiates were T.S. Eliot, W.H. Auden, D.H. Lawrence and Aldous Huxley. It shared its name with the German *Sonnenkinder*, the term used to designate the eugenically bred, racially pure *Lebensborn* children of Nazi Germany.

The intellectual side of Germany's culture did not fascinate Unity and, since the moment of their arrival, she continued to press Diana with the same question: 'When will we meet Hitler?' Knowing Unity's fondness for celebrity, Diana had sold the idea of Germany to her with the promise they would meet the new German Chancellor. Her sister longed to see Italy or France, and so far Germany was a poor alternative. Hanfstaengl was the only connection Diana had to Hitler and, despite his claim that he was a household name, no one outside of political circles seemed to know who he was.

The trip was slowly turning into a disaster; Diana knew about twenty words in German, she could ask a simple question but she did not understand the answer. Unity knew no German at all. Hanfstaengl did not give Diana his address; repeating the same motto, he assured her everyone in Germany knew of his whereabouts. However, this proved fruitless when Diana asked the doorman at her hotel to find him and they, too, could not track him down. Finally, Diana achieved success at Brown House, the Nazi Party's headquarters, and suddenly their luck began to look up when the illusive Hanfstaengl telephoned her hotel. 'You have come at exactly the right moment,' he cryptically told her, but in their current state of mind his words were of little consequence to the weary tourists. 'We are having our Parteitag tomorrow, I will get you tickets and a room in Nuremberg.' Having exhausted the sights of Munich, Diana and Unity accepted his offer.

Excitement was in the air when Hanfstaengl met Diana and Unity at the station, informing them the Parteitag would last four days, not one as they had imagined. It was a jamboree of Unity's dreams. Everywhere they looked they saw hundreds of men in uniform congregating around the old town and there were Nazi flags hanging in the windows; the sense of pageantry hypnotised her. Even Diana's dire spirits were elevated by the excitement, and both sisters were impressed to see Hanfstaengl in a party uniform of his own design. In return, he delighted in escorting the two beautiful women around Nuremberg.

The Parteitag of 1933 was not a militant display. There were no foreign visitors, no diplomats or prestigious guests, only the everyday German people who were riding a wave of joy and jubilation. Despite the event appearing low-key in comparison to Hitler's future rallies, the theatrics were advanced beyond the BUF's capabilities. Dramatic lighting, spirited music and vigorous young men in uniform served as a backdrop to Hitler as he stood below a 100ft spread eagle fixed upon a timber frame.

The German film-maker Leni Riefenstahl had been recruited to work on the special effects and Hitler ordered her to make a film of the event. *Victory of Faith* was an hour-long documentary screened for Hitler and party dignitaries in December 1933, and it was such a maverick piece of film making that the London *Observer* reported on it:

> The film is one long apotheosis of the Caesar spirit, in which Herr Hitler plays the role of Caesar while the troops play the role of the slaves. It is certainly to be hoped that this film will be shown in all cinemas outside Germany, if one wishes to understand the intoxicating spirit which is moving Germany these days.

In her autobiography, Diana described her invitation to the event as a chance encounter, a gesture of goodwill on Hanfstaengl's behalf. There were no strings pulled and no one exploited the connections with the BUF. However, Hanfstaengl had all of the characteristics of a snob and his English visitors were just the type of old-world aristocrats which he, and Hitler, admired.

Was Hanfstaengl working behind the scenes? It certainly seems that his inviting Diana and Unity was a calculated move, for a few weeks later a brochure of the Parteitag was published with photos of Unity wearing her BUF black shirt under a tweed suit. This photograph of Unity reached England and her parents were livid at Diana for introducing Unity to 'a murderous gang of pests'. This hardly mattered to Diana, who was still estranged from David and Sydney.

Although they could not understand the speeches, Diana and Unity were mesmerised by Hitler's oration, the dramatic pattern of his voice and the passion driving his political message. Had Diana been fluent in the language she would have listened to a speech driven by the topic of racial purity, largely motivated by recent events – the boycott of Jewish businesses, the book burnings and the *Arierparagraph*, which banned the hiring of Jews in a wide range of professions. Aside from the grotesque anti-Semitism, it is baffling how someone who loved books as much as Diana could support a party and a leader who ordered such a senseless undertaking. Those who listened to, and understood, Hitler's views were left in no doubt about his future plans for the Jews.

Perhaps given the language barrier, the overall impression of the Parteitag remained a positive experience for Diana, who 'witnessed this demonstration of hope in a nation that had known collective despair'. And recalling her previous queries on Nazism and the Jews that had enraged Hanfstaengl, Diana begun to wonder how such a political party, which seemed to have the respect and support of the German nation, could be harmful.

The thought of meeting Hitler did not conjure up the same thrill in Diana as it had in Unity. However, years later Diana felt the same level of excitement and confessed, 'I thirst for only a glimpse of him.' Determined to meet the star of the Parteitag, Unity implored Diana to follow up with Hanfstaengl, who offered a variety of feeble excuses, finally telling them: 'You mustn't wear lipstick, the Führer doesn't like it.' Finding this an odd statement, Unity defiantly announced, 'I couldn't possibly do without it.' Having previously exaggerated his importance in the Nazi Party, Hanfstaengl used it as an opportunity to dodge his promise of arranging a meeting with Hitler.

The exuberance of Nuremberg and Hanfstaengl's gracious hospitality added to the misery Unity felt when she returned to Swinbrook. She pleaded with David and Sydney to grant her permission to return to Munich, where she could study art and learn German. At 19, she had two failed seasons behind her and she displayed little enthusiasm in finding a husband, or even an admirer. She lacked Diana's grace, Nancy's ability to hold down a job and Pamela's contented nature, all of which added to her troublesome behaviour at home. After much deliberation, David and Sydney decided it might be good for Unity to experience a change of scenery. After all, the three eldest girls had spent a year in Paris, taking art lessons and becoming fluent in French.

With her rebellious behaviour and incessant need to shock, Unity found a kindred spirit in Diana. To the impressionable Unity, Diana was an esteemed example; her love for Mosley and her support of fascism strengthened Unity's political views. Although Mosley's propaganda palled in comparison to the Nazi Party, it thrilled Unity that her sister had a link to this ideology sweeping Germany, gaining worldwide attention and, at that time, respect. Diana was a proverbial bridge between Unity's connection to England and Germany, a place where she was certain she would find her niche.

Keeping it a secret from her parents, Unity joined the BUF and, through this hero worship of Mosley and Hitler, she coveted a small collection of militant materials. Among her prized collection were copies of *Blackshirt* and a badge which Mosley had personally given her. The words 'Hello, Fascist'[54] still thrilled her and, for someone who was viewed as an oddball, it made her believe that the Leader had singled her out. With this belief, Unity set forth to spread the word of fascism.

To Mosley, however, Unity was a liability. Despite his indiscretions, he was a shrewd man and, taking into consideration how the BUF respected Cimmie, he knew this allegiance with Unity might run the risk of making a mockery of the party. With Unity on her way to Munich, it seemed to be the best solution for everyone involved. She would be out of sight, out of mind.

27

THE GOLDEN MONTH
OF OCTOBER

With Mosley still abroad, Diana extended her travels to Rome, where she visited her friend Gerald Tyrwhitt-Wilson, 14th Baron Berners. Lord Berners had captured Diana's fancy the year before when they became acquainted through the great connector of people, Emerald Cunard. Aged 49 to Diana's 23, Berners was a contemporary of her parents but not a product of their uptight generation. Like her father, he held a seat in the House of Lords but had only attended once; he said he would never return because a bishop had stolen his umbrella.

Age never held any mystery for Diana and Berners possessed everything she admired in a human being. His talents ranged from charming painter to accomplished musician and, gifted with a sense of parody, he succeeded in writing 'screamingly funny' tales based on his friends and foes. Under the pseudonym 'Adela Quebec', Berners cast himself in the role of headmistress in his spoof novel, *The Girls of Radcliff Hall*. The novel, privately printed and distributed amongst friends, amused his admirers and troubled those who could not laugh at themselves. Cecil Beaton, for one, was outraged and bought fifty copies of the 100 printed and burned them all.

The daily routine was a sedate interval after the electrifying ceremony of Munich. Led by Berners, the culture-loving Diana indulged in guided tours of the city, with her friend wearing his tinted spectacles to divert attention from his eyes, which he believed were so kind that they would make him an easy target for beggars. As the afternoon sun palled, they enjoyed ices in the Piazza Navona and motored out to Frascati. For someone jaded by English society, it was refreshing for Diana to be exposed to something unknown.

In the mornings, Diana awoke to Berners sitting at his piano, composing music that seemed to match her mood. 'His music had a dying fall, there was a superficial gaiety in it accompanied by an underlying sadness.' She suggested he write twelve bars of a fascist march, which appeared in the *Daily Express*, simply 'because I asked him to'. Although apolitical, Berners did not mind Diana's leaning towards fascism; he was quite accustomed to the ideology, which had been the system in Italy for years. Rome, however, 'remained unchanged'. Diana's friends were extremely rich and with such riches came frivolity – and fascism, to this set, was the lesser of two evils when compared to communism. Fascism, they realised, posed no threat to their wealth.

After a morning of composing, Berners would move to the telephone located outside her bedroom door to make arrangements for their evenings. '*Pronto, pronto è Lord Berners*,' he shouted in fluent Italian, pronounced in his English accent.

When his guests arrived, Diana was amused by the Romans, whom she thought 'exceptionally beautiful to look at and also exceptionally spiteful about one another'. They sat on the balcony of his house at 3 Foro Romano, overlooking the Forum, which they used as their pleasure garden. Serenaded by the cook's canaries, Diana feasted on delicious sponge cakes of chocolate, sour cream, rum, angelica and candied cherries. Clever and witty, Berners made Diana scream with laughter, the gaiety lifting her melancholic mood, consumed by thoughts of Mosley and his devotion to Baba.

Berners, too, suffered from his own form of melancholy provoked by crippling bouts of depression, brought on by his bad heart. It was an illness which made him pessimistic and gloomy. Diana noticed that he could be talkative at lunch, keeping everyone entertained, and then down for the rest of the afternoon. If someone should come to dinner he would perk up again. This contrast in moods was confirmed when, towards the end of Diana's visit, they were joined by Desmond Parsons, a handsome young man governed by a pronounced lack of enthusiasm. It amused Berners when Parsons arrived promptly and announced: 'I had a *disastrous* morning in the Vatican.'

'I hope you like veal,' Berners said, without addressing Parsons' complaint.

'Oh yes,' said Parsons in sarcastic tones. 'I am a regular *veal fiend*.'

A fellow guest held the remedy for their glum spirits. M. Sandez, a Swiss millionaire whose pharmaceutical business bore his name, told them of a '*merveilleuse*' drug sold in Paris which promised to relieve symptoms of depression. Diana, sceptical of its claims, gently coaxed Berners: 'Don't worry, you'll come out of it; you always do.'

'My mother had the same depression and she died in the middle of one,' Berners replied.

That was the end of Diana's optimism and the three friends piled into Berners' lumbering Rolls-Royce with its interior lining sporting stencilled butterflies. Loathing to drive abroad, his chauffeur, William Crack, drove at a glacial pace towards the French border, occasionally taking wrong turns, which inspired Berners to tease him: 'William, I'm an old man and I've left you a lot of money in my will. I do think you might go the way I want sometimes.' By chance, their journey turned into a culinary adventure, stopping off at every three star restaurant on their way to Paris for the wonder drug.

Once the drug was in their possession, Berners and Parsons consumed it immediately. Assuring Diana it was 'quite harmless with no unpleasant side effects', they convinced her to sample it, too. She found it useless and it had no effect on her whatsoever. Berners and Parsons, however, manoeuvred around in a blissful state, ready for any joke. But this euphoria lasted only a day or two before their old familiar foe re-emerged.

When Mosley returned to England, he dedicated his attentions towards the BUF, which had been expanding at a rapid pace. This expansion was owed to the meagre membership fees which encouraged enrolment – 1s a month if employed and 4*d* a month if unemployed. However, uniforms were bought at the members' own expense. The uniforms were aimed at the youth of the nation who, according to Mosley, longed more than anything for something alive, something colourful.[55]

He found larger headquarters, settling on a former Whitelands Teacher Training College on the Kings Road in Chelsea, renaming it 'Black House'. The building could hold 5,000 bodies at full capacity and from the headquarters Mosley also ran a small printing press responsible for churning out BUF posters and leaflets. Using the unemployment crisis to drive his message of fascism, Mosley opened Black House to those in dire straits, for even the most menial of jobs guaranteed a bed and £1 or £2 a week in pay. Soon, 200 Blackshirts moved in, living under strict military conditions. Furthermore, centres and offices were set up around the country and the London staff became salaried.

Regular funding for the BUF did not come entirely from Mosley himself, for he had already plunged his personal wealth into the party. Private funding came from aristocrats who, in 1933, saw the movement as respectable. Lord Rothermere, founder of the *Daily Mail*, became the main financier, alongside the shipping magnate Lord Nuffield. A generous gift of £200,000 was pledged by Lady Houston. Left-wing supporters tried to uncover Mosley's secret backers but failed to find any hard evidence, and Mosley himself was secretive about such matters. Mussolini donated around £60,000 per year, paid monthly in a foreign currency lodged into a Swiss bank account, then transferred into the account of 'an individual in this country'. This individual was believed to be Bill Allen, an advertising magnate from Northern Ireland, who provided the perfect decoy for Mussolini's generous donations.

In the same vein as Hitler's creative collaboration with Leni Riefenstahl, Mosley had ambitions to consult with a British film studio in producing a film about fascism. During a visit to a film studio, he met Mary Russell Taviner (also known as Mary Russell Tavernan), a former actress turned producer, and for obvious reasons Mosley was interested in starting an affair with her. Like Baba, Taviner could be useful to this branch of BUF propaganda. Taviner made no secret of wanting to marry Mosley. She sent him lengthy, rambling letters, spiteful in their tone about Diana, whom she declared was 'of easy virtue'. During their meetings, Mosley played down his affair with 'that blonde lady' and he accused Diana of pursuing him – 'The type who will stop at nothing to satisfy their urge to possess,' Taviner warned him.

The fling with Taviner was becoming too risky, even for the philandering Mosley. He feared Diana and Baba would discover the true nature of their involvement with one another. Taviner began to stalk Mosley, often calling at Black House demanding to see him. But most alarmingly to Mosley, just when he needed support from Diana, she was not in the country. So used to having her at his disposal, this independent stance from Diana perplexed him.

Finally, after spending the summer apart, Diana and Mosley were reunited in early October. For their own personal reasons, they were relieved to be in one another's company again. Diana could hardly wait to tell him about Nuremberg and the physical displays of fascism at work in mending a broken country. And Mosley, unnerved by Taviner's behaviour and the complicated mess left behind from his affair with Baba, found Diana a welcome relief.

Unaware of Mosley's private turmoil over his affairs, Diana's attentions were spent elsewhere when a surprise note arrived from Swan Court. Had it emerged earlier, it might have given Diana a reason to think twice. It was from Bryan and his offer was simple and direct: 'If the situation ever changes you will let me know, won't you? A wire saying "Come" would enable me to make preparations to take you to China. All this is madness because it doesn't arise and is only a way of sending my love.' Eager to retain a friendship with Diana, Bryan bought her a generous birthday present of a watercolour painting by F. Nicholson, circa 1830. Bryan's offering, a comfort to any woman in Diana's predicament, was soon discarded. After all, Mosley had forsaken all others and returned to her.

In December, Nancy moved out of the Eatonry when she accepted Peter Rodd's proposal of marriage. The relationship with her parents was still tense, but Diana braved David and Sydney's scorn to attend Nancy's wedding, where Jonathan and Desmond served as page boys. Standing with her little boys, wrapped in cream cashmere shawls, Diana concealed her pregnancy, which, had it become known, would have further severed the fragile familial relations.

As she had once told James Lees-Milne, 'free love' would 'lead to endless misery and poverty among women'. And, having been deserted by their capricious lovers, they would have to maintain large families on nothing for years.[56] For a capricious lover such as Mosley, there was no question of marrying Diana, and he still used Cimmie's death as an excuse. Compassionate towards his grief, she consented to an abortion. A dangerous and illegal act in 1933.

28

THE FALL OF FASCISM

The rise of fascism had become another recreational topic of conversation for the upper classes. Alice Keppel, once mistress to King Edward VII, possessed 'immense superficial knowledge'[57] and in this frame of mind she ventured to Berlin to hear Hitler speak. For Emerald Cunard, one of Diana's earliest influences, it was another carefree fancy and an outlet for her to shock her contemporaries with her risqué machine-gun conversation. She, too, was pro-Hitler.

The British Union of Fascists peaked at 55,000 members and 1933 became the pinnacle year for the party. In a rare move in politics, Mosley established the women's section of the BUF, presided over by his mother and assisted by Mary Richardson, a suffragette leader. Several suffragettes had transferred their hero worship from Emmeline Pankhurst to Mosley, and Mary Richardson spoke for those women when she told *Blackshirt*: 'I saw in them the courage, the action, the loyalty, the gift of service and the ability to serve which I had known in the suffragette movement.' Whereas the Nazi Party fostered an image of wholesome domesticity in German women, Mosley, although he believed men and women should know their place in society and in the home, was promoting women in a man's arena – politics – where they were 'accepted as an independent, free-thinking individual'. Still, regardless of joining a movement which prided itself in masculinity, the women of the BUF condoned the Nazi view: 'If National Socialism can dignify motherhood and develop a healthier race for Germany, then a Fascist government can do it for England.'

This appealed to Diana, and it must have served to further validate Mosley's political message. At the heart of Diana's unhappiness in childhood was the constant reminder that she could not indulge in certain things because she was not a boy. This patriarchal point of view was not restricted to the home. David opposed the idea of having life peeresses sit in the upper house in the House of Lords, believing the sight of a woman in the House was 'lower than the belly of a snake'. And, as much as the BUF thrived on militant conformity, Mosley inviting women to join his party seemed an entirely modern and advanced concept. Diana saw it as progress and, therefore, it was right.

Appealing to the growing number of women joining the BUF, Mosley founded *The Fascist Woman*, a short-lived magazine which ceased publication in the autumn of 1933. Undeterred, Mosley kept up the momentum of the propaganda machine and launched *Fascist Week*,* a privately circulated newspaper.

Suffering from overwork, Mosley's old ailment phlebitis flared up and, to ease the burden of pain, he planned to escape to Provence at the first opportunity. And, still juggling several women, Mosley told Irene and Baba he was holidaying alone. Irene was satisfied for the time being that Baba's obsession and devotion would keep him from *that* Guinness woman. Ever the skilled deceiver, Mosley could see through Irene's plan and he played along, which pleased her immensely: 'I cannot get over Tom's consideration to Baba,' she wrote in her diary. Having successfully fulfilled his duty of taking Baba on holiday, it was his turn to escape with Diana.

The trip offered Mosley an opportunity to relax and he found a charming house near Grasse, which he rented from Sir Louis Mallet. A far cry from his jaunt across France with Baba, who demanded luxurious hotels, Diana was content to lounge in the sun by day and dine in front of a wood-burning fire by night. While Mosley slept, she went for long walks in the hills, encountering washerwomen beating their linen on oaken boards in the crystal-clear steams, their voices of Provençal dialect echoing together as they worked. She compared the animated scene to James Joyce's *Anna Livia Plurabel*. This level of simplicity was enough for Diana, for all she had wanted was Mosley to herself.

After two weeks of 'a sweet reunion', Diana returned to the Eatonry, where life continued on as before. She sat for Tchelichew, a famous artist in Paris but relatively unknown in London. He imagined Diana and her children with long golden hair and their faces gold with blue shadows and bright blue eyes. Her boys, aged 4 and 6, grew restless with the posing and the artist was unable to engage their attention as he spoke no English. They had to sit separately, accompanied by Nanny Higgs, who related their session to Diana: 'Mr Tchelichew was so kind, oh he was kind, but Desmond turned his head and wouldn't look, even

---

* The newspaper folded in May 1934.

when Mr Tchelichew gave him a sweet.' The children made matters worse when Tchelichew placed Desmond's hand lovingly on Diana's shoulder, which provoked a fit of jealousy in Jonathan and he threatened, 'I won't have Desmond hugging her. I won't sit.'

The daily routine of artists and friends calling to the Eatonry was reminiscent of Cheyne Walk. Her old, familiar friends Doris Castlerosse and Phyllis de Janze became regular callers; the two women shared a common link in that each relied on rich men for their keep. Diana was delighted when they brought along their Cartier boxes containing elaborate baubles from their admirers. And John Sutro, a wealthy member of Evelyn Waugh's circle, came to lunch every Sunday. Surprisingly, given Mosley's views, Sutro's Jewishness did not trouble Diana.

Although Diana could cherish a friend regardless of race or religion, such familiar feelings could not force her to change her outlook – and her outlook was firmly influenced by Mosley. She did not break off her friendship with Sutro, but she did sympathise with Mosley, who claimed the BUF only attacked the Jews because the Jews had attacked him first. In contrast to Diana's empathy towards Mosley, Irene recorded a painful incident in her diary, an example of his early hostility towards the Jews. He had forbidden Irene to entertain her Jewish friends, the Sieffs, at one of her musical soirees, threatening to remove the children from her care if she did. 'I was quite shattered by it,' she said.

The Jewish subject posed an interesting juxtaposition in looking at Diana's continued friendship towards those who possessed qualities the BUF and the Nazi Party abhorred. Her lifelong loyalty towards her homosexual friends, a quality reciprocated despite her admiration for Hitler, challenged the party's political message.

Homosexuality was classed as 'a degenerate form of behaviour' that threatened the nation's 'disciplined masculinity'. Joseph Goebbels emphasised the Nazi Party's intolerance when he announced: 'We must exterminate these people root and branch; the homosexual must be eliminated.' Heinrich Himmler estimated that there were 2 million homosexuals in Nazi Germany and he warned that if any SS man was found to be homosexual he would be arrested, publicly humiliated and sent to a concentration camp where 'they will be shot while attempting to escape', and those accused of homosexuality were forced to wear a pink triangle on their clothing. But this intolerance was not limited to the Nazi Party. Mussolini preached a similar message and declared homosexuality to be 'a social disease'.

This negative outlook was not confined to militant organisations trying desperately to convert society to their views. In Britain, homosexuality was a crime worthy of imprisonment. Unsurprisingly, Mosley was not averse to dismissing homosexuality, and he admitted to feeling wary of men who were attracted to their own sex, an attitude founded during his days at Winchester College. Later he adjusted his views 'on basic ground of liberty that adults should be free to do what they wished in private, provided they do not interfere with others'.

Professor Lindemann had warned her against the dangers of homosexuality becoming socially acceptable, yet, at the impressionable age of 17, Diana could rise above adversity to maintain she loved her friends regardless of their sexuality. This was a serving example of Diana's loyalty towards those she loved; she could tolerate anything regardless of social opposition, and it was merely another issue in her private life which conflicted with Mosley's beliefs.

For the first time in their relationship, Mosley invited Diana to Savehay Farm. In doing so, he must have been aware of the scrutiny he would have faced. The staff were outraged, though, given their place, they kept their opinions to themselves. The children's nanny, however, managed to manipulate her charges when she declared 'that fright Mrs Guinness' was responsible for their mother's death. Irene, not so silent in her views, agreed that Diana's presence at Savehay was offensive and a direct insult to Cimmie's memory. The loyal staff had scurried to alert Irene to the situation, and without hesitation she sent her car to ferry the children to Baba's house.

Since Cimmie's death, Mosley had fallen out of favour with the couple's once devoted friends. They were inclined to agree with Irene that he had been a 'cad' for inflicting needless suffering on his wife, who had devoted her life to him and his politics. Caring little for their criticism, he busied himself with the BUF, which had become his main priority. Though, as he warned Diana when she left Bryan: his politics came first, his wife second and his children third. Now that Cimmie was dead, Diana expected to move up a notch, but this hope was dispelled when he informed her that his children now came second and she would have to make do with third.

It was nothing short of a farce to imagine Mosley as a family man. The children were not his priority and he was particularly quick tempered and brutal towards his daughter, Vivien. Prone to attacking her in public, as he had done to Cimmie, the treatment had a devastating effect on her mental health. Irene did her best to boost Vivien's confidence and she often chastised Mosley for his cruelty, but after one callous outburst all she could muster was 'ugh!' This negligence trickled down to his sons. Nick's debilitating stammer had become worse and Micky would grow up barely knowing his father. By contrast, Diana thought Mosley 'so marvellous' with her boys: 'he knows what to say to children and jollies them along and makes things interesting for them.'

Despite the scandal that Diana openly courted when she left Bryan, those closest to her could not fault her as a mother. 'She was a remarkable lady and a marvellous mother. She was very beautiful, very funny ... She was very jolly and made everyone around her very happy,' Desmond said. When small, Jonathan and Desmond, whom Diana nicknamed 'the kittens', crawled into her bed every morning and with great patience she taught them to read. She made time to have tea with her sons every day and if she was at home Diana lunched with them, too. Shunning the rules of a traditional nursery, she often called in on the children throughout the day to play with them. And, on nanny's day off, Diana bathed and put them to bed, instead of leaving this to the nursery maid.

There was an ulterior motive on Mosley's behalf where his children were concerned. Vivien, Nick and Micky were his main source of income. Mosley's father, the previous baronet, had squandered the bulk of the family fortune, which left Mosley with an income eventually rising to £20,000 per year.[58] Although it was a generous sum, it was not enough to fund the BUF, support his mother, run Savehay and pay for his children's schooling and staff. But a window of opportunity presented itself when Cimmie's will was eventually published. Her property value for probate stood at £20,951, with the whole of her residuary estate to be held in trust for her children. Savehay was left to Mosley, who had been appointed executor along with the public trustee. The children were also bequeathed £10,000 per year from the Leiter Trust in Chicago, originally set up by Cimmie's paternal grandfather, the American millionaire, Levi Leiter.

Arguing that Savehay was the children's family home, Mosley successfully convinced the solicitor that he should be given the £10,000 per year, claiming that he could not afford the upkeep of the house on his own. Consequently, any cash Mosley could obtain (and this was largely derived from suing newspapers that printed defamatory information about the party) was invested into the BUF. In 1934 he brought a libel case against the *Daily Star* for reporting that his movement was ready to 'take over government with machine guns when the moment arrived' and was awarded £5,000 in damages.

Exploring another avenue to generate income, Mosley contemplated asking his children to refund him the money he had spent on Savehay when they came of age and were able to access their trust funds left by Cimmie. It did not alleviate his burden when Ma confided that Cimmie had sent a psychic message, warning that she did not want the children to associate with Mrs Guinness.

In April 1934, Mosley held a rally before an audience of 10,000 at the Albert Hall in London. It was a formal affair in the style of a gala evening and an orchestra had been engaged to play the 'Horse Wessel Lied' and 'Giovienzza', as well as 'Mosley',* a song especially composed for the event. A militant display had been choreographed; a procession of flags and banners were carried up the aisle, pausing before the spotlights as they were swung back to punctuate Mosley's appearance onstage. With his pronounced limp, his chest out and his head flung back, he took his place behind the lectern to address the spellbound audience. Watching from a private box, Irene's thoughts turned to Cimmie, whom she felt 'must be there and seeing all that, she would be glad'. Her thoughts were justified when the audience rose to their feet and erupted: 'Hail Mosley! Mosley! Mosley!' Encouraged by the enthusiasm of his supporters, he spoke to the captivated audience for an hour and a half.

Inspired by the success of the Albert Hall, Mosley planned to stage a rally at the Olympia – a venue significantly larger than the previous one. He planned a skilfully choreographed production reminiscent of a miniature Nuremberg Rally, with marching men, banners, spotlights and full militaristic paraphernalia. But regardless of his large following, there was growing unrest amongst the communists and anti-fascists, who were determined to stop Mosley at any cost. The *Daily Worker* published the BUF's schedule of talks and they encouraged their subscribers to take part in their anti-fascist marches by enclosing a map showing the route to the Olympia, bearing the warning: 'The challenge of Mosley will be met by the determined workers ... All roads lead to Olympia tonight!'

Planning ahead for trouble, 2,000 Blackshirts lined up to guard the platform and were scattered through the crowd of 12,000. A total of 2,000 free tickets were distributed on the day and 2,000 protesters also gathered outside Olympia, where 500 policemen struggled to control the angry mob. When Mosley took the stage, the heckling broke out and he warned that if it did not stop, his stewards would evict the troublemakers. The heckling soon turned into a brawl and people were removed from Olympia unconscious, with their clothing torn and blood gushing from their faces. Many of the anti-fascist protesters were Jewish, and it did not help Mosley when his BUF were viewed as the aggressors.

Distaste for fascism did not improve when, only three weeks later, news broke of Hitler's 'Night of the Long Knives' – the event in which the Nazis dragged

---

*   'Mosley: Leader of thousands!/ Hope of our manhood, we proudly have thee!/ Raise we this song of allegiance/ For we are sworn and shall not fail thee!'

Ernest Röhm, the chief staff of the SA (Sturmabteilung) and others from their beds and shot them dead for posing a threat to Hitler. The public pondered whether Mosley could be capable of doing the same should his party rise to a similar power. The BUF had briefly risen in glory – 'on the edge of respectability' – and in a flash was torn down and labelled as a paramilitary organisation led by a lunatic leader.

Diana had every intention of attending Olympia and prior to it she dined in the Eatonry's miniscule dining room which seated six – 'Diana's dining room is very nice, once you get in,' Emerald Cunard often teased her – with Gerald Berners and Vivian Jackson.[*] However, as the evening progressed, she retired to bed with a temperature. Although Diana had missed the Olympia meeting, it did not prevent her from defending Mosley: 'I have always regretted this. I wish I had seen it for myself.' The newspaper and eyewitness reports of violence, she declared, were untrue: 'If half of their stories had been true, the hall would have been strewn with dead and dying and the hospitals full of casualties.' Berners and Jackson went along to the meeting and they, too, agreed with her sentiments that 'no one was badly hurt', even though Jackson had been arrested and Berners stood bail.

To an extent Diana's claims were justified: no lives were lost and although the hospitals were busy dressing wounds, only one person, a fascist, spent the night in hospital. However, it did not distract from the fact Mosley had misjudged public support.

Mosley's message was simple. He often reminded Britons that they must foster home production by putting high tariffs on foreign imported goods. To do so, he warned, the home industries must put their house in order, otherwise they were not worthy of protection. It sounded like common sense, but Mosley's economical warning was overshadowed by violent brawls and his role as a strong leader became a ludicrous image in the public's mind. Many big industrialists were swayed by Mosley's ideals and they would have financed him but his high-handedness and tactlessness drove them away. All the while, Diana's loyalty to Mosley was unwavering; in her opinion, he was never at fault.

To many Britons, Mosley was a figure of hate and they felt the BUF must be stopped. He was banned from speaking on the BBC and Lord Rothermere, 'frightened out of his wits' of a boycott from the advertisers of his *Daily Mail*, withdrew his financial assistance. Furthermore, those respectable members who had once agreed with his manifesto cancelled their membership. The Conservative MP William Anstruther-Gray co-signed a letter to *The Times*, accusing the Blackshirts

---

[*]   Vivian Jackson's twin brother Derek married Pamela Mitford in 1936.

of 'wholly unnecessary violence'. Unity, who sided with Diana in her views, was 'longing to see him thoroughly beaten up. He does deserve it.'

Mosley warned Irene that if fascism failed 'his life was over and done with'. Diana could not risk losing him; if he left her it would prove her critics correct that he would eventually abandon her. Bolstering his ego became her priority, for if he gave up the BUF, he would likely give her up and settle into a rootless existence of casual affairs.

As much as Diana longed to be useful to Mosley, he rebuffed her, warning her that since Cimmie's death he 'had been haunted by the idea that she had worn herself out by political activities beyond her strength'. Cimmie worked tirelessly in her role as Labour MP for Stoke-On-Trent and, having been elected in 1929, she resigned in 1930 when Mosley left the Labour Party. She was mocked for her 'Hyde Park sentiments delivered in a Park Lane accent' and the toll of the campaign was blamed for a miscarriage she suffered shortly afterwards. According to Irene, Cimmie's political development was all for Mosley's benefit and because of this devotion to him she turned herself into an admirable speaker. After a maiden speech at Harrow, Cimmie told a women's meeting: 'I cannot speak. I only ask you to send my husband to the poll, as polling day is his birthday.' There was a roar of applause from the audience who were moved by Cimmie's sincerity and courage.

Paralleling her political interest in Mosley's work with Cimmie's efforts, Diana decided that her work for the BUF should be 'entirely connected with business and not at all with propaganda'. She believed him emphatically, obeying his warning as a testament of his love for her, and now all thoughts of ever campaigning or making a public speech filled her with dread. Diana's moment would come, but in the meantime she and Mosley fled to the South of France.

Life at Savehay had become unbearable for Irene, who tiptoed on the edge of a potentially explosive situation. She voiced her opinion in her diary: 'I resent the way I am looked on as a sort of governess, no thanks, no love, and Baba and Tom [Mosley] arm-in-arm all over the place and Ma and I looking like two waiting housemaids.' Provoked by Mosley's ill-treatment of her, Irene announced she was taking a holiday. With Irene's absence pending, Mosley was forced to resume his parental role. Relating the eldest children's comment: 'We don't cry when you talk to us about mummy, but we always cry when we talk about her among ourselves,' Irene convinced him it would be in the children's best interest to continue the family tradition of taking a house in Europe. Mosley rented a huge white house in Toulon perched high above the sea and, sparing little thought to Irene or Baba's wrath and his children's feelings, he invited Diana along.

When Irene and Baba learned of his plans they reacted with horror. Tensions flared, tearful arguments ensued and Mosley tried to pacify the ladies with his usual excuse: 'She's just a friend.' To prove this, he resorted to reverse psychology and invited Baba to join them in Toulon for the last two weeks in August. Mosley went to great lengths to pry into Diana and Baba's schedules for August, usually the month when the wealthy travelled extensively around Europe and the Mediterranean. Combining his skills at juggling many women at once (he had become a master at planning), and by sheer fluke of their travel arrangements, Mosley was confident he could handle this ominous schedule of holidaying with both women.

Diana was the first to arrive, appearing at the rented house with her maid. In her present situation and with her children in Ireland with Bryan, she did not need to plan ahead for extended trips. Her numerous trunks must have given off a sense of ambiguity, for Mosley wondered if she was planning to stay longer than two weeks and was momentarily relieved when Diana told him of her plan to travel on to Ravello. With his mind at ease, he and Diana settled into a relaxing routine and the children had no reason to feel suspicious of their father's 'friend'.

During the uneventful fortnight, Diana sunbathed with Mosley on the terrace and the children thought her a good sport when she climbed down the hundreds of rocky steps at the side of the house to swim in the Mediterranean Sea. Leaving the day before Baba arrived, Diana flew to Ravello to stay with Edward James in the Villa Cimbrone, overlooking the stunning beauty of the Amalfi Coast.

Bryan, too, had departed on his own travels at the end of August and, from the *Empress of Australia*, he sent Diana a sad note, inspired by his loneliness at sea. 'There is no one at all to be in love with ... I miss you so much. Sometimes they play our tune from *Carmen* at dinner, and I water the soup with tears in my eyes.'[59]

Diana had no time to mull over Bryan's sentimentality and from Ravello she travelled to Munich, where Unity had been living for several months *en pension* with Baroness Laroche. There was a promise to visit the Parteita, and another piece of news puzzled Diana as much as it impressed her – by a stroke of luck, Unity managed to fulfil her extraordinary mission and had succeeded in catching a glimpse of her hero, Adolf Hitler.

29

MUNICH: AN IDYLLIC LIFE

When Diana arrived in Munich, she was introduced to Unity's enviable lifestyle. There was nothing demanding about her daily routine of art classes, language lessons with Fraulein Baum, piano lessons, trips to tea shops for cake and coffee, evenings at the opera and bicycling to the nearby Englische Garten for picnics. Germany was good for Unity, Diana concluded, and her mind drifted back to the afternoon when she, then only two years younger than Unity's current age, had asked her father for permission to visit Germany. Diana must have bitterly reflected on his refusal. Had she been allowed to indulge in the same lifestyle, she might have shunned an early marriage, thus avoiding the complicated mess that followed. However, it was not Diana's nature to dwell on the past and she made up her mind to enjoy the present.

One element threatened to dampen their jovial visit. Putzi Hanfstaengl was less than enthusiastic about Diana and Unity looking him up. He claimed he had no tickets to the Parteitag and, despite his promise from the year before – Unity was determined to hold him to it – he blatantly refused to introduce them to Hitler. 'Goering and Goebbels expressed mock horror at the idea of my trying to present such painted hussies to Hitler,' Hanfstaengl later wrote in his memoir, *The Missing Years*.

It was a feeble excuse, but there was an ounce of truth in his statement. Although both Diana and Unity, with their blonde hair and blue eyes, were the epitome of Hitler's fantasies of an Aryan race, their heavily made-up faces contradicted his preference for a well-scrubbed, shiny complexion sported by the German women. Those conforming to Hitler's ideal took offence at what they judged as an outward display of shameless vanity, and they verbally attacked

Diana and Unity: 'Aren't you ashamed to stand in front of the Führer's house with painted faces?'[60]

Undeterred by having no tickets for the Parteitag and no lodgings, Diana and Unity ventured to Nuremberg. As they discovered on their arrival, about 700,000 people had flocked to the small town. It was what Unity dreaded the most, and even her normally buoyant optimism could not distract from the fact that every hotel in Nuremberg was fully booked. After an unsuccessful search for a room – any room, as they were not fussy – Diana implored Unity to admit defeat and return to Munich. 'Aren't you glad we came? Isn't it lovely? Do be glad we came!' Unity tried to jolly Diana along.

Unity further surprised Diana when she admitted her willingness to sit outside all night on the off-chance she would see Hitler and hear him speak. She tried to convince Diana to do the same: 'It doesn't matter about not having a room, does it? It's really all the better, because we can get such marvellous places for seeing the Führer go by tomorrow if we stay in them all night.' The thought of sitting outside on the street all night did not evoke a similar reaction in Diana. She had just about given up on their quest when Unity spied an elderly gentleman in a beer garden wearing a gold badge. Schooled on all things to do with Nazism, Unity knew straight away this badge meant the man was one of the first 100,000 members. Unity questioned him and he answered with pride: 'Yes, I am a very old member. I am number one hundred in the party.'

'Number a hundred!' she announced with more than a glimmer of delight in her voice. 'Then you must know the Führer.'

'Yes, I knew him in those days,' he confidently replied. Eyeing their bedraggled appearance and listening to Unity's tale of woe, the man felt sorry for the two stranded English women. He gallantly found tickets and located a room in a small inn. For Unity it played to her sense of destiny and Diana, who believed in a certain sense of predestination, felt inclined to agree.

Yet another surprise was in store when Diana and Unity presented their tickets. They were informed that the tickets they had obtained, through one of the earliest and most trusted members of the Nazi Party, afforded them the privilege of sitting in the exclusive section of the stands normally reserved for officials. Seated in the same stand was a young woman by whom Unity was intrigued. Having investigated every area of Hitler's life, and remembering her two chance encounters, she first noticed the woman in Hitler's court photographer Heinrich Hoffmann's shop, working as an assistant. And the second time she saw her, the same woman was seated in the back of a gleaming white Mercedes. Drawing on her findings, Unity suspected she was the mistress of someone important.

Now, seeing her for the third time at the Parteitag, Unity realised that the young woman was Hitler's mistress, Eva Braun.

At a given signal, in absolute silence, different groups of red flags filed into the centre of the arena, spreading out amongst the 'brownshirts'. Every move had a political significance. The brownshirts were the heart of Germany, out of which the Treaty of Versailles had torn her blood, and the endless stream of blood-red flags carried by the Gauleiters were the veins and arteries of National Socialism pumping their lifeblood into Germany's heart again.

Dizzy with the unexpectedness of finding herself in such an exclusive stand, Unity gathered her composure once Hitler took to the stage. He appeared as a mystic, descending to the lowest common denominator in the common man for whom he had a withering contempt, and yet he had hypnotic power over the masses he so despised. Hitler, in a trancelike state, came across as though from another world, he was of a higher being and the crowd were under his spell. The speeches transfixed Diana, and although she knew no German she could rely on Unity as her translator. Through this channel, Diana learned the gist of the topics discussed: the unemployment statistics had dwindled, new houses were built, plans for new roads were in progress and industry and agriculture were flourishing. It was everything Mosley hoped to achieve and, as with their luck in finding tickets, the coincidence of the topics discussed proved to Diana that fascism was a creed worth following.

When she went home to England, Diana decided to return to Munich where living was cheap and to take a small flat and learn German at the Berlitz School. If she could understand Hitler's speeches, she could relay the formula to Mosley. In the past Mosley had doubted Hitler's showmanship, but he was shrewd enough to realise the Führer's international appeal. He readily agreed and a plan was put in place. Diana set forth to Munich confident that she was fulfilling a higher purpose; all to assist her beloved in his quest for political power.

In Munich, Diana lived with a maid and a cook in a comfortable flat located on the Ludwigstrasse. She extended an invitation for Unity to escape her austere dwellings at Baroness Laroche's boarding house to occupy the spare bedroom. Together the sisters adopted a carefree lifestyle of sightseeing, taking German lessons ('You will feel such a fool if we meet him and then you can't understand everything he says,' Unity told her) and sitting for hours in Hitler's favourite restaurant, the Osteria Bavaria.

It was a common sight to see the 'two great blondes' pining for a glimpse of Hitler. Tom Mitford teased Unity by pretending to have met Hitler at the Bayreuth Festival, which she soon found out was untrue and became furious with him. Making a mockery of Hitler was strictly off limits.

Without revealing their tactics, Diana and Unity were confident and charming enough to secure press passes to the ceremony at the Theatinerkirche to commemorate the sixteen Nazis who died in the 1923 putsch. Despite their best efforts to get inside the arena, the passes only afforded them to stand outside the venue and, swamped by the crowd of journalists and photographers, they saw very little of the scene inside. Unity was jealous when she discovered that Diana's maid was the one who had the best view of Hitler and she vented her frustration by bombarding her with a series of trivial questions. 'What did you think of him?' she pressed, hoping for a detailed description.

'Well,' the unflappable maid began, 'he was quite different from what I thought he would be.'

'In what way?' Unity eagerly asked, hoping to provoke some excitement in the otherwise underwhelming response.

'He's got such beautiful hair,' was the maid's unexpected and disappointing answer.

To Unity's fury, Diana erupted into peals of laughter. She also confirmed the Führer's hair was indeed very neatly combed.

The sunny autumn days were gradually lapsing into a bitter, cold winter – another aspect which Diana thought was better dealt with in Germany. She did not find the winter climate unbearable because the German houses, unlike in England, had double glazing and efficient central heating. The icy air preserved an alluring smell, an aroma of brewing combined with the cigars the men smoked as they sat along the street cafés. Before sunrise there was a scuttle of quiet movement in the streets as hundreds of people walked to the station with their skis on their backs. From a distance, Diana could see the small figures speeding down the Alps with the blinding sunlight behind them, beaming off the snow and lighting up the baroque facade below. It was an idyllic setting, but with their plan to meet Hitler already wavering, Diana gave up her flat and returned to England, having spent five weeks in Munich.

Arriving home days before Christmas, and with her children spending the festive season with Bryan, Diana accepted Gerald Berners' invitation to stay at his country house, Faringdon. The house often played host to bizarre guests; one such oddity arrived in the form of a boa constrictor, brought by Luisa Casati, a famous Italian marchioness. 'Wouldn't it like something to eat?' Berners' mother, Mrs Tyrwhitt-Wilson, asked as the snake was retrieved from its basket.

'No, it had a goat this morning!' the marchioness said in a matter of fact voice as the snake slithered across the floor.

Mrs Tyrwhitt-Wilson eyed the reptile with contempt. 'It does seem so inhospitable,' she complained.

Inhospitable was not an adjective to describe Berners. His guests seemed to be a gathering of lost souls and on this occasion the oddity was in the form of Gladys, Duchess of Marlborough. Joking that she and Gladys were bonded together as one social pariah to another, the latter was in a far more precarious situation than Diana. Unlike Bryan, who wished to inflict no harm on Diana, Gladys's husband was resorting to harsh tactics to destroy her reputation and her domestic circumstances. Although estranged from the duke, she continued to live in his house at Carlton House Terrace and, in an attempt to evict her, he had the electricity turned off.

When her evenings were not consumed by Mosley, Diana visited Gladys, where they sat on the balcony overlooking the Mall, illuminated by the street lights. Leaving the house was an adventure, which Diana realised when she had to feel her way through the dark landing and down the staircase, until she eventually reached the front door, miraculously uninjured.

The sadness radiating off Gladys was painful for Diana to observe. Once a celebrated beauty, feted in the pre-war circles of Paris and Rome, Gladys's enormous, clear blue eyes were a reminder of her ethereal appeal, obscured by a botched plastic surgery attempt. The facial deformities were the result of an early attempt at face-lifting. Desiring a perfect Grecian nose, the plastic surgeon had advised Gladys to have a piece of paraffin wax inserted where the nose connects to the forehead. The wax gradually slipped from its place, and eventually her nose resembled a deflated balloon.

As much as Gladys's plight pulled on Diana's heartstrings, she was relieved when Berners provided lighter moments during her stay. Withdrawing to her bedroom on her first evening at Faringdon, Diana noticed a book placed on her bed. The dust jacket read: 'This is the hottest thing written in the last twenty years – sex, crime, violence ...' Intrigued, she opened the book only to discover it concealed a copy of the Bible. The laugher ensued over Christmas lunch when Berners presented a gourmet feast to his guests. Cutting into the Christmas pudding, Diana was surprised when buttons and thimbles spilled out. 'Nobody got a ring or anything nice like sixpence,' she recounted.

To the horror of Nancy and Jessica, David and Sydney's attitude towards Hitler and Germany had changed. Sydney was the first convert; she found 'great beauty and charm' in Munich's baroque architecture. And Unity reported to Diana that David, too, had admitted to being wrong in his judgement of Hitler. Debo, who was 14, wrote to Diana: 'I argue for fascism at school as all the girls are Conservatives.'[61]

Having turned her political compass to the far left, Jessica could no longer tolerate her family supporting such politics.

Loyalties were further divided when Jessica allayed herself with the Communist Party. Uncompromising in her political beliefs – a trait she shared with Diana and Unity – she had begun to view her parents, especially her mother, as 'an enemy of the working classes'. And the more she learned of Mosley, the more she loathed him. This sense of loathing transferred on to Diana, her once favourite sister. As far as Jessica was concerned, Diana was to blame for their parents growing admiration of Hitler and, in particular, Unity's fanaticism with him. A few years later, when she eloped with Esmond Romilly,[*] her second cousin and fellow communist sympathiser, she severed all ties with Diana.

Nancy retaliated by planning a book which parodied fascism. 'The Leaderteases', as Nancy referred to them, were no longer amusing to Diana. Inventing the whimsy title *Wigs on the Green*, as she had done with all of her novels, Nancy looked to her nearest and dearest for inspiration. Fearing Diana's wrath, and not overlooking her sister rescuing her from many a financial disaster – 'Thank you by the way for the lifesaving gift of £5' – Nancy knew better than to satirise her. She used Unity as her protagonist in the form of Eugenia, an ungainly girl in tatty clothing who worshipped the fascist leader, Captain Jack of the Union Jack Movement. Diana was appalled, but Nancy possessed enough gumption to argue: 'fascism is now such a notable feature of modern life all over the world that it must be possible to consider it in any context ...'

There was a fragment of truth behind Nancy's self-justification for writing *Wigs on the Green*, as fascism was indeed springing up in many contexts. W. H. Auden and Christopher Isherwood's anti-fascist play, *The Dog Beneath the Skin*, was published in 1935 and first performed by the Group Theatre in 1936. Gerald Berners and Diana dined with Auden, then a relatively unknown writer, and to be polite they attended a performance of the play. Diana remembered two things: the play 'was not very good' and the playwright 'was pale yellow, hair and suit, he had bitten nails and a dirty suit'.

Although Diana tolerated Auden and Isherwood's play, Nancy's betrayal also coincided with Diana's old friend Edward James (whom she had been in love with during her days as a debutante), who was going through a very public divorce from Tilly Losch. Diana was quick to leap to his defence, even though society

---

[*] Esmond Romilly's mother, Nelly Hozier, was the daughter of Lady Blanche Hozier. Nelly, too, was rumored to have been the daughter of Bertie Redesdale, thus if such rumours were true, Nelly was, in fact, David's half sister.

abandoned him for daring to challenge Tilly's suit on the grounds of adultery when she countersued Edward, claiming the marriage was a sham due to his homosexuality. 'After the divorce I discovered who my real friends in England were,' and when Edward tallied up those who supported him, he counted two women – one of whom was Diana.

Diana was sincere when she told Edward: 'Pa was very grateful to you for marrying Tilly, we were so afraid that Tom would.' However, not everyone in the Mitford family had feared a marriage between Tilly and Tom. Nancy became one of Tilly's many supporters; a sore point for Diana, whose feelings of love mellowed into a lifelong fondness for Edward. The divorce was granted in 1934 and Edward – now available – proposed to Diana, but she declined with the words: 'No fear.' Diana needed a stronger man, hence her continued devotion to Mosley. The publication of *Wigs on the Green* and Nancy's support of Tilly further embittered Diana, and the once close sisterly relationship cooled.

If the New Year of 1935 brought any eventualities in Diana and Mosley's life, nothing could compare to the news that Unity was about to reveal. On a Saturday afternoon in February, Unity stepped off the damp street into the Osteria Bavaria and, following her normal routine, she ordered some lunch and waited for the usual sighting of Hitler.

Hitler and his entourage entered the restaurant and they walked past Unity's table at the front – she always sat at that table because Hitler would have to walk past her to enter and to leave. Having stared at him the entire time, as she always did, Unity took the last sip of her coffee and cast the empty cup to one side. The waitresses at this point had become acquainted enough with this strange English girl to know to automatically refill her cup. There was something unique about this particular day. Before Unity gestured for the waitress, she looked up and to her surprise one of Hitler's cronies stood before her and announced in German: 'The Führer would like to speak to you.'

For anyone unfamiliar with the story, it would seem a remarkable fluke that Unity was chosen at random to meet the Führer, who went to the Osteria Bavaria to dine as a private citizen. However, this had been a carefully crafted plan, in the works for over a year. On 9 February, Unity saw the results of her dedication. 'I can't tell you all the things we talked about ...' Unity swooned in a letter to Diana. The topics included Noel Coward's *Cavalcade*, which Hitler thought was the greatest film he had ever seen, and he warned that the international Jews must never again be allowed to make two Nordic races fight against one another.

Unity wrote to Diana, urging her to come to Munich at once so that she, too, could meet 'the greatest man of all time'.

There was no question of what Diana should do and Mosley encouraged her to go to Munich at once. With the credibility of the BUF floundering and his public support at an all time low, he knew there was only one direction in which the party could go: it needed foreign support, and this, he hoped, would come from Germany.

Since the Olympia rally, Irene had become opposed to Mosley and the BUF. However, as much as her artistic nature clashed with her brother-in-law's ideology, she pointed the majority of the blame in Diana's direction. She wrote in her diary: 'Baba saddened me deeply by tales of Mrs Guinness's increased wriggling her way into Tom and the children and that she goes everywhere with him in a black shirt and has entree to Hitler and Goebbels for him.' The black shirt was an exaggeration and her perception was off, for it was Unity who was working to gain Mosley 'entree with Hitler' and, having met him a further two times since writing to Diana, she was introduced to his propaganda minister, Joseph Goebbels. However, unlike Hitler who was enchanted by Unity's gaiety, Goebbels was suspicious of her motives from the beginning.

Finally, the lifestyle of freedom that Diana had imagined when she left Bryan was coming true. Leaving her children behind, Diana set off for Munich via Paris in an elegant Voisin car – a present from Mosley – which ran into trouble as the heavy snow fell in the Black Forest. The chauffeur from the Voisin factory's grumbling was more than Diana could bear and, spying a peasant with a team of horses, she called for help and was pulled to safety. It would be the only hindrance during her trip.

There was nothing exceptional about Hitler when Diana finally met him on 11 March 1935. She observed that he 'appealed in equal measure to women and to exactly the sort of men he needed'. She claimed that she never heard Hitler rant, or indeed go off on a political tangent. He had simple tastes, apparent over luncheon at the Osteria Bavaria when he ordered 'eggs and mayonnaise, and vegetables and pasta, and compote of fruit or a raw grated apple, and Fachingerwasser'. Hitler was extremely polite to women and impressed Diana with his European manners: he kissed her hand, bowed his head and did not sit down until she was seated. This, she felt necessary to mention in her autobiography, given the 'acres of print about Hitler in which his rudeness and bad manners to everyone are emphasised'.

Hitler fascinated Diana with his greyish blue eyes, so dark that they often appeared brown and opaque, and like those who possess sinister intentions, he charmed her. The charm was in abundance; he admired Unity and Diana, the latter in her chic Parisian clothes. Unlike many in his company, the sisters were not intimidated by him and they conversed freely, often punctuating their sentences with Mitford jokes and witty nuances.

To dispel the myth surrounding Unity's head-over-heels infatuation with Hitler, Diana wrote: 'Unity was never awed in her entire life. She said what came into her head.' It was this candour which made the Führer laugh and in return 'he inspired affection'.

Two days later, Diana and Unity left for Paris, taking it in turns to drive the Voisin. Bryan was staying at the Rue de Poitiers flat with Nanny Higgs and the children. It was Jonathan's 5th birthday and, still friendly with Bryan, Diana joined them. Paris never appealed to Unity and after exhausting the museums she departed for Munich.

Unity was not shy in boasting about her connections to 'Cousin Winston' and the English aristocracy and, knowing Hitler's admiration for prominent people, she also told him of Mosley. Although Hitler publicly disapproved of co-habitation and adultery, he was fascinated to learn more. So, when Mosley received his invitation to visit Hitler in April, Diana must have, in some way, felt useful to him.

30

A SERIES OF UNFORTUNATE EVENTS

Harold Nicolson, Mosley's old friend who had supported the New Party but severed political ties when the BUF was formed, once remarked of Cimmie: 'She was not made for politics. She was made for society and the home.' It is not apparent if this statement was known by Diana, but it certainly paralleled with Mosley's reluctance for her to become involved with the BUF. Cimmie might not have been made for politics, but Diana was. The ease in which she communicated with Hitler – she was now fluent in German – would later act as a vital tool for Mosley and his BUF. For now, Diana remained in Paris with Bryan and the children while Mosley travelled to meet Hitler.

Before Mosley's departure, he made a startling anti-Semitic speech[*] in Leicester: 'For the first time I openly and publicly challenge the Jewish interests in this country commanding the press ... commanding the cinema, dominating the City of London, killing London with their sweatshops ...' This speech reached Julius Streicher, whose own hatred of the Jews was the most prominent among the Nazi Party. He wrote to Mosley to congratulate him on his rousing speech. Mosley's reply to Streicher was published in his newspaper, *Der Stürmer*: 'I value your advice greatly in the midst of our hard struggle. The power of Jewish corruption must be destroyed in all countries before peace and justice can be successfully achieved in Europe. Our struggle to this end is hard, but our victory is certain.'

---

[*] Government records released in 1983 revealed that Mosley planned to deport all Jews and abolish elections if his movement had come to power.

The meeting with Hitler was a small, intimate affair. The Führer invited the Kaiser's daughter, the Duchess of Brunswick, Frau Winifred Wagner and Unity. This was a milestone for Unity in particular, though her presence must have inspired an uncomfortable feeling in Mosley, who was no stranger to her extreme fanaticism and outbursts. Mosley found Hitler to be a 'calm, cool customer, certainly ruthless, but in no way neurotic ... with a gentle, almost feminine charm'. It was a careful, methodical response from Mosley; he hardly knew Hitler and the meeting was not enough to gauge whether there would be any sort of political friendship between the two. Prior to extending an invitation to Mosley, Hitler had sent his aide, Colonel Ross, to England for three weeks to observe the BUF. Ross reported there 'was a fine spirit and the movement had a splendid leader, but no organisation'.

The calmness did not extend to Unity, who was said to possess 'a masculine streak' when it came to politics.[62] She was tipped into a frenzy of excitement at being in the company of both Hitler and Mosley and, caught up in the moment, she immediately wrote a letter to Julius Streicher, asking for it to be published in his newspaper. 'The English have no notion of the Jewish danger. Our most dangerous Jews work only behind the scenes ... I want everyone to know I am a Jew hater.'[63] It was a dangerous and immature gesture, but Nancy brushed it off with the usual flippancy she resorted to when dealing with Unity: 'Good gracious that interview you sent us, fantasia, fantasia,' she teased. Trying to justify Unity's comments, Diana defended her sister's outlook by attaching it to loyalty, and this affinity with Hitler, she explained, provoked her to believe 'the enemy of my friend is my enemy'.

Unsurprisingly, the written attack was not well received outside of those with anti-Semitic feelings and it established Unity as a notorious anti-Semite. Mosley, too, had garnered such a reputation by his own hand with his speeches. Diana had refrained from making such public comments against the Jews – she had many Jewish friends – but she had become guilty by association.

On a humid evening in July, Mosley telephoned Diana, inviting her to spend the night at Savehay to sleep in the cool, country air. Having suffered sleepless nights from the intolerable London heat, she accepted his invitation. Before she could motor down to Denham, she attended a dinner party at the Dunns, where she sat next to the press baron, Lord Beaverbrook, and consumed liberal amounts of champagne.[64] Rather tipsy and drained from the hot weather, she returned to the Eatonry to change into her coolest outfit: a white satin jacket and a long, white skirt. It was after midnight when she finally set off in the Voison with her timid spaniel in the back seat. She approached the junction where the five roads meet between Belgrave Square and Cadogan Place, unaware that a Rolls-Royce was speeding in her direction. It crashed into the side of the tiny Voison and its impact caused Diana's head to hit off the windscreen, smashing the glass, which sliced through her face.

Some of the residents were out for a midnight stroll and, alerted by the noise of the collision, they began to gather around the wreckage. The small crowd of onlookers attracted the attention of two policemen, one of whom dragged Diana's limp body from the car and laid her unconscious head in his lap. Her cut face and the satin coat, saturated in blood, inspired two elderly ladies walking their dog to a lamppost to caution: 'Don't look, it's *too* horrible.' And then, certain Diana was dead, they added, 'Poor thing! So young, too.'

As she lapsed in and out of consciousness, Diana weakly begged the policemen to take her and the dog home. 'All right,' they humoured her. When she came round again, they were carrying her up the steps of St George's Hospital on Hyde Park Corner. 'Where's my dog?' she asked them. 'He's all right, he's gone home,' they lied. The dog had spent the night at the police station. Throwing Diana's limp body onto an examination table, one of the policemen announced: 'We've brought you another street accident.'

After a quick check-up, the doctor roughly examined her limbs and concluded she had suffered no broken bones. In fact, her nose and jaw were broken and her face was badly severed and bleeding heavily. In her semi-conscious state she could hear the medical staff talking over her. 'Where's the thin thread?' the irritated young doctor asked the nurse.

'Night sister's locked it up,' came the reply.

'Well, haven't you got a key?'

'No, and she's gone off.'

Due to this blunder, the doctor opted to use a coarse, thick thread. Warning Diana it would sting, he added that they could not provide her with anaesthetic, but did not elaborate why. Thoughts of Mosley ran through her mind. She began to fret, what if he was worried and what would he assume when she failed to show up? She was certain the accident would be reported in the morning newspapers and he would wonder if she was dead or alive. In a lucid moment, Diana asked the doctor if she could telephone Mosley. 'Oh, no,' replied the doctor. 'You certainly can't. You wouldn't be able to stand up for one thing.'

'But I *must* telephone,' Diana reasoned. 'You can carry me on the stretcher to the telephone.'

'We'll see,' the doctor punctuated his response by stabbing the needle into the side of her nose. The thread, which felt as thick as rope, was ripped through her skin. After two stitches, Diana could just about stand the pain. 'This stings,' the doctor added.

Diana bargained with the doctor, 'If I don't scream will you let me telephone?' He agreed and the entire procedure was carried out without a whimper from Diana, who felt the payoff of getting to telephone Mosley was worth the suffering. It was after two o'clock in the morning when Diana reached Mosley, who was fast asleep in bed. 'I'm at St George's Hospital and I'm quite all right,' she shouted down the static telephone line.

Diana was not all right. She had four stitches along her nose and ten in her chin. Her face was fully bandaged up with two slits for her eyes to peer out of. When she returned home to the Eatonry, Bryan came over immediately. 'You must see Sir Harold Gillies,' he told her. 'I'm going to get hold of him *now*.' His careful consideration and quick thinking saved Diana from permanent facial deformity. The renowned plastic surgeon, Sir Harold Gillies, arrived at Diana's bedside and was horrified at what he saw when he removed the hospital bandages. He could not operate for one week due to the swelling and he replaced the haphazard, coarse stitches with two stitches of silk thread strong enough to hold the gashes together. Diana was warned not to laugh or talk more than she was obliged to.

Sir Harold had no way of knowing the exact dimensions of Diana's once symmetrical face because photographs had never managed to capture her beauty to its full potential. Once again, Bryan saved the day when he remembered the life mask of her face which he had commissioned in 1930, and he gave it to Sir Harold for reference when it came to repairing her nose and jaw.

In what seemed like famous last words, Cecil Beaton wrote to Diana: 'My last vision of you was a radiant one ...' Panicking that her perfect face had been ruined forever, her loved ones also shared his sentiment. It hardly mattered to Bryan; he still loved her unconditionally.

One week later, Diana was admitted to the London Clinic to undergo reconstructive surgery on her face. Bryan's past words to Diana – recalling her diphtheria – in the painful letter he wrote leading up to their divorce, 'Who did you want when you came to?' began to ring true. When she came to, Bryan was at her bedside, not Mosley, for he had fled to Naples with Baba.

It would have pained both women to acknowledge it, but Diana and Baba were not dissimilar. Both were dominant in the marital home and over their husbands; Fruity Metcalfe, like Bryan, felt helpless when he tried to prevent his wife from seeing Mosley. There was not a shred of remorse in Mosley, who looked upon such extra-marital rendezvous as 'terrific fun' and as such, he claimed, they should be treated as a joke.

Ever the manipulator, Mosley and Baba agreed to treat Irene with the utmost kindness. An act that, she thought, was sincere in its delivery. But this courtesy towards Irene had been a motive between the lovers to convince her to ask her friend, Lady Rennell, if she would rent out her villa at Posillipo in Naples for the entire month of August. With baby Micky in Irene's care, Baba, Mosley and his two children boarded a small plane at Croydon airfield for Italy. Unlike the Toulon holiday, where Mosley had exercised an approach of veiled honesty with Baba and Diana, inviting each one to spend two weeks separately with him and the children, he refrained from divulging the details of this trip. Diana, recovering in the London clinic from her surgery, was unaware that Mosley was with Baba. And Baba, who was in Naples, did not know arrangements had been made for Diana to come to the villa.

Since forming a positive opinion of Hitler during a visit to Germany, David had thawed towards Diana. He was at her bedside when a wire arrived from Mosley, its words lifting Diana's spirits when she read: 'Hurry up and get better!' She looked at her father and wailed, 'I shall never get well here because I hate it so much.'

'What do you want to do?' David asked with his usual no nonsense approach.

'I want to fly to Naples, but they say I must stay another week.'

David admired gumption and he agreed with Sydney's disapproval of hospitals and clinics. He must have been unaware that the wire was from Mosley, for he still loathed him, and so agreeing with Diana he hatched a plan for her escape. Knowing the routine of the staff, Diana advised David to arrive in his car before dawn when the night nurses were at breakfast and the day nurses were still asleep. Diana dressed quietly and David assisted her down the stairs – they did not dare to risk taking the lift, given the din it would have caused in the long and echoing corridor. He whisked Diana off to Croydon Airfield and she caught a plane to Marseilles, changing in Rome for Naples.

The villa, a 'crazy jumble of styles', was perched high above the sea overlooking the bay of Naples and Mount Vesuvius. Diana thought it an absurd house and she was baffled by its architectural design. It was a physical example of the frivolity of the upper classes before the First World War. At the Roman embassy, twenty years before, Gerald Berners and his friend Gerry Wellesley had held a competition to see who could design the most hideous house and the price for such an achievement would be hung pride of place on the wall of the Chancellery. During a routine visit, Lady Rennell happened to see the drawing. 'My dream house!' she cried, and promptly asked if she might borrow the drawing. She used the design to create the Posillipo villa.

Although a fan of irony, the ridiculousness of the villa did nothing to lighten Diana's mood. There was a sense of urgency behind her visit, although 'fiasco' would have been a better description. For the second time in two years, she was pregnant with Mosley's child.[65] Arriving jet-lagged from her early start and connecting flights, Diana looked battered and bruised from the accident and surgery, only to see Baba, tanned, snake-hipped and aloof. It must have given Diana a sense of how Cimmie had felt three years previously when she was pregnant with Micky and, feeling wretched, had been confronted by her husband's beautiful mistress.

Diana's timing could not have been worse; she arrived in the middle of a formal dinner party given in honour of Baba's friends, the Crown Prince and Princess of Italy. She did not enter the room, but sent James, one of the footmen, who whispered in Mosley's ear: 'Mrs Guinness has arrived.' Between stage whispers, Mosley coolly told Baba that he had wired Diana not to come until Thursday. 'Lie!' Baba seethed. Knowing that Baba would not directly challenge him in front of their guests, Mosley slipped out of the dining room to find Diana in bed. 'I didn't know you were coming,' he said to her.

'I'm so sorry,' Diana replied. 'But I did send a wire.' Five minutes later the wire arrived.

Leaving Diana to rest, Mosley returned to Baba, who had bid goodnight to their guests. Dodging her wrath and remaining calm, he convinced Baba that he had been unaware that Diana was coming and that he, too, was furious with her and had ordered her to remain in her bedroom. Furthermore, Mosley managed to paint a pathetic picture of Diana, portraying her as a besotted ex-lover who would not leave him alone. Baba accepted his story and Mosley explained in a most chivalrous manner that Diana might as well stay and convalesce. To Diana, Mosley justified his affair with Baba as a form of recompense to Cimmie, who adored her younger sister. Before Diana could react, Mosley whisked Baba off on *Vivien*, his 30ft, three-cabin motor yacht, to Sorrento and Amalfi, where they 'honeymooned' in luxurious hotels, leaving his children and their nanny on board. Afterwards, Baba flew to Tunis and Mosley returned to the villa.

In Mosley's absence, Diana had been left in the care of the servants. She disliked the afternoon sunlight, as the heat irritated her wounds, and her mood at having been abandoned for Baba was understandably sour. Such an expert at arranging his love life to suit whatever predicament he was in at the time, Mosley managed to hide Diana from his children and he did not bother to tell them of her arrival. Following his usual morning routine, Nick approached Baba's bedroom door – the room Diana now occupied – but was halted by Cimmie's maid, Andree. 'Where are you going?' she questioned him.

'To say good morning to Auntie Baba,' he replied.

'It's not Auntie Baba in there,' Andree hissed. 'It is Mrs Guinness.'

Naivety prevented Nick from discovering the sordid details of his father's affairs. He had been used to Diana's presence since the holiday in Toulon and he was accustomed to his father bringing Aunt Baba along on their trips, too. He did not realise at the time that his father was simultaneously sleeping with both women.

Diana regained her strength and had recovered enough to tackle the hundreds of steps leading to the beach to join Mosley and the children. She chose to ignore Baba's presence and she never mentioned the topic to Mosley. The children approached her with caution, intimidated by her beauty and peculiar speaking voice with its swooping intonations. Sometimes Mosley would imitate this and she would smile.

The older children noticed that, unlike their late mother, Diana never argued with Mosley and they appreciated the harmonious atmosphere she created. It was different from the life they had shared with him at Savehay before Cimmie died. As a father, Mosley could be 'a mixture of unpredictable tyrant and indulgent parent'. One moment he roared in 'incendiary rage' at some frustration or at an unsuspecting servant. At other times, he adopted the eccentric ritual of wandering naked round his rose garden, composing his political speeches. Easily riled, he did not suppress displays of violence in the presence of his children. One occasion scarred them when, irritated by the barking of the family dog, he 'discharged both barrels of a shotgun from his study window at the animal'. There was a vast turnover of staff, especially male servants, who could not tolerate their master's rudeness. Concealing this side of his character in front of Diana, the older children were beginning to wonder if she was, in fact, good for their father. It certainly made life more bearable, for the duration of the holiday, anyway.

Throwing herself into Mosley's family life, Diana made an effort with the children and presented herself as a playmate. It was a contrast to Baba. Even though they loved their aunt, she did not have an easy manner around children and often banished them from grown-up life. Their father's 'friend' Diana, they decided, was just as fun as their beloved aunt Irene.

Despite this vision of Diana as an attentive stepmother, it still did not inspire Mosley to marry her. And so, for the second time in two years, she aborted his child. Again, Diana had to go through the indignity of approaching an understanding doctor who would carry out the procedure. In those days, a sympathetic gynaecologist would perform an abortion if the pregnancy was in its early stages. It was expensive, but it was the preferred option for women in Diana's position who could afford it. For poor and uninformed women there was still the backstreet abortionist. Either way, it was still a criminal act, carried out in secrecy and putting the woman's life at risk.

The aftermath of the abortion triggered a change in Diana. Although she loved Mosley and would have done anything to please him, for her own physical and mental health she could not continue to terminate each pregnancy at his request. The obvious solution would have been to cut her losses and leave him, as he was still seeing Baba and had no intention to stop. She could not give him up. The only alternative was to force Mosley to commit to her and, avoiding marriage as best he could, he agreed to an engagement. Words were of little consequence to Mosley and to him the engagement signified nothing. As for Diana, it gave her hope.

31

THE IMPORTANCE
OF UNITY MITFORD

Once she had become an established member of Hitler's inner circle, Unity
delighted the Führer with tales of the 1933 Parteitag and how she and
Diana were discouraged from meeting him because of their make-up.
Hitler laughed and said it was typical of Putzi Hanfstaengl, who had 'bored him over
and over again with old American women not to introduce just for once somebody
he would have liked to see'. Hanfstaengl, Diana came to realise, 'was an inveterate
gossip and just the sort of man one doesn't want set loose on hostile foreign journalists'. Under ordinary circumstances, Hanfstaengl would have 'been dropped years
before but Hitler kept him on for old times' sake, he was a bit of a joke'. Aside from
Hanfstaengl's error, Hitler was further amused by their gate-crashing of the 1934
Parteitag, through obtaining tickets from the old Nazi member 'Number 100'. This
determination impressed and flattered him. He impulsively promised Unity that she
and Diana would be among his guests of honour at the 1935 Parteitag.

Hitler extended invitations to other members of the Mitford family, ordering
Heinrich Himmler to contact Nancy and her husband Peter Rodd to invite them
to Germany to view a concentration camp, all expenses paid. Germany's first concentration camp had been opened at Dachau in March 1933 by Himmler and its
first prisoners were political detainees arrested after the burning of the Reichstag.
Loathing fascism and refusing to visit 'the nasty land of bloodbaths', Nancy commented: 'Now why? So I could write a funny book about them?'

Nancy and Jessica were the only two to shun a private audience with the
Führer, much to Unity's dismay. Pamela visited and found him very ordinary, 'like
a farmer in his brown suit'. And Deborah, aged 16, was more observant of his

monogrammed towels and his incessant ringing of a service bell which nobody answered. For Unity, Hitler was the equivalent of a messiah.

In England, another politician was eager to have an audience with Diana. Such gracious hosts during her visits to Chartwell, it had been years since Diana last saw her beloved cousins, Winston and Clementine Churchill. After a session of small talk in the drawing room of their flat near Westminster Cathedral, Churchill wanted to hear about Herr Hitler. Among the political topics they discussed were Italy, foreign sanctions and the Abyssinian War. Echoing Mosley's point of view, Diana asked if it would be dangerous for a British fleet in the Mediterranean, where it was easy for Italian aircraft to attack the ships if provoked. 'No,' stated Churchill, 'an aeroplane cannot sink a battleship. Their armour is impenetrably thick.' Diana thought he was naïve, but having no proof with which to contradict him, she refrained from arguing her point.

Diana was further encouraged in her opinion of Churchill and the Tories being short-sighted in international politics when Gerald Berners returned from Rome with stories detailing the fury against Anthony Eden and England's policy of sanctions. The Duchess of Sermoneta told Berners that she wished she could open her veins and banish every drop of her English blood. In Diana's opinion, England was the aggressor abroad – a view she held long after the Second World War.

Diana's political point of view was in the minority and Mosley was still preaching a message about the danger of international Jews. During his meeting with Hitler months before he was interviewed for the *Fränkische Tageszietung,* which printed a chilling verdict on 24 June: 'Mosley very soon recognised that the Jewish danger may well work its way from country to country, but fundamentally it poses a danger to all the peoples of the world.' It played to the brutal anti-Semitism in Germany and that same year, in September 1935, the Nuremberg Laws were passed and further sanctions were placed on the Jews. It became a crime to marry anyone with Jewish blood, Jewish names were erased from war memorials and the most basic human rights were stripped from the Jews.

History has shown that a percentage of Britons and politicians admired Hitler when he came to power.[*] But, as 1935 wore on, many Britons changed their views and looked upon the German National Socialists as a terrifying movement, one that must be stopped. In the same vein, Mosley and the BUF were treated with similar disdain, especially when he changed the party's name to the British Union of Fascists and National Socialists, abbreviated to BU.[**]

---

[*]   The American publication *TIME* magazine voted Hitler as 1938's Man of the Year.

[**] It shall be called BU from hereon in.

Hitler provoked disorder and yet, at the same time, claimed he was the only one who could maintain order. It was a significant move that he had mastered in the early days of his political career when he needed to prove to the desperate German population that he was a competent leader. Mosley, however, could not achieve the same; he created disorder, but he did not have the means to stop it. Chaos rang out wherever the BU marched and the name Mosley was associated with thuggery.

Diana resented that she had been absent from Mosley's most damning public displays; first at Olympia and then for his ill-judged march down Cable Street – an event that would happen in the near future. Was it this absence that clouded Diana's judgement? For, once Irene witnessed the true nature of Mosley's fascist meetings, she revoked all support for her brother-in-law. Eager to keep Diana away from his meetings where Baba was present, Mosley related the details to Diana in person. She trusted Mosley, and hearing his version of the truth – he was never at fault, he always maintained the Jews attacked first – was enough for her to support his ideology without pausing for a moment to consider the opponents' view.

Away from the political mania of Mosley and Hitler's message, there was a core difference in its delivery. Hitler preached racial purity, whereas Mosley's original manifesto was always directed at the British economy. Using the economy as his focal point, Mosley convinced his poor and unemployed followers that Jews were stealing their jobs. 'Fascism was, essentially, a national creed – both its strength and its weakness – and therefore it took, in every country, a completely different form,' he said in defence of his ideology. 'We could not run a great empire made up of every sort of race and have a racialist policy. That was out of the question.'[66]

For a nonconformist like Diana, who loathed restrictions and violence, and who once thought the repressive confines of Swinbrook too much to bear, it was astonishing that she could go along with Mosley's point of view. What did unemployment mean to her? She had never had a job or, at least since marrying Bryan, she had never had to live off a small income. Diana was blindsided by the events that happened after her initial disenchantment with the British government and the physical signs of the economic depression in 1931. From 1931 onward, Diana was led by Mosley and he had altered her thinking to believe that he was the only saviour for the working classes. Possessing an unbending will – a trait in all of the Mitford offspring – Diana could see no alternative.

True to his word, Hitler kept his promise and in the summer of 1935 Diana and Unity were treated as his guests of honour at a party given on the eve of the

Parteitag. During an eclectic mix of folk dancing and rampant anti-Semitism, Streicher interrupted one of the numerous speeches to introduce the ladies at the top table: Leni Riefenstahl, Frau Troost and the 'precious specimens' Unity and Diana.

The informal celebrations lapsed and finally it was time for the Parteitag, the event Unity and Diana had anticipated most. As Hitler's guests, the sisters received the most hospitable treatment. They stayed at the Grand Hotel and arriving at the stadium they were given excellent seats next to Eva Braun, where they listened to Hitler's official speech on the Nuremberg Laws. Lost in translation, Diana could have pleaded ignorance during the 1933 Parteitag, but two years had passed and, now fluent in German, she understood every word of Hitler's speech and she later commented:

> The anti-Jewish laws were passed in Germany in the thirties with the object of inducing the Jews to leave the country. As Arthur Koestler has written: 'The Old Testament laws, racial and economic against the stranger in Israel could have served as a model for the Nuremberg Code.'

Her loyal support of Hitler and Mosley did not begin and end in Germany during its season of militant displays. Returning to England, Diana attended a rally at Hyde Park organised by the British Non-Sectarian Anti-Nazi Council against German cruelties and promoting the boycott of German goods. The acting leader of the Labour Party, Clement Attlee, and Mrs Despard, the 91-year-old Irish suffragist, declared that there should be similar demonstrations throughout Europe. Responding to the audience's triumphant cheers, Mrs Despard called for a show of support for the proposal. A sea of hands agreed with this notion, but one lone hand, Diana's, rose to vote against it.

Except for a few jeers, the crowd ignored Diana's defiance and laughed at what they viewed as ignorance. Not to be ignored, Diana further expressed her views when, during a rendition of the National Anthem, she raised her hand in a fascist salute. It was a provocative gesture and the angry crowd charged forth to Diana. Moments from being attacked, she was pulled to safety by two passing members of the BU. Several newspapers reported on Diana's stance against Attlee's speech. Given Unity's association with Hitler, printed almost daily in British newspapers, and Diana now attracting similar attention there was no relenting. It was a bold statement and one that confirmed her place in Mosley's life.

With support for the BU dwindling in London, Mosley began touring across the country on speaking engagements. He turned his political sights to the north of England, where he had a growing support from the unemployed whose livelihoods were crippled by the decline of the mining and steel industries. His schedule often made it impossible for the two to meet, even though Diana was prepared to join him at a moment's notice. With this in mind, she thought it was logical for her and Mosley to not only live together, but for both of them to relocate somewhere closer to his work.

The idea lingered in her mind, but for the present time Diana was busy with her frequent trips to Germany. Unity's persistence and fanaticism finally served a purpose and she was the key person to promote the BU to Hitler, something she was only too enthusiastic to do. There was a motive in Mosley's encouragement: he needed funds and having perplexed his usual sources it could only come from one place – Hitler.

32

A LIFE TOGETHER

rene was not happy. She resented the loose chatter amongst the Mosley children, whom she had grown to think of as her own offspring, especially 'the blessed one' Micky. The children informed their nanny and Irene that Mrs Guinness planned to move her sons into Savehay. Further wounding to Irene was the gossip circulating around the nursery that a governess would soon take her place and, as such, Mosley planned to get rid of her in the autumn. 'It was all that awful Diana,' Irene wrote in her diary before she escaped on holiday.

Diana harboured no ambition to move into Savehay; its upkeep was entirely paid for by the Mosley children's trust fund. She also sensed the disapproval from the servants and how it would reflect on Mosley himself if his mistress suddenly imposed on the family home. But Irene's perception was not entirely wrong. Diana did want to live with Mosley, in their own home in the countryside, close to his speaking engagements and a safe distance away from the temptation of Baba.

Wootton Lodge, an early seventeenth-century house, captured Diana's fancy. 'How beautiful,' she remarked when an estate agent produced a photograph. Declaring the house a white elephant, the estate agent warned her there was no hunting, few pheasants and no profitable farmland. It hardly mattered to Diana, who did not wish to generate a profit from the country pile, and she convinced Mosley to view the house.

With Mosley behind the wheel, they motored down a mile-long avenue lined with beech trees, leading to the majestic three-storey house surrounded by wooded hills and the springtime bluebells in bloom. Diana envisioned living there forever, she imagined her children tobogganing down the sloped grounds in winter and Mosley fishing in their private stream in summer. Wootton's owner,

Captain Unwin VC, stood on the steps of the house, cordially greeting Diana with, 'How do you do, Mrs Guinness ...' and, casting a gimlet eye over her companion, the elderly sailor added, 'and Sir Oswald, too, I see.' Leading the couple on a tour of the house, Captain Unwin explained to Diana and Mosley that he could no longer afford to run the place. If he hinted at any discomforts in living in such an old, draughty house, they went over Diana's head. She was smitten by the large rooms, all containing sash windows and eighteenth-century panelling – the type of interior she loved most.

Mosley, too, was enthusiastic about Wootton and Diana sensed this was because he wanted her 'miles away from all inties [intellectuals] and different nationalities'. When they signed the lease, Mosley agreed to pay the rent of £400 a year and Diana agreed to pay the servants' wages and the indoor utilities. She also tapped into her allowance from Bryan to install central heating – a necessity in ensuring their comfort during the icy cold winters even though, as she would learn, the oversized rooms were almost impossible to heat.

With her usual flair for running a house, Diana engaged a cook, a gardener and enticed Cimmie's footman James to come to Wootton with his wife. Unable to dissolve her lease on the Eatonry, Diana continued to pay the yearly rent of £300 until it lapsed at the end of the war. Budgeting her annual allowance of £2,000 to pay the servants' wages and the indoor expenses left Diana with little disposable income for decorating Wootton. The furniture from the Eatonry barely filled one of the rooms and Mosley did not offer to help and, given his lack of interest, she never asked him to.

After considering several avenues where she could find the extra money, Diana reluctantly sold the exquisite ruby and diamond bracelet which Bryan had given her during their marriage. It fetched £400, enough to furnish Wootton. Immediately after selling the bracelet, Diana wrote to Bryan and confessed what she had done. It must have pained Bryan that Diana, who had previously rebuffed his offer of a generous allowance, had to resort to such measures in this arrangement with Mosley.

Mosley, too, made sacrifices. He gave up his flat on Ebury Street and took a lease on a newly converted nightclub at 129 Grosvenor Road, overlooking the Chelsea riverfront. Inspired by Grecian décor, Diana used a blue colour scheme to decorate the rooms, with the dramatic pillars in the drawing room painted white. Even Irene was impressed by Diana's sophisticated eye and remarked: 'Diana Guinness's taste is lovely.' That was about all the praise she could, and would, ever divulge. During her visit to the flat, Irene approached Mosley about his situation with Baba, Diana and the children. Talking for an hour and a half, Mosley eased her worries with his usual charm and persuaded her that he had everything under control. '[It] eased my poor heart,' she wrote in her diary. 'He said I had been a help and I left at 3.45 praising God.'

In early 1936, Mosley began to plan his customary holiday with Baba and they decided on the Île de Porquerolles. Before he departed, Mosley asked Irene to take the children up to Wootton – 'absolutely torture to me' – for she did not care to see the 'vile Mrs Guinness'. A pang of guilt must have struck Mosley's conscience and he decided to tell Baba ahead of their trip that Diana would be joining them. Baba refused to go to the Île de Porquerolles and their relationship cooled. Mosley knew how Irene would react – she would immediately blame Diana – and owing to her involvement with the children, he was anxious not to disgruntle her.

Irene was concerned with another aspect of her sister's tangled love life. Baba had started an affair with the American millionaire Jock Whitney, and her inability to run away to the United States with him to start a new life plunged her into a deep depression. 'How she cried!' Irene recorded in her diary after spending the day with Baba. Meddling in Baba's affairs was second nature to Irene and she only ever had one objective: to eradicate Mrs Guinness from Mosley's life. She sent her footman over to Mosley's flat with a note regarding his treatment of Baba and, sensing her words would draw blood, she escaped to Savehay with Micky. At midnight, Irene accepted a call from Mosley, asking her to meet him the following day for lunch.

Over lunch, Irene found Mosley in a most congenial mood and she seized the opportunity to demand that he retract his invitation for Diana to join him on the Île de Porquerolles. He agreed. Triumphant with the results and hastily predicting that Mrs Guinness had been usurped, Irene rushed to Baba's house on Cowley Street to deliver the good news. 'In she came at four, exquisite and perfect, and after all I had done for her she merely said it was all too late and she was not going. What a woman!'[67] Baba, for once, had the upper hand and the trip was cancelled.

After a laborious round of speaking engagements across the north and the Midlands, not to mention the violence which became part of his speeches – once Diana had to press herself against a wall to avoid the stampede of his opponents – Mosley fell ill with appendicitis. The medical emergency, given Cimmie's morbid outcome, was cause for great concern amongst Irene and Baba. With his usual zeal, Mosley pulled through and to recuperate from the operation he arranged a trip to Sorrento, where Diana vouched for the healing tranquillity of its Mediterranean climate.

Mosley, Ma and his eldest children boarded a small boat at Naples and, without prior warning, Diana appeared. It was a potentially explosive situation. Ma was possessive of her son, seeing Cimmie's death as a way of getting him back: 'When my son married Lady Cynthia, she took her place by his side. Now she is dead and there must be someone to help him in this work and I am going to do my best to fill the gap,' she told the Women's Section of the BU. The gap she spoke of was not a vacancy for Diana. A straight talking, uncultured philistine, Ma loathed Diana, and Diana's angelic politeness towards Ma only riled her further. 'Unutterably awful and affected,' she told Irene.

In Mosley's absence, the spirit of the BU was kept alive with young Blackshirts marching through the East End of London, yelling: 'The Yids! The Yids! We've got to get rid of the Yids!' They stopped at nothing to intimidate the Jews of the East End, painting the BU symbol onto street walls with the slogan: 'Perish Judah!' The *Blackshirt* magazine also busied itself with a staunch anti-Semitic theme, with its endless debates on whether all Jews should be exiled to Palestine or Madagascar. Irene was crushed by Mosley's blatant anti-Semitism. It was a recruiting tactic for which he told her 'one must have a scapegoat'. A scapegoat – or channel as he preferred to call it – was indeed the thing Mosley desired most.

The blissful climate of Sorrento, without the threat of Baba, put Diana in an accommodating mood. Returning from the trip, she briefly stopped at Wootton and said goodbye to her two little boys. Desmond was complacent, but Jonathan, whom she was known to show favouritism towards, was inconsolable. Without a backward glance, Diana left for Berlin to join Unity and the Führer, to pitch to him an idea that might relieve the BU of their financial woes.

33

THE UPPER HAND

The expensive villas on Schwanenwerder, an island on the Havel River in Berlin, once belonged to a colony of wealthy Jews. Under the Nuremberg Laws, the Jews were driven off the island or forced to part with their property for a meagre sum. Among those profiting from this scheme was Hitler's minister of propaganda Joseph Goebbels and his wife Magda. The Goebbels' villa at Inselstrasse 8, where Diana and Unity had been invited to stay, previously belonged to the Jewish banker Schlitter, who had since fled Germany.*

For one so dedicated to fanaticism, Unity relished the idea of an island dedicated to Nazism. A swastika flag decorated the water tower, originally hung to intimidate the Jewish residents. Plans were underway to transform one of the larger villas into a Reichsbräuteschule, a concept thought up by Himmler to train young women to be 'perfect Nazi brides'. Not only were the future brides taught domestic matters, they were also educated in 'special knowledge of race and genetics'.

On her first visit to Schwanenwerder, Diana was enchanted by the scene of natural beauty and although it was referred to as an island it was a peninsula, surrounded by water and concealed by oak, birch and pine trees. The grounds of the Goebbels' villa contained three houses: the main house, Kavaliershaus, as well as an annex for guests and farm buildings that had been partly renovated into a cinema. The blonde-haired Goebbels children, ponies and sheep dogs ran around the garden which sloped down to the edge of a reedy lake,

---

* Hitler had also given Unity a flat in Munich which had belonged to a Jewish couple who had 'gone abroad'.

where a white motorised yacht was moored on the jetty. It was this display of wholesome domesticity that was often filmed and shown as part of the weekly newsreels in German cinemas.

Diana was fond of Magda who, with her dyed blonde hair, matched Hitler's ideal of Aryan womanhood, but she would soon discover the falseness of this image. Magda moved around the villa wearing a sorrowful expression, for she was desperately unhappy in her marriage and had remained with her husband because Hitler refused to let them part. She sought solace in her many little children. It seemed she was constantly pregnant and producing a child at a rate of one per year – a promise she had made to Hitler.

As much as Magda understood the pains of suffering such melancholy, she was alarmingly without a sense of empathy. Although she permitted her household staff a free reign, there was always a vast turnover of employees and Magda was forever in search of nannies and cooks. Once, she hired a young maid who forgot everything and if she didn't forget, she got it wrong. When Magda scolded her and threatened to dismiss her, the maid ran to the kitchen, turned on the gas tap and lay under it. Fortunately, she was discovered in time. Magda showed little kindness towards the girl and said: 'If a person's so out of control that she wants to kill herself for a justified scolding, I have no sympathy.'[68]

The household ran on a strict schedule; at seven o'clock in the morning Goebbels' manservant came into his bedroom to wake him up, bringing with him a small tea trolley of black coffee, a plate of three different vitamin tablets and two slices of wholewheat bread, each cut into quarters. After breakfast, it then took Goebbels exactly forty-five minutes to dress.

Magda, too, adhered to an unchanging routine. She woke up at the same time every morning, regardless of whether she stayed up late or felt unwell. When she brushed her hair, she counted every stroke and spent the same amount of time brushing her teeth from right to left and top to bottom. It was a foolproof routine, which allowed her to get ready in an astonishingly short time. Always immaculately turned out, she never had a hair out of place. It was also a compulsive ritual for Magda to change her clothes for lunch and to reapply her make-up. This provided her with an armour to distract from how deeply insecure she felt.

There was a common thread running through Unity and Magda's lives. They each idolised Hitler, and this sense of belonging to the movement, along with her own personal power and luxurious lifestyle, made it easier for Magda to bear her husband's cruelty. Goebbels admitted: 'I don't treat her well. Must devote myself more to her. She is so kind underneath. But sometimes she has her moods; like all women. Then you have to show her your teeth.'[69]

This militaristic way of life took its toll on Diana and she felt an air of contempt from Goebbels, avoiding him as best she could. He was jealous of her access to Hitler and was suspicious of Mosley. In many ways, Diana's physical presence made Goebbels feel inferior; standing at a diminutive 5ft 4in tall, Diana and Unity towered over him, his head was much too large for his body and 'in his emaciation he resembles Ghandi'. Unlike 'the two great blondes', his appearance did not conform to the Germanic racial categories and he 'would be taken at first sight for an Italian or even a Jew'. An ethnologist once produced a treatise on a Germanic group referred to as Nachgedunkelnter Schrimpfgermane – approximately translated as 'dwarf Germans who later became darker in colour' – and he placed Goebbels in this category.

However, Diana found Magda easy to talk to and she often spent the afternoons chatting to her and admiring her small children. Unlike Diana and Unity, she was not witty and never made jokes but she liked to laugh at other people's nuances. Magda seemed to be more of an empty vessel, absorbing the atmosphere of those around her and reflecting it as best she could. She was quick to dismiss people with whom she had little in common, but felt an intense loyalty to those she was close to. Like Unity, Magda was deeply superstitious and often had her fortune told by gypsies; they predicted she would die an unnatural death between the age of 40 and 45. This she told Diana during her stay at Schwanenwerder.

Diana's perception of Goebbels proved correct. She was right in believing him to be a spiteful man, prone to exaggeration. He wrote in his diary that Diana came to him pleading for the Nazi Party to loan Mosley £100,000. This was contradicted by Diana's own diary in which she wrote the best Hitler could offer her was £10,000. Goebbels also claimed that Diana had used her visit to the Olympic Games as an opportunity to ask Hitler for more money, which Goebbels took great pleasure in refusing her. If his diary entries are to be believed, then Diana asked once and was successful, but was consequently turned down after that.

As for Unity, many of Hitler's staff – Goebbels included, and particularly his intelligence team – were baffled at his tolerance of this boisterous English girl. What purpose did she serve? It was a simple theory: the Nazis courted young, upper-class English girls to see whom they knew – it was a question of networking, and Unity knew everyone. Diana, however, really did know everyone and she did not exaggerate her closeness to whomever Hitler was interested in. In cynical terms, it was a friendship of convenience.

Hitler's in-house doctor, Dr Theodore Morell, offered a different theory to this closeness between Hitler, Unity and Diana: 'In 1936 ... he could still laugh out loud and often did. He was a good natured man. The stories of violent tantrums are hugely exaggerated: I often had to admire how much he had himself under control.'[70] Dr Morell simply confirmed this ease with Unity and Diana was down to Hitler's approachability.

More extraordinarily, Diana succeeded in establishing a close relationship with Hitler away from Unity, whose giddiness and comical remarks often distracted from the seriousness of whatever he and Diana were discussing. Hitler admired her intelligence and he could easily talk politics with her. Mosley's preference for leadership lay with Mussolini, whom he thought more virile, and he openly referred to Hitler as a 'terrible little man'. But he was wise enough to notice that Hitler, quite taken with Diana, could be useful and she became his channel to him: 'It was a habit of Hitler to convey to me his views of events through Diana.'

Finally, this gave Diana a sense of power and a central role in the BU. Baba, too, admired Hitler and had travelled to Berlin for the 1936 Olympic Games, but she was always juggling several affairs and could not be relied upon to provide any real substance for Mosley's cause. Although it was the one thing Baba and Mosley had in common, she was not as tactful as Diana or as focused to set out on a mission and see it through. Hitler became Diana's mission and soon Mosley would see that. With Diana on Mosley's side, he and the BU might have a future.

The energy surged through the streets of Berlin ahead of the Olympic Games. Prior to the games, signs were placed around popular tourist attractions stating 'Jews Not Wanted'. However, in a rare moment of defeat, Hitler withdrew his regulation that Jews and black people were forbidden to participate when several nations threatened to boycott the games.* Despite the impression of a peaceful nation bracing itself to host the Olympics, it was a chilling reminder of how deceptive Hitler could be. Only two days after the games, Captain Wolfgang Fürstner, head of the Olympic village, committed suicide when he was dismissed from the military service because of his Jewish ancestry.

It was an opportunity for Hitler to camouflage the Nazi regime and to impress foreign visitors. Streicher's anti-Semitic newspaper, *Der Stürmer*, had been removed from news kiosks, though it continued to be published. The streets of Berlin underwent a massive clean-up and Hitler ordered the arrest of all Romany

---

* Prior to the games, Jewish athletes were disqualified from the teams selected to compete. To appease the international countries competing, Hitler consented to Helene Mayer, the fencing champion who was half Jewish, to represent Germany.

Gypsies, to be detained in a concentration camp close to a sewage dump in the suburb of Marzahn.

Overlooking the controversy surrounding the games, many international brands viewed it as an ideal platform for advertising. Guinness, in particular, was one brand who was eager to capitalise on this, and they drew up advertising posters of SS men holding a pint of beer and bearing the slogan: 'Es is zeit fur ein Guinness.' The English offices were reluctant to be associated with Nazi Germany and they opposed the advertising campaign. They subsequently clashed with the brewery at St James's Gate in Dublin, who were busy negotiating with a Berlin importer. The recent breach of the Versailles Treaty in March with the remilitarisation of the Rhineland caused some to feel suspicious of the future of Nazism and, because of that ill-feeling, the English offices exerted their authority and the deal did not go ahead.

Another exciting form of commercialisation was under way – the games were the first to have live television coverage and for some it was a display of majesty. For others it was a chilling reminder that Nazism was a disease spreading at a rapid pace.

Hoping to instil calmness in those Britons panicked by Hitler, Lloyd George championed the cause of the Nazis. He had visited the German ambassador to Britain (later the foreign minister of Nazi Germany), Joachim von Ribbentrop,* and Hitler in Berchtesgaden, where he, too, became smitten with the Führer's personality. Reporting back to the British people, Lloyd George assured them: 'Hitler is a born leader of men with a magnetic dynamic personality. The Germans have no longer the desire themselves to invade any other land ... They have definitely made up their minds never to quarrel with us again.' The veil of deception eventually evaporated and soon Lloyd George sensed the dangers of Hitler, but this vocal misjudgement would remain a blemish on his political career.

In spite of the escalation of terror spreading through Hitler's opponents, the excitement of the Olympics still inspired optimism in some – one being Deborah Mitford, who wrote to Unity: 'Would you send me a letter with a German stamp with an Olympic Games on it ... DON'T FORGET.'[71] But as the theatrics dazzled the onlookers in Germany and abroad, more quietly the concentration camps were filled and the road to war was paved.

Irene abhorred the wave of ceremony sweeping through Berlin, turning the heads of foreign visitors. Provoking further agitation, Irene received an official

---

* Leading society hostesses entertained von Ribbentrop, most notability Nancy, Lady Astor, who helped to make Nazism fashionable amongst the smart set. When war was declared in 1939, Lady Astor violently opposed Hitler.

invitation from Hitler. 'I did not want to be the guest of the German government,' she later explained. When she learned many prominent English people were going to Berlin for the Olympic Games, she reluctantly agreed to go, too. There was nothing remarkable about Irene's presence in Germany. However, it is a unique insight when considering her point of view on what she had witnessed in contrast to Diana, Unity and Baba's positive impression of the Olympic Games and of Hitler.

Flying alone to Nuremberg, Irene was jolted into the hall of the National Hotel, where she was crushed in a bedlam of Blackshirts, brownshirts, generals, officers of the army and navy, and journalists. She observed the spectacle of the city, overrun by Nazi propaganda, and she gathered her thoughts upon hearing Hitler speak. Unlike Diana and Unity, she was not so captivated as to overlook the sinister points of his speeches. She understood him perfectly, having spent a year in Dresden prior to her debutante season. When Irene met the Führer, she felt his dark eyes knifing through her soul and far from being charmed by his manners – an attribute Diana constantly praised – she recoiled when he kissed her hand and silently critiqued his unkempt hair. Hair cream, she advised, would tame the wandering strand that hung over his low brow. Despite the Nazi's trademark hospitality, the meeting had left her cold.

Further astonished by the German hospitality which Diana so loved, Irene did not mince her words when she was invited to a dinner given for the German head of all the sports and physical training in Germany. When elderly German women in white linen coats distributed packets of sausages, Irene turned to an SS man and scolded him. She suggested that he, a strong man, should be delivering the sausages and that Nazis only used their women for breeding and cooking. Disgusted at what she had witnessed, Irene fled.

Every day, Diana and Unity motored to the games in a procession of Mercedes cars following the Führer. Fortunately for Diana, who disliked sports, she and Unity were seated in a separate section from Hitler and his party, free to wander from the stadium that held 100,000 spectators. Jesse Owens, the black American runner 'who dashed along faster than anyone else', captured her attention and it was a 'pleasure to watch him' but, except for this fleeting spectacle, Diana was bored.

Diana's spirits were lifted when the games were finally over and she and Unity were treated to the Bayreuth Festival, which was 'as heavenly as the Olympic Games were boring'. An avid music lover, it was the most divine experience of Diana's summer; she listened to 'The Ring', which she knew from Covent Garden, and for the first time she heard *Parsifal*. Confiding to Hitler, Diana said she liked it least of Wagner's operas. Hitler reminded her 'that is because you are young. You will find as you get older you love *Parsifal* more and more.' A prediction, Diana discovered, that came true.

It was a summer of endless suppers with Hitler in a restaurant near Festspielhaus, the venue where Diana met Frau Winifred Wagner, a great friend of the Führer. British-born Winifred Wagner took a critical view of the overexcited Unity, but she held her grandfather Bertie Redesdale in high regard. Unity must have been unaware of Frau Wagner's disapproval, for she wrote to her mother: 'She's such a nice motherly person.'[72]

When the celebrations drew to a close, Diana decided it was time to talk business, and away from the festivities she finally had a chance to speak with Hitler alone. Preoccupied all throughout the Olympic Games, the two-week-long sporting event seemed like a lifetime to Diana. She had dreamt up a canny operation which, if Hitler agreed to it, would provide the floundering BU with funds and also net a profit for the Nazi Party. Hitler might have been a generous host to Diana but he was not so lenient as to pour money into a foreign political party without gaining something in return.

Mosley always claimed his party received no foreign aid, he even denied the generous handouts from Mussolini, which by 1936 had stopped. He was also keen to dispel any evidence that Hitler invested in the BU, but MI5 files reveal that Hitler *had* given money to the party. When such files came to light and were shown to Diana in her later years, she simply dismissed the accusation in that typical Mitford way: 'Oh well, if it's in the documents, then it must be true.'[73] It *was* true and it was exactly the reason Diana travelled to Berlin. Before this significant visit in 1936, her earlier trips had been for pleasure and to see Unity. Her later trips, however, were calculated and encouraged by Mosley, who desperately needed money. Diana was on a mission and she was determined the Führer would oblige her request.

Diana thought up the concept of a radio station, Air Time Limited, which would transmit to British airwaves. In Britain, the BBC had a monopoly over the airwaves and, since Mosley was banned from speaking on air, Diana had to think up creative ways to launch her plan. Any independent radio station would have to be founded on foreign soil, and she had carried out enough research to realise that similar stations had been successful. One such station, the International Broadcasting Company, had secured a licence from the French government to operate Radio Normandie, broadcasting to Great Britain from France. The basis of this radio station idea was surprisingly apolitical; Diana's scheme involved selling household goods and she had ambitions to manufacture a cosmetic line. She knew where her pitch lay: Germany needed hard currency and her household items, sold in sterling, would draw the type of profit beneficial to them both.[*]

In *Mein Kampf*, Hitler spoke of the importance of marriage, it was an institution which he regarded as holy, and one of the central themes of Nazi propaganda was family values. But this self-righteousness did not stop Hitler's own hypocrisy; publicly he proclaimed he was a bachelor married to the German nation, though privately, as Diana and Unity discovered, he was involved with Eva Braun. As much as Unity boasted that she knew every aspect of Hitler's life, she did not imagine that he was sleeping with Fraulein Braun.[74] Even Diana dismissed that Hitler was capable of having a sexual affair with anyone.[75] As such, she sensed Hitler's disapproval of her arrangement with Mosley. With this in mind, would his opinion be swayed towards the BU if she and Mosley were to marry? This gave Diana an incentive to discuss marriage with Mosley, and, for the first time, he considered the idea a possibility.

---

[*] Unsurprisingly, Goebbels was dead against the plan. He resented giving up one of his wavebands, but also hated the idea of broadcasting from German territory that would not be under his control. Hitler was the only one who could overrule Goebbels and Diana decided to approach him directly. She skilfully scheduled her visits to Berlin to coincide with Hitler and remained in her hotel room until a phone call would come through late at night. Suffering from insomnia, the Führer would summon Diana to his private apartment where he would talk politics with her. Twice Diana received a letter (in 1937 and 1938) refusing her proposal but she persevered and on the third attempt, in 1938, she succeeded. Unfortunately for Diana, her meticulous planning had gone to waste – with the declaration of war in September 1939, the plan fell through.

34

DECLINE AND FALL

Warning signs of conflict raged through Europe. Hitler was denouncing every international control and stamping the Treaty of Versailles into the ground. Such arrogant disregard towards foreign sanctions and tense peace talks overshadowed his twenty-five year Peace Pact – but did anyone believe it? Many Britons asked: 'Are we safe?' The reassurance they craved did not come from the steadfast monarchy when, in January 1936, society was thrown into despair with the death of King George V.

The new monarch, King Edward VIII, with his casual approach to dressing and modern views on socialising, hinted that the old traditions were waning. Such trivialities were looked upon as frivolous and nothing more than a privileged man doing what he pleased. However, for the old guard, an air of uncertainty lurked. For those who had grown up in the generation of the Bright Young Things, it signalled a change for the better. Baba and Fruity moved in Edward's fast-paced circle and, with his ascent to the throne, Fruity assumed the king would reward him for his loyalty and elevate him to the role of an equerry. Baba predicted that the new king had other pressing matters to deal with, and she was right – it came in the form of the twice married, once divorced American socialite, Wallis Simpson.

Polite society had always frowned upon public displays of adultery and it was a social rule that divorced women could not pay Court. They were viewed as wanton and indecent, and no self-respecting woman would challenge her husband for a divorce, regardless of infidelity on either part. Such things were simply kept behind closed doors and the married couple continued on as before. In 1936, Edward disregarded society's rules and his public rendezvous with Mrs Simpson shocked the nation. He often escaped with his married mistress on Colonel Guinness's yacht, but this hardly surprised Diana, who knew her former father-in-law could be capable of hypocrisy. But now, such taboo subjects were forced into the forefront of everyday life.

Unlike Diana, who was treated with scorn both publicly and privately when she left Bryan, the British government enforced sanctions on the newspapers, prohibiting them from printing photographs of the king and Mrs Simpson together. Hitler, too, was aghast when he learned of the affair through Diana and Unity. It challenged the Nazi principle of family life, and he also ordered the German press to steer clear of reporting on the affair. Public reaction was catastrophic and the ordinary people who looked to their monarch as an example reacted violently and chalked on the granite walls outside Balmoral: 'Down with the American whore.'

While the general public were staging a minor revolution over the king's indiscretions, the MPs scurried to limit damage and Ramsay MacDonald echoed the aristocracy's motto: 'The people of this country do not mind fornication but they loathe adultery.' Mosley capitalised on the attention the scandal was attracting and openly supported the king. He commented: 'The people will resist any attempt to hustle King Edward off the throne.' And he demanded a public vote before abdication was even considered.[76]

While Fleet Street was preoccupied with the king and Mrs Simpson, the plans for Diana and Mosley's impending marriage were discussed. Mosley warned Diana that politics were rough and with her being alone for long periods of time at Wootton the best thing for her safety would be to keep it a secret. The reasoning behind this discretion were Irene and Baba – Mosley was still appeasing one and sleeping with the other. As such, the wedding would have to take place outside of England. Paris was decided upon, but Diana discovered the notice of the marriage would be posted up on the wall at the consulate, easy for prying eyes and journalists to discover – so in theory it was no better than a London registry office. Diana sought the advice of the Munich consul and she learned the procedure was much the same. Hitler stepped in and offered to order the Berlin registrar to keep the marriage quiet and, while she stayed at the Goebbels' villa at Schwanenwerder, he helped her with the official forms. The wedding was arranged for October.

Magda, now a devoted friend to Diana, promised to oversee everything from the purchasing of rings to hosting the wedding breakfast at Schwanenwerder. This pandering to Diana embittered Goebbels and he continued to address her as Mrs Guinness or 'Ms Ginest' – the spelling of her name varied depending on his temper – and this formality highlighted that he felt no friendliness towards her. He loathed the idea of the marriage – 'that's not all right with me' – and he was livid that Hitler had a hand in such a thing. Whilst Goebbels sulked, Diana busied herself with shopping for her wedding outfit. And, as before with the Albert Hall and Olympia, she was absent for the most damning move of Mosley's political career.

On 4 October 1936, Mosley led the BU through the East End of London, home to a vast Jewish community and communist supporters. Independent Labourites and Jewish ex-servicemen marched in their own parade, escorted by a heavy throng of police, to repeated cries directed towards the fascists: 'They shall not pass!' Although Mosley obeyed the police, halting the parade and changing direction of the march at their command, it was a needless act used to provoke a reaction.

One hundred thousand anti-fascists gathered, building roadblocks near the junction at Christian Street in a bid to prevent the BU from getting through. In an arrogant display of authority, Mosley arrived in an open-top Daimler to inspect his men and was almost the target of a missile, which narrowly missed him as he exited the car. A riot broke out. Lorries were overturned and bricks, stones and glass bottles were hurled through the air. Women in the doorway of their terraced houses threw rubbish, rotten vegetables and contents of chamber pots at Mosley and his fascist supporters, about 3,000 in total – clearly outnumbered by opponents who raised their fists in communist salute and shouted: 'Kill Mosley!'

It became known as The Battle of Cable Street and, to avoid bloodshed, Mosley agreed to abandon the march and his men were dispersed towards Hyde Park. The anti-fascists continued to riot, despite the 6,000 designated policemen sent to control the violence. A total of 150 demonstrators were arrested and 175 people were injured, including policemen, women and children. Of course, Mosley's most loyal supporters, Diana and Baba, were unapologetic: it was the Jews and communists who created the disorder, certainly not Mosley.

Mosley had, in fact, acted in accordance with the law and legally he could not be faulted. It still did not prevent parliament from passing the Public Order Act, prohibiting the wearing of Blackshirt uniforms and regalia, as well as giving the police the power to ban fascist marches. The most damaging clause lay in forcing movements like the BU to reveal the source of their funding. Accusing the government of 'surrendering to red terror', Mosley made comparisons to pre-Nazi Germany. He cited that Germany, when trying to suppress Hitler before he attained power, adopted the same tactics only to discover that the law aroused sympathy for, and interest in, the Nazi cause. Mosley was still confident he could convince a nation to follow his political ideology.

With the world's newspapers reporting on the movements of Hitler, the abdication crisis talks and the disgraceful fall of the BU, Mosley escaped to Germany.

35

A TOKEN GESTURE

U nity had become Diana's chosen confidant. Long past the days of confiding in Nancy, Diana had severed ties when her eldest sister carried out the treacherous act of mocking and writing about Mosley. Since moving to Germany and staying with Diana during her brief spell of living in Munich, the two sisters established a bond based on trust and their mutual admiration of fascism. Unlike Nancy, Unity did not criticise Diana's devotion to Mosley, for she, too, had become involved with a married man.

Janos Von Almasy's introduction to Unity came through Tom Mitford who, in 1928, had stayed as a paying guest with the family of Janos. Descended from the Hungarian Counts Almasy, Janos played up to his role of a minor European aristocrat. At twenty-one years her senior, a 'dashing Nazi' and highly connected, it was the Nazi connection which Unity found attractive. He was married to Marie Esterhazy, the sister of Prince Esterhazy. His wheelchair-bound wife had been paralysed from the waist down by poliomyelitis in her childhood. It was a common rumour that Janos had married Marie for her enormous dowry and, since their marriage, they resided at Bernstein Castle in Austria. On his desk there was a skull wearing a Jewish yarmulke and a piece of polished serpentine, a soft gemstone from the castle's quarry, chiselled with Hebrew lettering said to contain a curse.

Unity had become a frequent guest at Bernstein Castle and together she and Janos holidayed in Venice, as had Diana and Mosley in the beginning of their affair. Described as dark and sinister looking, perhaps not unlike Mosley, Janos was an enthusiastic occultist, a keen astrologer and necromancer in the Wallenstein tradition. Mosley was also no stranger to the occult; one of his closest allies and spokesman on military matters, J.F.C Fuller, had been a disciple of Aleister

Crowley, the libertine founder of the religious cult Ordo Templi Orientis (known by mainstream culture as OTO). Impressing Unity with his spiritual experiences, Janos charted Hitler's horoscope, which he warned 'portended catastrophes, collapse and death at his own hand'. Far from distracted by her romance with Janos, Hitler still remained the central protagonist in Unity's life.

Taking Unity into her confidence, Diana entrusted her with the most important secret of all: she and Mosley were to be married. The ceremony was shrouded in secrecy, but she cared little if the press learned of their union. However, Mosley was still desperate to keep the news from Irene and Baba. Having convinced her that discretion was key, he also made clear that it was under such circumstances that he would marry her. As always, she obeyed. But Diana ignored one of his rules when she told her parents, whom she felt would see him in a different light if they were no longer living in sin.[*] She also longed for a relationship with Deborah, who had been forbidden from visiting the Eatonry and Wootton because of their living arrangements.

Hitler arranged everything; the marriage would take place on 6 October, just two days after Mosley's disastrous march through Cable Street. It was a contrast to Diana's wedding to Bryan, where every detail was overseen by her formidable mother-in-law, Lady Evelyn. Now, hidden in a bedroom in Berlin, Diana was carrying out what Bryan had declared as 'sacred' with the most calculated deception.

But what of Bryan? In a non-conspicuous setting, he first met the woman who would become his second wife in 1925, a year before he had first set eyes on Diana. Echoing their initial meeting, he first caught a glimpse of Elisabeth Nelson, aged about 13, as she moved in a chattering crowd of young girls as they came in late to supper. He had been invited to the Nelson family home at Princes Gardens, Kensington, as the guest of Elisabeth's older brother, Ronan. After an uneventful dinner, Ronan took Bryan rollerskating and he left without making the acquaintance of Elisabeth.

In July 1936, Bryan met Elisabeth for the second time when they were both present at her cousin's house. Elisabeth had just returned to England with her sister Biddy after a year of helping Ronan on the family's ranch in Wyoming. The pattern of their courtship followed that of his early days with Diana. Elisabeth came to Biddesden and afterwards Bryan drove her to London, taking her to see Tchekhov's *Seagull*. As he had done with Diana, Bryan fell in love with Elisabeth in

---

[*]   Deborah was still forbidden to visit Diana because of the secretiveness of the marriage – to her parents it was equal to living in sin. Diana commented: 'My darling Kit [Mosley] is more to me than all the visitors who are not allowed to come here.'

the theatre; he felt 'a sense of affinity' to her, which had nothing to do with her physical looks. 'I had indeed seen, admired and mutely loved others before my marriage to Diana, and I had less mutely admired others while recovering from the shattering experience of its breakup.'[77]

Bryan had only seen Elisabeth three times before she set off on a drive down the Rhine to Salzburg, from where she sent him a postcard inviting him to stay at their family home in Argyll. With the thought of proposing to Elisabeth weighing heavily on his mind, Bryan went to St Martin-in-the-Fields to pray about his decision. Without warning, and before shyness overwhelmed him, Bryan proposed to Elisabeth whilst standing in a burn. They were married in a quiet ceremony at the Chelsea Registry Office on 21 September 1936. 'A much better wife for him than I was,' Diana modestly said.

Standing in the bedroom window of the Goebbels' Berlin home in Hermann Goeringstrasse, Diana strained to see through the bright autumnal sunlight and she spied a familiar figure striding across the park-like square. Emerging from the trees, she could see it was Hitler, closely followed by an adjutant carrying a box – her wedding present, a photograph of the Führer in a silver frame adorned with 'AH' and an eagle – and a bouquet of orchids. Filled with optimism, she confided to Unity that it was the happiest day of her life: 'Everything was perfect.'[78]

Dressed in a simple golden tunic draped over a long black skirt, Diana joined Mosley downstairs in the drawing room in front of Unity, Hitler, Magda and Goebbels. The ceremony was brief, with the registrar saying a few words in German, of which Mosley understood not one word. They exchanged rings and signed their names on the document. In a few minutes, the deed was done; it was cold, clinical and, most importantly, convenient. Hitler stepped forward and offered to look after the marriage certificate, promising to keep it in a drawer. It was the last time either Mosley or Diana would see it.*

Afterwards, the party drove to Schwanenwerder, where the Goebbels gave a luncheon for twelve. Magda's little girls, Helga and Hilde, with their bright-blonde hair and blue eyes – so much like Diana's own sons – rushed in and out, presenting her with the flowers they picked in the garden. Diana wrote to Unity: 'I could write forever about that part of the day ...'

The other part of the day did not evoke similar feelings of happiness in Diana. 'I cannot describe,' she confessed to Unity, how Mosley 'spoiled the day for me'. The atmosphere had grown tense when Hitler dominated the conversation and

---

* Diana and Mosley were remarried again in 1974 after Mosley needed the certificate to make a French will. Unable to locate their certificate from 1936, they remarried at the Caxton town hall.

Diana and Unity were clearly hanging on his every word. For someone who was used to being a type of führer in his own home, Mosley reacted with jealousy. He understood no German, Hitler did not speak English and, sensing Mosley's displeasure, Diana tried to translate.

When they were alone he argued that Hitler was no better than Ramsay MacDonald. Diana was furious with his comparison – she felt MacDonald a weak politician who 'had a vanity that most found disturbing' – and they quarrelled. The row made them late for dinner at the Reichskanzlier and it caused Diana further pain and embarrassment to keep Hitler, who had gone to so much trouble, waiting. Mosley's 'awful childish behaviour and the way in which he tried to say everything he could to wound' her, had cast a dark cloud over the day. His viciousness was enough to shock Unity[79] and she pitied Diana, who was known to cry easily at such displays of brutality.

After a long day, the newlyweds retired to the Kaiserhof, where they argued again over the same issues. Diana displayed her anger through heavy silence and Mosley instigated a fight. Having exchanged bitter words, they went to bed in a dudgeon. Perhaps it was a premonition for what was yet to come.

36

LADY MOSLEY

Mosley did not discriminate when he cast a veil of secrecy over his marriage to Diana; his own children were also unaware and in the near future they would read about it, along with the general public, in a newspaper. Baba, too, learned of the marriage whilst glancing at a newspaper on the train to Paris and she inwardly seethed. Irene was in America when the news broke and when she returned to England to confront Mosley she possessed enough tolerance that it eventually brought out the best in her. Listening to Vivien's unselfish views on the marriage and how Diana made Mosley happy, Irene agreed that her niece should continue to be loyal to her father. However, this mellowed composure broke when Irene sternly warned Mosley that he must never again betray his children's trust.

Hidden away at Wootton, Diana managed to keep her pregnancy a secret. It was an easy feat; Deborah was still prohibited from visiting her, Pamela had married Derek Jackson and was busy with her own life, and Jessica had been estranged from Diana since her elopement with Esmond Romilly. Following the publication of *Wigs on the Green*, Mosley banned Nancy from visiting the house and, exerting such an influence over Diana, she did not challenged his authority. She, too, agreed that there was 'so much spite and disloyalty that I couldn't really love her'. If she was lonely, she did not complain; the prospect of having Mosley's child meant her 'happiness was complete'.

In November 1938, Diana gave birth to their son, Alexander. Afterwards she sat up in bed in the Grosvenor Road flat, looking out at the dark waters of the Thames with its distant wharves blanketed in snow, the remnants of a wintry storm that had swept through London. During her afternoon nap, the 'stupid puritanical' nurse took the baby from her side and placed his basket on the balcony outside. Awakening to the baby's piercing cries, Diana feared the seagulls would swoop down and attack him. This fear, brushed off as irrational by the sinister nurse, consumed her waking thoughts and she willed herself to remain awake lest the baby's freezing body should be carried off by the hungry scavengers.

The British press constantly speculated about a secret marriage between Diana and Mosley, and each time they denied it. Since establishing himself as a journalist, Randolph Churchill attempted to exploit his connection to Diana and pestered Tom Mitford for a scoop on the marriage, but it was to no avail. Fleet Street had smelled a rat when Wallis Simpson sent the newlyweds a congratulatory telegram, which the telegram office intercepted and rerouted to Whitehall. However, without access to the wedding certificate there was no proof.

Mosley felt it was time to officially announce the marriage and used the opportunity to print a notice of his son's birth. The press were sharpening their poison pens and the inevitable happened. After almost two years of complete secrecy and lies, their marriage became front-page news.

In a bizarre turn of events, Irene, who still loathed Diana, ventured to Wootton for a meeting with the woman whom she felt had destroyed Cimmie's happiness and contributed to her untimely death. It was a peaceful meeting, though Irene's acid wit did not overlook the underwhelming tea of bread, butter and thin slices of Christmas cake. She also noticed how 'badly decorated' Wootton was, with its tiny windows 'so one suffocated' and the framed photographs of Hitler and Goering on the mantelpiece which she 'longed to smash into atoms'.

The women spoke of domestic matters and, perhaps for the first time, Irene really heard Diana's voice. They had never exchanged a word before and she found the tone and rhythm of the Mitford drawl to be ridiculous. She listened as Diana chatted about the baby, and Irene, who adored children, softened at the sight of Alexander whom she thought 'big and strong for his age, more like a baby of nine weeks than over just one month old'. They further discussed Diana having to hire a new cook and Vivien's impending debutante ball, which Irene stressed she would oversee.

As the New Year of 1939 crept in and the uncertainty of war loomed, Irene went with the Mosley children to Wootton in case tensions should advance and England found itself under attack. Further currents threatened to pull Mosley asunder when the children's solicitor reminded him that he could no longer avoid his parental responsibilities. The solicitor would not consent to a house that was not the children's family home being partly maintained by their trust fund money. Mosley appealed on the grounds that the nursery world had transferred to Wootton but the solicitor still rebuffed his plea.

Ever the opportunist, Mosley asked Irene to subsidise the running of Wootton. Although she had dedicated her life to the Mosley children, Irene could not oblige Mosley's request and she felt as though she were sinking further into the cesspit of the Mosleys' life together. Her nerves were on edge because of Diana's pro-German comments, so casually made as they listened to Anthony Eden's anti-Nazi broadcasts on the wireless. Irene sensed her days at Wootton were numbered.

When Britain declared war on Germany the dynamic of Mosley and Diana's life changed, though they were yet to realise it. During the phoney war, Mosley had campaigned for peace and, having witnessed the atrocities of war first hand, he declared himself a staunch pacifist. The Earls Court Peace Rally in 1939 was the largest yet and Mosley continued to campaign openly with considerable support.

Although genuine in his delivery, Mosley's association with the BU's director of propaganda, William Joyce (dubbed by the press as Lord Haw-Haw), aroused suspicion in his motives. Later appointed as deputy leader of the BU, Joyce was a key player in changing the party's policy from campaigning for economic revival through corporatism to a focus on anti-Semitism. When he sacked Joyce in 1937, Mosley turned the BU's focus away from anti-Semitism and towards activism, but it was too late to reform the party's image. The British government, who viewed Mosley as a friend of Hitler, had little tolerance for his efforts. Diana maintained this was because Winston Churchill was 'more interested in war than anything else in the world'. Echoing the government's views, the masses believed Mosley's peace campaign was an ulterior motive to help Hitler invade England.

News of the attempted suicide of Unity Mitford (on 3 September 1939) overshadowed any attempts on Mosley's behalf to prevent a war. She had once romanticised an idea that a strong German army combined with the English Navy would 'rule the world' and, excited by this idea, Unity had commented to Diana: 'Oh if we could have that, and what wouldn't be worth doing to help the cause of friendship between the two countries even a little.' Her dream ended in disappointment and Unity declared that she could not witness England and Germany – the two countries she loved – go to war with one another. To her, death was a pleasant alternative.

Prior to Unity's suicidal feelings, Hitler had given her a pearl-handled pistol for her protection, and it was with this same gun that she hoped to end her life.[*] It was a clumsy shot and the bullet lodged itself in her brain. Still, it was not enough to kill her, but it succeeded in rendering her lifeless. Diana felt this was a crueller

[*] The old bullet became infected and Unity died in 1948, aged 33.

blow to Unity, whose 'glittering personality' her family, including the communist Jessica, loved. Lying unconscious in a Munich hospital, it was several weeks before the family knew of Unity's whereabouts or the true nature of her suicide attempt. It was four months before Sydney could fetch her daughter home from a clinic in neutral Switzerland, where Hitler had arranged to pay for Unity's medical treatment. The two never met again. News of the invalid returning to England and evading questioning by Scotland Yard horrified the public. Diana and Mosley's names were at the forefront of the press reports and once again their association with Hitler was emphasised.

Diana bore the brunt of Unity's actions; she was seen as the instigator, the clever sister who introduced the highly impressionable Unity to the dangerous lifestyle she so loved. Nancy and Jessica blamed Diana and political ideologies further destroyed the family. David publicly opposed Hitler in a rousing speech he gave in the House of Lords and Sydney resented his views, for she still felt a fondness towards Hitler. After almost forty years of marriage, their differing politics caused David and Sydney to separate.

Diana and Mosley's luck was on a downward spiral. Realising he could no longer afford the upkeep of his Grosvenor Road flat, Mosley gave up the lease. He and Diana found smaller premises in Pimlico, settling on Dolphin Square, London's most modern and ugly block of flats. They moved into two adjacent flats – separate bathrooms were essential – on the seventh floor of Hood House.

In between their tumultuous financial situation, Diana had given birth to their second and last child, a son named Max. A short while later, they gave up the lease of their beloved Wootton and moved back to Savehay. It was something Diana was not enthusiastic about, but she had made her life with Mosley and where he went she blindly followed. Cimmie's preference for chintz décor was not to Diana's taste and she tore down the flouncy curtains and replaced them with her understated grey silk ones from Wootton. Diana's elegant world did not blend with Cimmie's lavish and influential touch. The memory of the deceased lady of the house still weighed heavily on the staff, including Nanny Hyslop, who had cared for the Curzon girls and now for Cimmie's offspring.

It was the first time 7-year-old Micky had lived with his father, though hidden in the nursery he hardly saw him. Quite tellingly, on one of Mosley's visits to Irene's house, he asked to see Micky, who had just gone up to bed. The nanny encouraged the boy to call out an affectionate greeting to his father but he defied her orders, explaining he was unsure how to address the man, given he had only met him 'about four times' in his life.

Nanny Higgs came to Savehay with Max and Alexander, much to the disapproval of the former nanny. Nanny Hyslop knew Mosley was too cowardly to dismiss her, yet she realised he was cruel enough to allow her to suffer from too much pressure, overwork and constant humiliation, all in the hope of breaking her spirit. The nannies clashed and spent the entire winter at opposite ends of the landing, with each one not uttering one word to the other. Nanny Hyslop also felt no obligation towards Diana and coolly addressed her as 'Lady Mosley' whenever circumstances prevailed for her to speak to the new mistress of the house.

37

FATE

On the morning of 23 May 1940, Diana's day started like any other. Differing from her unremarkable routine, she planned to go up to London to visit Desmond, who was in a nursing home with a gland infection. She mentally went through her list of what needed to be done for the day. Before setting off to London she would have to feed Max and, while they were in town, Mosley suggested they motor over to their flat at Dolphin Square.

As their chauffeur-driven car pulled up outside the flats at Dolphin Square, Diana and Mosley spied four men lingering at the entrance of Hood House. 'They must be coppers,' she muttered as she looked in their direction.

'Sir Oswald Mosley?' said one of the men.

'Yes?' Mosley asked, as he and Diana exited the car.

'We have a warrant for your arrest. Can we go upstairs to your flat?'

Mosley possessed enough arrogance to feel above the law, and he confidently led the four policemen and Diana into the small lift, where they stood uncomfortably close as it climbed seven floors. Once inside the flat, Mosley asked, 'But what is the charge?'

'There is no charge,' came their reply.

Diana was thrown into a state of turmoil, but she had enough control over her emotions to calmly ask where they were taking him. Brixton Prison, she was told. Not to fret, they added, she could visit him the next day. Still believing it to be a mistake and he would be released, Mosley embraced her and from the window she watched the policemen take him away in the car.

Gathering her composure, Diana asked Perrot, their chauffeur, to drive her to the nursing home. She calmly told Desmond and his governess, Miss Jean Gillies, what had happened and added they were not to worry. She still believed it to be an error. Desmond remained calm, though at almost 8 years old and ill in bed, he probably did not grasp the severity of the situation. Still, something about the visit struck Diana as odd and she felt an undercurrent of nervous tension surging through the room.

As she drove back to Savehay, Diana was alone with her thoughts. She immediately telephoned Nick's housemaster at Eton to tell him about the arrest. Her stepson's feelings were not far from her mind, and when she asked his housemaster if he thought Nick would suffer because of it, she was told: 'Oh no. You see he's grown up – he's 17 – and he's got his friends and that's that.' She listened to this stranger's voice as he advised her over the telephone to worry about her own son, Jonathan, who was a boarder at Summer Fields.

Diana was momentarily relieved when she discovered that Jonathan was protected from victimisation because his last name was Guinness; surely his schoolmates would not realise that his mother was the notorious Lady Mosley. It must have crossed her mind if she, too, would have been spared had she kept to her immoral status as a divorcee, thinly disguised behind the title Mrs Guinness. Surely that would have been the lesser of two evils. Diana was unnerved when her 10-year-old son informed his mother that he was not surprised about Mosley's arrest. With Mosley's anti-war protests, Jonathan thought it was only a matter of time before the British government saw him as an enemy towards their patriotism.

Relations with her stepdaughter Vivien had thawed, and since the marriage to Mosley, they had fallen into an easy-going friendship. That evening, Diana and Vivien dined together and their conversation revolved around Mosley's arrest earlier that day. They spied the wooden gate opening on the side of the lawn and within seconds, policemen pushed through it. Diana instinctively knew they had come to search the house and she raced to her bedroom to hide her photograph of Hitler under the mattress on top of which her baby slept.

After nine o'clock, Sydney telephoned, the news of Mosley's arrest had been broadcast over the wireless. 'What's the charge?' her mother asked.

'No charge!' said Diana, whose anxiety dilated into a cold fury.

'Disgraceful!' cried Sydney.

'Yes, disgraceful!' Diana wailed.

Mosley's arrest raised several questions. Who would make decisions for his children? And was Diana, as their stepmother, in a position to automatically become their legal guardian? Irene was eager to preserve her rightful place in the children's lives and she approached Mosley on the subject. After a visit with his client in Brixton Prison, the lawyer warned Irene that Mosley was adamant he would have nothing more to do with his children if their guardianship was revoked from him, and he added that Savehay would be out of bounds to them. Irene's lawyer stepped in and suggested they share joint guardianship of the children. Irene realised the setbacks of Mosley's incarceration would lead to Diana's potential input and she declined. The judge leaned towards Mosley and was willing to dismiss all questions of guardianship, but Mosley refused. He only 'wanted entire control of the boys – he was not interested in the girl'. The judge revoked his sympathies and Irene was granted guardianship.

The once jolly and courteous Cousin Winston, always so fond of Diana, had joined the band of friends who publicly denounced her. Churchill told his Cabinet that he opposed Mosley's anti-war views and explained the reasoning behind his arrest without trial – known as Defence Regulation 18B.* His message was brief – if he bowed to Mosley, sooner or later Mosley would set up a British government 'which would be Hitler's puppet'.[80] It was a bitter pill for Diana to swallow; she still remembered Churchill's enthusiasm for inviting her to his flat for tea, pressing her for information on Hitler and speaking of his great rise to power.

Her old acquaintance, Nancy Astor, who had also been a friend to Mosley and trusted confidante to Cimmie, addressed the House of Commons: 'Is it wise to lock up the man and leave his wife free when the wife is more notorious than the man?'[81] Lady Astor's question was met with riotous applause, mirroring the overall public opinion on both Diana and Mosley.

Public opinion or, as Diana put it, 'the views put forward by politicians, press and BBC', was that she was as bad as him, if not worse, given the patronising view of women in that era. How could this beautiful, young woman, who was also a mother, entertain an ideology as contemptible as fascism? This question burned in people's minds and in the House of Commons.

However, it was not Churchill and her old friends that Diana needed to worry about. Nancy had actively shopped her sister to Gladwyn Jebb at the Foreign

---

*   Defence Regulation 18B, often referred to as simply 18B, was the most famous of the Defence Regulations used by the British government during the Second World War. It allowed the internment of individuals suspected of being Nazi sympathizers. Winston Churchill, originally a strong supporter of the regulation, later recognised its danger to democratic freedom, prompting him to describe it as 'in the highest degree odious'.

Office. 'I am disturbed about my sister,' she told Jebb. 'She's madly pro-German and I think something should be done to restrain her activities.'[82] Jebb did not overlook this piece of information, though it would be a conclusive piece from another source closer to home that would ultimately seal Diana's fate.

Diana had been notified that the War Office was going to requisition Savehay and would need it by 1 July. The best thing, Diana decided, would be for everyone to split up. Vivien, Micky and Nanny Hyslop went to Irene's, while she and her four sons made plans to live with Pamela at Rignell Farm. Diana then promptly paid off the remaining staff who had not already joined the war effort. Preparations were made to store furniture and trunks of clothing, and necessities were placed in the hall for their departure to Rignell. She was husbandless and soon she would be homeless. What more could happen by way of bad luck?

Casting her mind back to her visit with Desmond at the nursing home, Diana remembered that of the three present in the room, Jean Gillies seemed the most agitated. It was something she had not forgotten, and soon she would know why. Colonel Guinness had been paying Gillies to spy on Diana and to record in her diary the amount of times she had visited Nazi Germany and had spoken of Hitler. Satisfied that he had garnered enough evidence to sink Diana, Colonel Guinness wrote to his friend Lord Swinton, Chairman of the Security Executive – a committee so secret that he was one of the very few who knew of its existence.

As Colonel Guinness had hoped, Gillies' diary had a familiar theme: Diana's frequent trips to Germany, her casual references to Nazism and, on one occasion, she had apparently taught Jonathan and Desmond how to give the Nazi salute. But the most damning piece of evidence appeared when Gillies recalled that, on 27 September 1938, Mosley had commented that Hitler was perfectly justified in invading Czechoslovakia. When the *Athenia* was sunk, both Mosley and Diana agreed it was 'a good beginning'. And Diana had said of Poland: 'Surely now the goddess of wisdom has forsaken them and they will realise their colossal folly before it is too late.' The ink was barely dry on the paperwork when plans for Diana's arrest were put into place.

On 29 June, Nanny Higgs brought Max, who turned 11 weeks old that day, to Diana for his two o'clock feed. Afterwards, she changed her baby son and placed him in his pram in the garden where she sat next to him to read her book. A maid's voice interrupted the peaceful scene – if it weren't for the endless trunks gathered in the hall it would have seemed like any other sunny day. The nervous tone of the maid's voice alerted Diana that the man and two women callers were not friendly visitors or journalists. She looked up to see them intruding across the lawn, a policeman and policewoman, announcing they had a warrant for her arrest. 'Now what happens?' she asked, desperately trying to conceal the panic in her voice, 'I've got a tiny baby and I'm feeding him.'

'You can take him with you,' stated the policeman, unmoved by her plea.

As her mind raced, Diana gathered her composure and asked which jail she would be going to.

'Holloway,' they said.

Holloway, in London, was far too dangerous for a baby, Diana decided. She knew the bombing of the city was not too far in the future now that France was in Germany's hands. Diana explained that she would leave Max with his brother, and the policewoman followed her upstairs. 'How much luggage should I take?' she asked.

'Oh, only enough for the weekend. You'll be out on Monday,' the policewoman told her.

Diana packed a change of clothes and a pocket edition of Lytton Strachey's *Elizabeth and Essex*. Fighting back tears so as to not upset the children, she handed baby Max to Nanny Higgs and kissed 18-month-old Alexander goodbye. They watched from an upstairs window as the police escorted Diana to the car.

After what seemed like an endless journey from Denham to London, the police car drew forth to Holloway prison, its grim building within sight. Outside the prison gates, a poster warned: 'YOUR FREEDOM IS IN DANGER.' Led through the entrance, Diana passed the stone dragons with their menacing fangs exposed. The jingle of keys and caterwauling of female inmates grew louder as she walked down the long and echoing corridor.

Diana underwent the routine fingerprinting, followed by the humiliating inspection for fleas and venereal disease. When it was time for a delousing bath, she protested, saying she had had a bath that morning. Satisfied with Diana's response, the sinister-looking female doctor with dyed hair and long finger nails painted blood red, examined her, noting her weight and asked if she was pregnant.

Once the procedure was complete, Diana was taken to reception – prison jargon for a four-by-four wooden box with a roof of wire netting. She later learned that this was a practical joke on the prison authorities' behalf, for there was no reason why she could not go straight to a cell. The filth seemed contagious, it coated everything: the walls, the floor, utensils and the thin, damp mattress on the floor were saturated in dirt.

The phantom weekend stay had passed and Diana realised that her internment under Regulation 18B meant she could be held for as long as the government saw fit. Her mind turned to Mosley in his cell at Brixton and to the small children she had left behind. As much as she ached for 'the sweet baby', she was glad she had not brought Max to Holloway.

Alexander and Max were entrusted to Pamela, who preferred her dogs and had little patience for young children. Faithfully writing to Diana, Pamela updated her on the progress of the babies. Alexander, she wrote, toddled through a field of thistles. With her letters rationed, Diana could not respond immediately, which added to her worries for her children. 'His poor little legs,' Diana said of the incident, before reasoning, 'it's not her fault she doesn't like babies ...'

Each day followed the same pattern as the next. She fell into the rigorous prison schedule of scrubbing floors and sitting in her cold, concrete cell on Holloway's F-wing, the window so dirty not even a glimmer of sunlight could shine through. She slept sitting upright against the wall and refused everything by way of prison food. Women from the BU arrested under Regulation 18B rallied to Diana's cell. They had never met her before, but given their loyalty to Mosley they became subservient, offering to clean her cell and anything they could do to ensure her comfort. This embedded a level of resentment in Diana — in their own small way these strangers attempted to ease her burden, while her acquaintances in the government did not.

Finally, three months later, the familiar clinking of keys alerted Diana and she sprung forth, hoping that the internment had come to an end. She was disheartened to learn it was not so, but Diana remained optimistic that she might be able to argue her case when she was brought before the Advisory Committee for questioning.

Sitting before the Advisory Committee, Diana was pale and thin, her appearance worn from the rough conditions of prison life. She instantly sensed their feelings of hostility towards her. 'Have you reflected during your detention why you were detained?' they asked.[83]

'Yes often,' Diana truthfully replied.

'What conclusion did you come to?'

And, with more than an ounce of truth in her answer, Diana said: 'It was because I married Sir Oswald Mosley.'

Following the ineffective appointment with the Advisory Committee, Diana was led back to her cell. Adopting her familiar position beneath the dirt-encrusted window, she realised that any hopes of freedom were pointless. She was no longer frightened. It had nothing to do with courage, 'it was simply that I hardly cared whether I lived or died'.

After a separation lasting a year and a half, Diana and Mosley were finally reunited. This unusual arrangement came about when Tom Mitford dined with Winston Churchill and asked him to find a way for the Mosleys to be together. Sending word to Holloway, Churchill ordered the governor and prison commissioner to find a solution. A former parcels house on the grounds of Holloway, renamed the Preventive Detention Block, became Diana and Mosley's prison abode where they lived with another couple; a prominent BU member, Major de Laessoe and his wife.

Detached from the main part of the prison and its unbending routine, the Mosleys and the de Laessoes lived an almost self-sufficient existence. The men took responsibility for the boiler, each taking it in turns to stoke the coals so at least the women could have the luxury of hot water. Tending to the small patch of soil, formerly used as a victory garden, Diana transformed the few mouldering cabbages into edible kitchen produce and grew Jersey pea-bean and fraises des bois. They borrowed dozens of books on gardening and set to work, maintaining their vegetable patch and battling the weeds. Food was scarce and there was little variety, but compared to the oily greyish water in which swam a few bits of darker grey gristle and meat served from the prison cauldrons, it was fine cuisine.

In some ways prison life had become bearable and Diana was able to find a few pleasantries for which she could be grateful. As the seasons changed, she wandered around the yard every day, in fog and snow, rain and wind, and in the airless heat of a London summer, Diana sunbathed on the small patch of lawn. A visiting priest, astonished at the scene, commented to a prison warden: 'It's the garden of Eden out there, Lady Mosley in her little knickers.' The newspapers kept the public informed of Diana's prison life and those who were appalled at the lenience shown towards the couple referred to the parcels house as 'Lady Mosley's Suite'.

A wardress brought two convicts to clean the parcels house. 'You don't want petty pilfering so I'm sending sex offenders; they are always clean and honest,' she said. Diana was forbidden to talk to them, but once out of the wardress's sight she conversed freely. One convict was a bigamist, though she confessed it was a mistake and told Diana that she had been sentenced to nine months. Diana said she was lucky, at least she knew that she would be released when the nine months were up. 'We seem to be here for life,' she added.

Visiting rules had become more lenient. Deborah came, now married to Lord Andrew Cavendish, and sprinted across the yard with her two whippets. Pamela and Unity visited and Sydney brought the two Mosley boys. As much as Diana delighted in seeing her two toddlers, she was faced with the reality that in her long absence she had become a stranger to them. Alexander and Max stayed overnight, but after the second visit they did not want to leave. Alexander clung to Diana's skirt and had to be torn away, he wailed and begged to stay with his mother. It was an agonising decision but in the best interests of her children, Diana agreed the visits must be stopped.

Mosley's physical health was failing and his old ailment, phlebitis, caused him great agony. Tom, now abroad with his regiment, could no longer serve as Diana's channel to Churchill. Recalling Randolph's message relayed through Tom, that Churchill wanted to release her, Diana asked Sydney to appeal to Clementine. But Clementine did not converse seriously about the imprisonment and offhandedly remarked that the Mosleys were better off in prison, since if they were to be released the furious populace would be after them. Sydney said Diana was willing to take that chance.

Their fate was ultimately sealed when Dr Geoffrey Evans' medical report on Mosley's declining health managed to sway the prison commissioner's decision, warning the Home Office that if Mosley developed so much as a chill or influenza in his present condition 'he would not answer for the consequences'. Diana, too, had suffered ill-health and was weakened from a bout of dysentery. Major de Laessoe gave Diana a pill from his medicine chest. He promised it had cured him from the same affliction during his days in the African bush. The ancient pills had become more potent over time and Diana almost died from opium poisoning. But when she came to and gathered her strength, her thoughts turned to Mosley and his suffering.

On a cold morning in November 1943, Diana stood at the stove making Mosley his morning porridge when a wardress rushed into the dimly lit kitchen and announced: 'You're released!' After three and a half years of imprisonment with-out trial, Diana had given up hope. Confirming that the news had been broadcast over the wireless, the wardress convinced Diana that it was true. Abandoning the porridge, she flew to Mosley's bedside to deliver the good news.

A penance had been served and Diana, 'filled with inexpressible joy', believed Mosley was to be saved, the family would be reunited and their life could begin anew. She had come to the end of a dark tunnel and, seeing a glimmer of sun-shine, Diana thought the nightmare was over.[84]

Diana's marriage to Bryan had been a gilded cage. On that afternoon in 1932 when she told Bryan, 'I am in love with the Leader ...', she, at the age of 22, was prepared to give up her marriage in exchange for freedom. The condemnation Diana expe-rienced since her marriage to Mosley in 1936 and the hardship she would suffer was all too apparent. She had brought it on herself. 'I was in love with him, I was in love with life and to me they were more or less identical.' She could not bear a metaphysical prison with someone she did not love or respect and, although she resented Holloway and the banishment of her liberties, she had Mosley, and their prison reunion was 'one of the happiest days of her life'. It was not only passion that fuelled this attraction to Mosley; together with a profound faith in his ideals, Diana believed they were made for each other.

EPILOGUE

I n the summer of 1983, Diana made a rare visit to London. She cut a lonely figure
as she sat in an armchair in the House of Lords, where she planned to lunch
with Frank Pakenham, the 7th Earl of Longford. Sitting in contemplative silence
in a place that had once denounced her as the enemy, she heard the sound of
footsteps approach. Looking up she could see an elderly gentleman, frail, with
unruly white hair, dressed in corduroys and carrying a plastic bag. He tottered to
the cloakroom and removed a filthy macintosh, hanging it on a hook. There was
something familiar about his unassuming manner – an alarming contrast to the
intimidating grandeur of the House of Lords. A flood of memories jolted Diana
from her pensive mood and she quietly called out, 'Bryan?' The unique drawl disturbed him and without a moment's hesitation he rushed to Diana and kissed her.

'Which of you is it?' Bryan's eyes searched her face.

At that juncture Frank Longford loomed. 'Look who's here and he doesn't know
me,' Diana said with a mischievous grin. The former husband and wife laughed as
though not a trace of bitterness existed and they were old friends. It had been
the first time Bryan had met Diana in fifty years that he had not wept. Their long,
eventful lives had been lived; the sting of past events long forgiven and forgotten.

Bryan's ominous statement, 'which of you is it?', often inspired the same question in those who loved Diana. There was Diana, the kind and tolerant friend.
And Lady Mosley, who had not only endorsed National Socialism[85] but remained
loyal to the memory of her friendship with Hitler and his politics. Although Diana
admitted to being horrified at the Holocaust – 'I thought it appalling, wicked,
monstrous' – it could not force her to denounce the man who had charmed her
as a young woman and who had led the world into war. 'What about the Gulag?

Stalin killed many more than Hitler. Or the thirty million the Chinese killed in the so-called Cultural Revolution,' she responded when asked of her views. 'The fact is, we live in a cruel world.'[86]

As for Mosley, he had aimed very high, he had gambled and he had failed. He formed the Union Movement, which called for a single nation state to cover the continent of Europe and he later attempted to launch a National Party of Europe. In 1958, Mosley made a brief return to Britain to stand in the 1959 general election at Kensington North, where he unsuccessfully campaigned for the repatriation of Caribbean immigrants as well as a prohibition upon interracial marriages. He stood again in the 1966 general election at Shoreditch and Finsbury, but this, too, resulted in failure. He returned to France, where he and Diana had been living in semi-exile since the 1950s.

Although Diana had dedicated her life to Mosley for forty-eight years, he never remained faithful. She never admitted it, but suspicion about his infidelity plagued her. And, although she retained the view that 'monogamy was supremely foolish', Diana remained faithful to him. She promoted Mosley's beliefs after he had abandoned them, and continued to praise his political folly long after his death in 1980. 'Unrepentant' until the end, she died in Paris at the age of ninety-three.

NOTES

1 'Legs like gateposts from playing hockey, and the worst seat on a horse of any woman I ever knew.' Nancy Mitford, *The Pursuit of Love*. As read by Pamela Mitford in *Nancy Mitford: A Portrait by her Sisters*. BBC, 1980.
2 *James Lees-Milne: The Life*, Michael Bloch.
3 Letter from Diana to James Lees-Milne, September 1926, *James Lees-Milne: The Life*, Michael Bloch.
4 Letter from Diana to James Lees-Milne, 19 March 1927. Source as above.
5 Extracted from Daphne Du Maurier's diary, as published in *Daphne Du Maurier and her Sisters: The Hidden Lives of Piffy, Bird and Bing*, Jane Dunn.
6 'I think in his own character he is a person who enjoys war, and always saw himself as a great leader.' Notes of a meeting held at the Berystede Hotel, Ascot, on Wednesday, 2 October 1940.
7 Letter from Diana to James Lees-Milne, February 1927, *Diana Mosley: A Life*, Jan Dalley.
8 Michael Bloch describes this incident in *James Lees-Milne: The Life*. This episode of Milne's life had been omitted from his memoirs, *Another Self*.
9 Letter from James Lees-Milne to Diana, 1927. *James Lees Milne: The Life*.
10 'Know then that one alone can give me breath/ To mutter charms so delicate, so true/ That my poor soul torment unto the death/ The fragile heart that quivers at the view/ My feeble head is raised to hang the wreath/ Of poesy; thus much your sight can do/ Beauty's last balm more hurtful is than that/ Which kills with ugly shaft the jaded cat.' *James Lees-Milne: The Life*, Michael Bloch.

11 Letter reproduced in *Diana Mosley*, Anne de Courcy.

12 In *Another Self*, James Lees-Milne wrote that Unity, Jessica and Deborah looked at him and chanted: 'We don't want to lose you/ But we think you ought to go.' The accuracy of his account was questioned by his biographer, Michael Bloch. I have chosen to accept Nancy's version of the visit by drawing on her letters in *Love from Nancy: The Letters of Nancy Mitford*, Charlotte Mosley (ed.).

13 As explained by Deborah Devonshire in *Wait for Me*.

14 As told to Anne de Courcy in *Debs at War*.

15 '... about which I can remember nothing since my thoughts were not following the words.' Bryan Guinness, *Potpourri from the Thirties*.

16 The entire poem is printed in *Potpourri from the Thirties*, Bryan Guinness.

17 Murtogh D. Guinness (1913–2002) spent his life travelling the globe, collecting and preserving antique mechanical instruments and automata. His collection spanned to some 750 items and were awarded to the Morris Museum in New Jersey, USA.

18 The full letter is printed in *Diana Mosley*, Anne de Courcy.

19 *Potpourri from the Thirties*, Bryan Guinness.

20 'I remember at the time considering that this set was entirely alien to us and to our friends ...' *Potpourri from the Thirties*, Bryan Guinness.

21 As opposed to his idol worship of Diana, Evelyn Waugh did not 'idolise Nancy, he respected her'. Dr Barbara Cooke, research associate on the *Complete Works of Evelyn Waugh*.

22 Recalled by Diana in *A Life of Contrasts*.

23 Diary entry dated 14 August 1929, *Potpourri from the Thirties*, Bryan Guinness.

24 Letter to Diana dated 1929, *Letters of Evelyn Waugh*, Mark Amory (ed.).

25 Jonathan Guinness sold the manuscript of *Vile Bodies* at auction in 1985 for £59,400.

26 A letter dated 12 August 1930, *The Letters of Lytton Strachey*, Paul Levy (ed.).

27 Complete poem printed in *Potpourri from the Thirties*, Bryan Guinness.

28 The scene was related in a letter to Carrington, dated 28 May 1930, *The Letters of Lytton Strachey*, Paul Levy (ed.).

29 Diana told her second son, Desmond Guinness: 'Of course we'd have had you one day, darling, but just not then.' *Diana Mosley*, Anne de Courcy.

30 As told to Anne de Courcy, author of *Diana Mosley*.

31 *A Life of Contrasts*, Diana Mosley.

32 Complete poem printed in *Potpourri from the Thirties*, Bryan Guinness.

33 *Carrington: Letters and Extracts from her Diary*, David Garnett (ed.).

34 '… when I told him of the Cochran's suggestion he poured gallons of cold water on the project; he even went to Cochran and talked him out of it.' *A Life of Contrasts*, Diana Mosley.

35 Diana often said: 'Sometimes I think the Church of England is the fount of all evil.' *The Mitfords: Letters between Six Sisters*, Charlotte Mosley (ed.).

36 'The absurd figure of Ramsay MacDonald pretending to lead it [the country] as prime minister were a despairingly inadequate combination.' *A Life of Contrasts*, Diana Mosley.

37 *The Glasgow Herald*, 22 September 1928.

38 *James Lees-Milne: The Life*, Michael Bloch.

39 *Another Self*, James Lees-Milne.

40 *A Life of Contrasts*, Diana Mosley.

41 *Another Self*, James Lees-Milne.

42 Extracted from Lady Cynthia Mosley's letter in *Mosley*, Nigel Jones.

43 Letter to Mark Ogilvie-Grant, 20 June 1932, *Love from Nancy: The Letters of Nancy Mitford*, Charlotte Mosley (ed.).

44 As told to Anne de Courcy, author of *Diana Mosley*.

45 'I felt quite sure he would find the sort of wife he needed.' *A Life of Contrasts*, Diana Mosley.

46 A letter from Nancy to Diana, 25 January 1933, *The Mitfords: Letters between Six Sisters*, Charlotte Mosley (ed.)

47 'I explained to my furious parents that as M had never been faithful to her, his wife would think nothing of it; to her I was just another girl he fancied.' *A Life of Contrasts*, Diana Mosley.

48 Source as above.

49 The comment was recorded in Irene Ravensdale's diary, published in *The Viceroy's Daughters*, Anne de Courcy.

50 Source as above.

51 Letter published in full in *Diana Mosley*, Anne de Courcy.

52 'Baba Metcalfe, Cimmie's sister, was a sort of surrogate Cimmie in my eyes.' *A Life of Contrasts*, Diana Mosley.

53 'Lady Mosley added that she had reported to him what she heard: that Diana had said she was out to get him and that those who knew her said she was the most determined minx and talked freely to everyone.' *The Viceroy's Daughters*, Anne de Courcy.

54 On the eve of Diana's divorce from Bryan, Mosley called at the Eatonry where Nancy, Pamela and Unity had gathered. Pamela quickly departed, but Mosley looked in Unity's direction and greeted her with: 'Hello Fascist!' He also gave her a BUF badge.

55 Quotes in the *Glasgow Herald*, 13 December 1983.

56 A letter from Diana to James Lees-Milne dated September 1926, *James Lees-Milne: The Life*, Michael Bloch.

57 'No sensibilities as far as I could see; nor snobberies; immense superficial knowledge and going off to Berlin to hear Hitler speak.' Virginia Woolf's diary, published in *Mrs Keppel and Her Daughter*, Diana Souhami.

58 Lord Curzon wrote in a letter to his wife, Gracie: 'The estate is in the hands of trustees who will give him £8–10,000 a year straightaway and he will ultimately have a clear £20,000 per annum.' *The Viceroy's Daughters*, Anne de Courcy.

59 Letter printed in *Diana Mosley*, Anne de Courcy.

60 Published in the notes of *A Life of Contrasts*, Diana Mosley.

61 A letter from Deborah to Diana, 4 October 1943, *The Mitfords: Letters between Six Sisters*, Charlotte Mosley (ed.).

62 'She had quite a masculine streak in her. She would go off to BUF meetings in Oxford, donning her black shirt which couldn't be taken seriously. She enjoyed doing it to provoke.' Statement made by Unity Mitford's friend, Claud Phillimore, *Feminine Fascism: Women in Britain's Fascist Movement, 1923–45*, Julie V. Gottlieb.

63 Printed in *Der Stürmer*, July 1935.

64 '... because of the heat she drank champagne liberally.' *Diana Mosley*, Anne de Courcy.

65 Jessica Mitford made reference to this in a letter to Unity: 'I went to see Cord [Diana] after her operation, she looked terribly ill. I kept nearly having to leave the room because she and Muv would keep talking about an awful thing called the afterbirth.' Month unknown, 1934. In chronology, the letter is placed between 4 August and 19 September, *The Mitfords: Letters between Six Sisters*, Charlotte Mosley (ed.).

66 Transcript from a television interview with William F. Buckley, 25 March 1972.

67 Irene Curzon's diary in *The Viceroy's Daughters*, Anne de Courcy.

68 *Magda Goebbels*, Anja Klabunde.

69 Joseph Goebbels' diary entry, 11 May 1936. Published in *Magda Goebbels*, Anja Klabunde.

70 *The Secret Diaries of Hitler's Doctor*, David Irving.

71 A letter from Deborah to Unity, (month unknown) 1936. Deborah also signed off her letter with: 'Well DON'T FORGET about the Olympics stamp.' *The Mitfords: Letters between Six Sisters*, Charlotte Mosley (ed.).

72 *Winifred Wagner: A Life at the Heart of Hitler's Bayreuth*, Brigitte Hamann and Alan J. Bance.

73 Nigel Dorril said of the documents proving that Mosley had received funding from the Nazis: 'When I showed Diana what I had found, not long before she died, she said in that typical Mitford way: "Oh well, if it's in the documents, then it must be true." Oswald Mosley was a financial crook bankrolled by Nazis'. Article by Ben Fenton, *Telegraph*, 20 March 2006.

74 Hitler's doctor confirmed that Hitler and Eva Braun had a sexual relationship. Following their suicide in 1945, Gretl Mittlstrasse, when questioned by authorities, confessed that Eva would send her to Hitler's in-house doctor who would give her medication to suppress her period during Hitler's visits at the Berghof. *The Lost Life of Eva Braun*, Angela Lambert.

75 '... I don't think sex was a big appetite in him.' Diana Mosley to Duncan Fallowell, *The Independent*, 17 August 2003.

76 *Reading Eagle*, 9 December 1936.

77 *Potpourri from the Thirties*, Bryan Guinness.

78 'I felt everything was perfect.' A letter from Diana to Unity, 7 October 1936, in *The Mitfords: Letters between Six Sisters*, Charlotte Mosley (ed.).

79 'I do hope Kit [Mosley] is less nasty by now ...' A letter from Unity to Diana, 7 October 1936, in *The Mitfords: Letters between Six Sisters*, Charlotte Mosley (ed.).

80 'We should become a slave state, though a British government which would be Hitler's puppet would be set up, under Mosley or some such person.' Winston Churchill's address to his Cabinet in his room in the House of Commons.

81 Lady Astor's speech referred to a raid on the Anti-Vivisectionists Society.

82 Diana discovered this betrayal after Nancy's death.

83 Diana was questioned by the Advisory Committee during a meeting held at the Berystede Hotel, Ascot, on Wednesday, 7 October 1940.

84 Described by Diana in *A Life of Contrasts*.

85 Diana was interviewed by Sue Lawley on 'Desert Island Discs'. When asked of Hitler and the Holocaust, Diana answered: 'Having been in Germany a good bit it was years before I could really believe such things happened.' Sue Lawley asked: 'And do you believe it now?' Diana replied: 'I don't really, I'm afraid, believe that six million people were killed, I think this is just not conceivable. It's too many – but whether it's six or whether it's one makes no difference morally. It's completely wrong. I think it was a dreadfully wicked thing.' Originally broadcast on BBC Radio, Sunday, 26 November 1989.

... To interviewers she would respond with practised ease.

Diana Mosley, Anne de Courcy

SELECT BIBLIOGRAPHY

Amory, Mark (ed.), *The Letters of Evelyn Waugh* (Ticknor & Fields, 1980).

Amory, Mark, *Lord Berners: The Last Eccentric* (Sinclair-Stevenson, 1998).

Bloch, Michael, *James Lees-Milne: The Life* (John Murray, 2008).

Chisholm, Anne, *Frances Partridge: The Biography* (Weidenfeld & Nicolson, 2009).

Conradi, Peter J., *Hitler's Piano Player: The Rise and Fall of Ernst Hanfstaengl, Confidante of Hitler, Ally of FDR* (Gerald Duckworth & Co., 2005).

Dalley, Jan, *Diana Mosley: A Life* (Faber & Faber, 2000).

De Courcy, Anne, *Diana Mosley* (Chatto & Windus, 2003).

De Courcy, Anne, *The Viceroy's Daughters* (Orion, 2000).

Devonshire, Deborah, *Wait for Me! Memories of the Youngest Mitford Sister* (John Murray, 2010).

Garnett, David (ed.), *Carrington: Letters and Extracts from her Diaries* (Jonathan Cape, 1970).

Gottlieb, Julie V., *Feminine Fascism: Women in Britain's Fascist Movement* (I.B. Tauris, 2000).

Guinness, Bryan, *Diary Not Kept* (The Compton Press, 1975).

Guinness, Bryan, *Potpourri from the Thirties* (The Cygnet Press, 1982).

Hamann, Brigitte & Alan J. Bance, *Winifred Wagner: A Life at the Heart of Hitler's Bayreuth* (Granta Books, 2005).

Hanfstaengl, Putzi, *Hitler: The Missing Years* (Eyre and Spottiswode, 1957).

Hastings, Selina, *Evelyn Waugh: A Biography* (Houghton Mifflin, 1994).

Hayward, Allyson, *Norah Lindsay: The Life and Art of a Garden Designer* (Frances Lincoln, 2007).

Holroyd, Michael, *Lytton Strachey: The New Biography* (Chatto, 1994).

Irving, David (ed.), *The Secret Diaries of Hitler's Doctor* (Focal Point Publications, 1983).

James, Edward, *Swans Reflecting Elephants: My Early Years* (Weidenfeld and Nicolson, 1982).

Jones, Nigel, *Mosley* (Haus Publishing, 2004).

Jovanovich, William, *The Temper of the West: A Memoir* (University of South Carolina Press, 2003).

Klabunde, Anja, *Magda Goebbels* (Little, Brown & Company, 2002).

Lambert, Angela, *The Lost Life of Eva Braun* (St Martin's Press, 2007).

Lees-Milne, James, *Another Self* (Faber & Faber, 1970).

Levy, Paul & Penelope Marcus (eds), *The Letters of Lytton Strachey* (Viking, 2005).

Lovell, Mary S., *The Mitford Girls: The Biography of an Extraordinary Family* (Little Brown, 2001).

Mitford, Jessica, *Hons & Rebels* (Gollancz, 1960).

Moran, Mollie, *Aprons and Silver Spoons: The Heartwarming Memoirs of a 1930s Kitchen Maid* (Penguin, 2013).

Mosley, Charlotte (ed.), *Love from Nancy: The Letters of Nancy Mitford* (Hodder & Stoughton, 1993).

Mosley, Charlotte (ed.), *The Mitfords: Letters between Six Sisters* (HarperCollins, 2007).

Mosley, Diana, *A Life of Contrasts* (Hamish Hamilton, 1977).

Mosley, Diana, *Loved Ones* (Sidgwick & Jackson, 1985).

Mosley, Diana, *The Pursuit of Laughter*, (ed. Martin Rynja) (Gibson Square Books, 2009).

Mosley, Nicholas, *Beyond the Pale: Sir Oswald Mosley and Family, 1933–80* (Secker and & Warburg, 1983).

Mosley, Nicholas, *Efforts at Truth: An Autobiography* (Minerva, 1996).

Mosley, Nicholas, *Rules of the Game: Sir Oswald and Lady Cynthia Mosley* (Secker & Warburg, 1982).

Mosley, Sir Oswald, *My Life* (Nelson, 1970).

Mulvagh, Jane, *Madresfield: One House, One Family, One Thousand Years* (Blackswan, 2009).

Nicolson, Nigel (ed.), *The Harold Nicolson Diaries: 1907–1964* (Weidenfeld and Nicolson, 2004).

Patey, Douglas, *The Life of Evelyn Waugh: A Critical Biography* (Wiley-Blackwell, 1998).

Pryce-Jones, David, *Unity Mitford: An Enquiry into Her Life and the Frivolity of Evil* (Dial Press, 1977).

Pugh, Martin, *Hurrah for the Blackshirts! Fascists and Fascism in Britain between the Wars* (Jonathan Cape, 2005).

Ravensdale, Irene, *In Many Rhythms* (Weidenfeld and Nicolson, 1953).

Soames, Mary, *A Daughter's Tale: The Memoir of Winston and Clementine*

Churchill's Youngest Child (Doubleday, 2011).

Soames, Mary, *Clementine Churchill* (Revised and updated edition, Doubleday, 2002).

Taylor, D.J., *Bright Young People: The Rise and Fall of a Generation 1918–1940* (Chatto & Windus, 2007).

Wilson, A.N., *Betjeman* (Hutchinson, 2006).

INDEX

abortion 144, 169, 170

Acton, Harold 41, 87

Albert Hall, the 51, 150, 190

anti-Semitism 38, 135, 138, 163, 164, 172, 174, 179, 183, 198

Aryan ideology 38, 154, 181

Asthall 15, 16, 17, 18, 19, 20, 21, 22, 24, 33, 34, 37, 43, 73

Asthall Manor 12, 16, 25, 27, 31, 33, 89

Astor, Bill 31, 35

Astor, Lady Nancy 184, 203

Bailiffscourt 54, 55, 58, 73, 74

Baldwin, Stanley 21, 24

Batsford 12, 99

Batsford Park 12, 63, 89, 99

Battle of Loos, the 11, 103

Berlin 69, 132, 134, 145, 179, 180, 183, 184, 185, 186, 187, 189, 193, 194

Berners, 14th Baron/Gerald Tyrwhitt-Wilson 140, 141, 142, 151, 157, 158, 159, 167, 172

Betjeman, John 90, 91

Biddesden 77, 89, 90, 91, 93, 95, 96, 112, 115, 125, 131, 132, 193

Blackshirt 139, 145, 179

Blackshirts, the 113, 114, 121, 130, 142, 150, 152, 179, 185, 190

Bloomsbury Group/set 71, 83, 86, 87, 96, 115

Bracken, Brendan 22, 111

brats 19, 23, 37

Braun, Eva 156, 174, 187

'Bright Young Things' 41, 72, 83, 84, 188

Brighton 54, 129, 131

Britain 105, 106, 115, 136, 148, 184, 186, 198, 210

British Government 173, 189, 198, 202, 203

British Union of Fascists (BUF) 113, 114, 115, 116, 118, 121, 130, 137, 139, 142, 143, 145, 146, 147, 148, 149, 150, 151, 152, 161, 163, 164, 172, 174, 179

British Union of Fascists and National Socialists (BU) 172, 173, 174, 175, 179, 183, 186, 187, 190, 191, 198, 206

Buckingham Street 67, 71, 72, 73, 78, 79, 81, 82, 87, 93, 97, 115, 122

Bury St Edmunds 49, 69, 77, 99

Byron, Robert 56, 64, 98

Cable Street 173, 190, 193

Carrington, Dora 84, 86, 87, 88, 91, 92, 95, 96, 99

Castlerosse, Doris 111, 113, 147

celebrity 7, 29, 72, 83, 136

chaperone 21, 23, 27, 28, 29, 31, 35, 47, 48, 65

Chartwell 19, 20, 21, 22, 23, 24, 26, 28, 37, 38, 39, 47, 68, 106, 172

chauffeur 43, 44, 51, 55, 58, 61, 69, 78, 142, 161, 201, 202

Cheyne Walk 97, 98, 108, 111, 118, 119, 121, 123, 124, 125, 147

Churchill (née Ogilvy), Lady Clementine 10, 11, 17, 19, 20, 21, 22, 23, 37, 47, 79, 172, 208

Churchill, Diana 19, 22, 37, 47, 59, 80, 111

Churchill, Randolph 17, 19, 20, 43, 59, 65, 81, 100, 111, 119, 132, 197, 207

Churchill, Sarah 37, 38

Churchill, Winston 17, 19, 20, 21, 22, 23, 24, 28, 37, 65, 98, 106, 159, 172, 198, 203, 206, 208

communism 69, 141, 150, 159, 190, 199

Communist Party, the 24, 159

concentration camps 147, 171, 183, 184

Conservative Government/Party, the 21, 23, 24, 49, 68, 69, 99, 100, 103, 106, 152, 158, 172

Cours Fénelon, the 26, 27, 29, 35

Cunard, Lady Emerald 70, 132, 140, 145, 151

Curzon, Baroness Irene 103, 113, 114, 121, 122, 125, 128, 129, 130, 131, 143, 146, 147, 148, 150, 152, 153, 161, 167, 169, 173, 176, 177, 178, 179, 184, 185, 189, 193, 196, 197, 198, 199, 202, 203, 204

Daily Mail, The 36, 121, 143, 151

de Janzé, Phyllis 91, 147

debutantes 20, 32, 35, 43, 44, 45, 47, 49, 51, 56, 66, 68, 72, 132, 159, 185, 193, 197

divorce 116, 118, 119, 121, 127, 129, 131, 132, 135, 159, 160, 166, 188

Dublin 49, 76, 77, 84, 184

East End 114, 134, 179, 190

Eaton Square 124, 125

Eatonry 125, 127, 129, 130, 132, 144, 146, 151, 164, 166, 177, 193

Ebury Street 107, 120, 124, 130, 177

education/school 10, 13, 14, 16, 18, 20, 22, 23, 26, 27, 28, 32, 33, 36, 39, 47, 55, 67, 71, 91, 102, 103, 149, 156, 158, 180, 202

Edward VII, King 9, 145, 188

England 7, 27, 30, 31, 33, 45, 77, 84, 115, 137, 139, 142, 145, 156, 157, 160, 164, 172, 174, 175, 189, 193, 196, 197, 198, 199

Eton 13, 16, 21, 30, 36, 47, 48, 58, 59, 202

Europe 40, 69, 89, 90, 106, 110, 134, 135, 152, 153, 161, 163, 174, 188, 192, 210

fascism 105, 106, 113, 114, 115, 138, 139, 141, 142, 143, 145, 150, 151, 152, 156, 158, 159, 171, 173, 174, 190, 192, 203

First World War, the 9, 25, 46, 103, 134

France 10, 110, 131, 132, 133, 136, 146, 152, 186, 205, 210

Freeman-Mitford, David 9, 10, 11, 12, 13, 14, 15, 17, 18, 21, 22, 23, 25, 27, 29, 32, 33, 35, 39, 40, 41, 42, 43, 44, 45, 47, 55, 56, 57, 58, 59, 60, 62, 63, 67, 76, 79, 87, 89, 99, 119, 120, 121, 122, 132, 135, 137, 138, 144, 146, 158, 159, 167, 199

Freeman-Mitford, Deborah 13, 33, 34, 36, 63, 68, 73, 119, 171, 184, 193, 196

Freeman-Mitford, Jessica 10, 13, 33, 34, 36, 63, 73, 119, 122, 158, 159, 171, 196, 199

Freeman-Mitford, Nancy 9, 11, 13, 14, 17, 18, 20, 24, 26, 29, 31, 35–6, 39, 40, 41, 42, 43, 44, 47, 49, 54, 58, 72, 73, 75, 77, 78, 87, 95, 111, 118, 119, 120, 123, 125, 138, 144, 147, 158, 159, 160, 164, 171, 192, 196, 199, 203

Freeman-Mitford, Pamela 9, 11, 12, 13, 15, 18, 24, 31, 34, 35, 42, 44, 54, 60, 90, 95, 112, 138, 151, 171, 196, 204, 205, 207

Freeman-Mitford, Sydney 9, 11, 13, 14, 15, 17, 18, 21, 22, 23, 25, 26, 27, 28, 29, 32, 33, 34, 35, 36, 38, 42, 43, 44, 45, 50, 52, 53, 54, 55, 56, 57, 59, 62, 63, 64, 65, 68, 80, 87, 114, 119, 120, 132, 137, 138, 144, 146, 158, 167, 199, 202, 207, 208

Freeman-Mitford, Tom 9, 11, 13, 16, 17, 19, 33, 36, 37, 39, 40, 47, 48, 63, 69, 70, 73, 88, 102, 111, 112, 119, 122, 126, 128, 132, 134, 146, 156, 160, 161, 192, 197, 206, 207–8

Freeman-Mitford, Unity 13, 34, 36, 93, 98, 132, 133, 136, 137, 138, 139, 152, 153, 154, 155, 156, 157, 158, 159, 160, 161, 162, 164, 171, 172, 173, 174, 175, 179, 180, 181, 182, 183, 184, 185, 186, 187, 189, 192, 193, 194, 195, 198, 199, 207

General Strike, the 23, 24, 106
General Webb 89, 90, 91
Germany 52, 69, 70, 106, 115, 133, 134, 135, 136, 137, 138, 139, 145, 147, 154, 156, 157, 158, 171, 172, 174, 175, 180, 183, 184, 185, 187, 190, 191, 192, 198, 204, 205
George V, King 9, 45, 188
Gillies, Jean 202, 204
Goebbels, Joseph 147, 154, 161, 180, 181, 182, 187, 189, 190, 194
Goebbels, Magda 180, 181, 182, 189, 194
Graham, Captain Miles 128, 130
Great Depression, the 25, 124
Grosvenor Place 50, 51, 60, 61, 79, 121, 123, 124
Grosvenor Road 177, 196, 199
Guinness, Bryan 49, 50–3, 54, 55, 56–7, 58–61, 62, 63, 64, 65, 67, 68, 69, 70, 71, 72, 73, 74, 76, 77, 78, 80, 81, 83, 84, 85, 86, 87, 88, 89, 90, 92, 93, 94, 95, 96, 97, 98, 99, 100, 101, 102, 107, 108, 109, 110, 111, 112, 113, 115, 116, 117, 118, 119, 120, 121, 122, 123, 124, 125, 126, 127, 129, 131, 132, 133, 135, 143, 144, 148, 149, 153, 157, 158, 161, 162, 163, 166, 173, 177, 189, 193, 194, 208, 209

Guinness, Grania 51, 54, 55, 61, 73
Guinness, Jonathan Bryan 80, 81, 84, 94, 111, 112, 122, 125, 131, 144, 147, 149, 162, 179, 202, 204
Guinness, Lady Evelyn (née Erskine) 49, 50, 52, 54, 55, 56, 57, 58, 60, 61, 62, 63, 64, 65, 67, 68, 69, 73, 74, 79, 121, 131, 193
Guinness, Murtogh 54, 55, 61, 73

Ham Spray 86, 87, 91, 95, 100, 115
Hampstead 58, 74, 78
Hanfstaengl, Ernst 'Putzi' 132, 133, 134, 136, 137, 138, 154, 171
Hartnell, Norman 41, 63
Heath House 50, 58
Helleu, Paul César 26, 29, 30, 31, 32, 34, 35, 38, 43, 48, 70, 98, 132
Higgs, Nanny 80, 122, 147, 162, 200, 204, 205
Himmler, Heinrich 147, 171, 180
Hitler, Adolf 38, 96, 106, 115, 132, 133, 136, 137, 138, 139, 143, 145, 147, 151, 153, 154, 155, 156, 157, 158, 159, 160, 161, 162, 163, 164, 167, 171, 172, 173, 174, 175, 179, 180, 181, 182, 183, 184, 185, 186, 187, 188, 189, 190, 191, 193, 194, 195, 197, 198, 199, 202, 203, 204, 209, 210
homosexuality 35, 38, 42, 86, 102, 147–8, 160
honeymoon 65, 91, 168
House of Commons, the 103, 203
Hyslop, Nanny 199, 200, 204

imprisonment/arrest 147, 148, 151, 171, 183, 190, 201, 202, 203, 204, 205, 206, 207, 208 Brixton 203, 205; Holloway 205, 206, 208
Italy 105, 115, 136, 141, 167, 168, 172

James, Edward 48, 50, 153, 159
Jews, the 38, 133, 134, 135, 138, 147, 150, 160, 163, 164, 172, 173, 174, 179, 180, 182, 183, 184, 190, 192

In your armoury, eternal one, do you have
A hammer still and not a wedge
For me, this earth-surplus,
Not blessed and yet blessed?

In four lines, 'question-singing, answer-speaking', the
aporias of human existence rhyme and form a word that will
much appeal to Kraft: 'earth-surplus' ('Erdüberzähligen').

'In him the mystical is nothing more than the victorious
faculty of perception of a liberated, thoroughly reasonable
man,' said Peter Handke of Wagner and the 'frequent moments
of happiness in his language'.

Reason and order, the service and submission of an anthologist, the objectivity and restraint of an editor, are all at work
in Kraft, virtues which allow others to stand out – Karl Kraus
or Rudolf Borchardt, the lyrics of the century before last –
with no historical-philosophical theses, no theories, no daring
images or metaphors. With Kraft we get only presenting,
highlighting, rediscovering.

Kraft's life as an anthologist made his existence profoundly
solitary. He did not belong with the scholars at the Hebrew University nor to Pilegesh. For his first two decades in Jerusalem he
was cut off from any possibility of effect in Germany, France or
England and, for reasons of language, from operating in Israel.

In his first years in Jerusalem he worked as librarian at the
Centre de Culture Française. The beginning of the Second
World War brought his pension payments from Nazi Germany
to an end. For his family of four it was the beginning of years
of adversity and deprivation, with half their home rented out
in order to secure their meagre subsistence.

first and foremost as an anthologist and editor, who wanted others to share in his discoveries, most of them written in short forms, as in Nestroy's aphorism: 'Only do not hasten to fulfil the will of the Evil One, before the old God can send an angel.' Christian Wagner was another he rediscovered for the German people. On 31 August 1935 he noted in his Jerusalem diary: 'Christian Wagner as lyric poet of the Third Reich! What a time!' In that month Nazi Germany celebrated the hundredth birthday of the poet, 'who died at a great age in 1918', as Kraft remarks in the foreword to his anthology. He belongs to the nineteenth century. And he goes on to say:

> The inclusion of German lyric poetry after 1900 would have brought *others* centre stage, alongside the well-known poets – and even those would be differently selected. The time for that has not yet come. For now, the image of the German lyric up to 1900 functions as our present, because the actual present is not yet far enough away for it to be allowed to be a distinct self. Whoever experiences the present as past, makes a mistake; the solution is to experience the past as the future.

This apologia for the nineteenth century is surprising at a moment when the twentieth century was already at least half over. What future in the past is Kraft talking about? Few poets show us more clearly than Wagner, who combines piety with the experience of nature, morality with freedom, mysticism with a daylight-clear consciousness, as in his short poem 'Do you have', which Kraft includes in his anthology as part of a comparatively large selection from the poet from Warmbronn: